875X

3-7-68

THE COMMON MARKET

By the same author

ENERGY IN EUROPE 1945–1980

THE
COMMON
MARKET

W. G. JENSEN

Ph.D.

LONDON

G. T. FOULIS & CO. LTD

1-5 PORTPOOL LANE, E.C.1

First published September 1967

© W. G. JENSEN   1967

SBN : 85429 072 9

Printed in Great Britain by

The Whitefriars Press Ltd., London and Tonbridge

TO MY WIFE

1448233

Contents

CHAPTER 1

A common heritage?

Why is it, the sceptic may ask, that it was only amid the ruins of the postwar world that the men of Europe, made cruelly conscious of the fact that the age of power and glory of the individual nation States of Europe had passed for ever, began to speak of union and abandonment of sovereignty? Was not the transition from the rampant table-thumping nationalism of the thirties to the pious Europeanism of the later forties and fifties a little too rapid to carry real conviction? Was it possible not to suspect that the real reasoning, the real purpose, the real objective behind the strident calls for unity in Europe represented the harnessing of the dreams of a band of romantic idealists to the economic and political aspirations of individual States? And if this indeed was the case, if European idealism, like patriotism, was merely a tool of Governments and politicians, what was then left of the noble proclamations of aims and longings shared by the ordinary men and women of Europe? And if those questions were relevant then, are they not more so today when the burning and vital question which faces the European Community is whether or not their real and ultimate aim is complete European unification?

The peoples of Europe are many: Teutons, Latins and Slavs, to name only the three largest ethnical groups – and immediately new questions come to mind. The Common Market admittedly embraces peoples of Latin and Teutonic origin. But what of the others? What, for example, of the peoples of Eastern Europe? What links or association, if any, should there be with them? Do we recognize that they also share a common faith, common aspirations and common factors of government and social organization?

So the more we scratch the surface of the question, the more confused the picture becomes. Of course, we can remember common ideals, objectives and achievements – with some, if not with all. But we remember also the wars we have fought, the wounds we have suffered, and the gulfs that have on occasion yawned, so utterly unbridgeable, between us. We have only to turn back the pages of

1

history to read how our ancestors spoke of Philip II of Spain and the peril of the Armada, of the ambitions of Louis XIV, of the insatiable power-lust of Napoleon, to realize, with amazement perhaps, that the words they used were often little different from those we in our turn used to describe the dark menace of Hitler. And if we lay aside our own history books and turn for a moment to those of our neighbours, in what light then are our own policies and objectives seen . . . the perfidy of Albion – ironic, perhaps, from the lips of a man so often described as 'the Corsican monster', but used nonetheless with telling effect and echoed by many down the years. Where, then, are the things that are common to us all? Where are the magnets that impel us to come together and forge the links and similarities that are, reputedly, stronger than the enmities and differences that divide us?

Since the present is to a very large extent the mirror of the past, it is to the history of our Continent that we must turn. Celts, Huns, Goths and Saxons emerged in turn from the steppes of Asia to occupy the forests and plains of Europe, but only a romantic visionary could find in the tribal ties of almost two millenia or more ago the origins of a common heritage. No, the first real intimation of a common weal, of a common single State, came with the Roman armies and the universal rule of Rome.

The legacy of Rome

It is perhaps too easy to forget that the whole of Europe South of the Danube and West of the Rhine, including therefore Belgium, England, France, Holland and Spain, formed for four centuries or more a part of the Roman world. For the first time in relatively modern history the greater part of Europe was one and indivisible – a single world, moreover, in which large numbers of the subjects of the Empire lived contentedly. Rome brought to them not only peace and prosperity, but also the virtues and advantages of Roman law, Roman roads and houses, Roman organization and Roman civil values. Above all, Rome gave Europe a common language so that Romans, Spaniards, Britons, Germans and Gauls . . . and leaving to one side a score of other peoples from Eastern Europe, the Middle East and North Africa . . . could converse easily and naturally together. The Roman stamp on Europe was deep, permanent and comprehensive. It was not merely a question of conquest but of instituting a new way of life, orderly and civic, which, if often rough and sometimes disregarded, began nevertheless to inculcate in the peoples of the Roman Empire a new regard for the individual human being and a nascent sense of human dignity.

When the Roman Empire in the West collapsed in the fourth and fifth centuries A.D. to be followed by the terror, anguish and suffering of the Dark Ages, men looked back wistfully to a time of unity, law and justice that, while it had become remote in time, remained in their minds as an ideal and a hope for the future. Nor was this a completely empty dream, for the final and most precious legacy of Rome was the religion of Christ which was eventually to spread to the farthest corner of the old Empire and to give our Continent a new cohesion and sense of oneness. At the same time the evidence of history suggests very strongly that the spread of Christianity contributed materially to the downfall of the Roman Empire. The Emperor Julian, known to history as the Apostate, was probably one of the few who fully understood the basic incompatibility between the power of Rome and the gospel preached by Christ. But his efforts to hurl back the surging tide of conversion to the new religion, although brilliantly conceived and executed, were shattered by his early death after a rule of little more than two years. The story told of his last words : 'You have conquered, Galilean', while almost certainly apocryphal, constitutes an accurate recognition of the victory of the Christian God. Paradoxically, it was the triumph of Christianity that kept alive, however faintly, through the fearsome centuries that followed the collapse of the Roman Imperium, the embers of European unity and a sense of corporate belonging.

The Christian succession

One cannot, I believe, stress too much the fundamental influence of Christianity in promoting a sense of oneness throughout the European Continent. The insignia, structure, purpose and methods of the Christian Church were in its early years basically similar in all the countries of Western Europe. The recognition of Latin as the universal language of the learned, the unquestioned acceptance of the Christian faith and all it stood for, and the known and valued common heritage of Rome, all contributed to the breaking down of barriers between one state and the next. Of equally vital importance was the gradual but general application of the feudal system which reinforced, almost unconsciously, the links between the ruling classes throughout Western Europe.

It is both evidence of, and a tribute to, the political genius of Charlemagne that he, more than any other ruler of his time, fully recognized the potential cementing impact of Christianity and strove to mould it to his own ambition by his dramatic coronation by the Pope in Rome in A.D. 906 and his assumption of the title of Holy Roman Emperor – which, in one form or another, was to survive through a thousand years of European history. Of course, in time, the Empire came, inevitably – and justifiably – to be regarded as no more than a cloak to cover the national or dynastic ambitions of Austria or Spain, but the fact remained that for several hundreds of years men continued to look upon the Emperor as a ruler who, in some rather vague and indefinable way, constituted, together with the Pope, one of the permanent and massive pillars of European society.

It is ironic to look back and see that in the eleventh and twelfth centuries Europe, with a largely common social structure – even if it was based on the feudal system of which serfdom was of course an integral part – a common language (among the educated classes), and a shared sense of Roman inheritance, was in many ways more intimately unified than it has ever been since or, indeed, is likely to be again in the foreseeable future. Within such a system built upon the permanent exploitation of the serfs by a privileged minority, it is not surprising that latter-day notions such as patriotism made little sense and scarcely existed. There was, not surprisingly in the conditions of the age, a far greater affinity between a French and a Spanish nobleman than between a French lord and his bailiff. At no time was this sense of brotherhood-at-arms more clearly demonstrated than in the first Crusades. The undoubtedly genuine fervour of many of the early Crusaders sprang not only from their Christian convictions but in some part also from their sense of belonging to a common European and Christian fraternity.

But if such emotive feelings existed at the time of the first Crusade, and the words of Peter the Hermit and the pathetic tale of the children's pilgrimage carry conviction over the centuries, they were soon lost or absorbed in the rivalries between the kings and princes of Europe and, above all, by the inexorable development of the nation state. Already, by the end of the twelfth century, England and France had become identifiable nation states with aspirations that were often – though by no means always – national rather than personal or dynastic in character. The rise of the nation state marked the inevitable decline and eventual dissolution of the feudal and baronial systems and, in so doing, shattered the old universal social order. The Western European world which, socially, hierarchically and emotionally, had come so close together in the tenth and eleventh centuries, began now to drift apart at a gradually accelerating pace until, by the seventeenth century, the pattern of individual nation states with widely varying social, spiritual and political and economic structures and conceptions left few obvious traces of the faith or order of life that had once been common to all.

And yet, although the notion of European identity or corporateness, of an outlook on life that was essentially similar, was no longer present, the old idea – or ideal – was never wholly forgotten. Throughout the centuries there had been men, often admittedly little more than proverbial voices crying in the wilderness, who have dreamed, spoken and written of the advantages of partial or complete unification. After all, even in the heyday of the nation state, were not European similarities far, far greater – and more obvious and compelling – than European differences? Thus, if in the eyes of many good prelates and churchmen the word 'christianitas' meant in fact little more than the geographical area of Europe – with the word 'Europe' itself being seldom used or heard – as early as the beginning of the fifteenth century, in 1406, the Frenchman Pierre Dubois wrote his now historic proposal for a European Confederation. Dubois's proposal, however, as the title of his book, *De recuperatione Terre Sancte,* made abundantly clear, was designed with the sole aim of recovering the Holy Land from the hands of the infidels. The same objective lay behind the impassioned appeal for European co-operation when in 1454 at the Diet of Frankfurt a man named Ænea Silvio Piccolomini, better known to students of religious history as Pius II, called the rulers of Europe to arms, as in the heroic days of the first Crusade, not this time to recover the Holy Land but to defend the lands of Central Europe against the menacing and encroaching advance of the Seljuk Turks. His words, spoken more than 500 years ago, have an almost modern ring : 'Formerly, when they (the Saracens) defeated us, it was in Asia or in Africa . . . in lands over the sea. But today they are striking at us in the very heart of Europe . . . in our homeland, our very own house and dwelling-place.' Almost at the same time an exiled French nobleman called Marini, living at the Court of Georg Podiebrad, King of Bohemia, persuaded his host to suggest to a number of his fellow Christian sovereigns that they should join together in the establishment of a European defensive alliance against the Turks. Podiebrad, suspected in Rome of heretical Hussite leanings, seized upon his guest's plan with alacrity and, improving upon it, drafted a 'Treaty on the Establishment of Peace throughout Christendom', which some historians have gone so far as to hail, a little exaggeratedly, as a precursor of the League of Nations.[1] By posing as the champion of Christendom against the heathen invaders, Podiebrad hoped to leave the Papacy with no alternative but to commend his efforts while at the same time providing useful prestige for his kingdom and placing at least an indirect responsibility upon his neighbours to assist him in ensuring the defence of middle Europe against the Turks.

[1]The draft treaty consisted of a preamble and 23 articles. Two of these, Articles 16 and 18, were of particular interest. Article 16 : 'Moreover, in order to ensure due execution of all that is written . . . every one of us shall have his envoys . . . come not later than next Sunday Reminiscere in the year of Our Lord 1464 to the city of Basle in Germany; where they shall be in constant residence for the immediately following quinquennium and in our name and the name of the other members or those desirous of being admitted into the union shall form, constitute and represent a body, corporation or regular college. And after the end of such a quinquennial assembly in Basle, the same assembly shall be held and sit for the next immediately following quin-quennium in the city of N. in France, and for the third quinquennium in the city of N. in Italy in the same manner and under the same conditions as resolved and decreed above. . . . The assembly shall have its own special council whose president shall be N. as its father and head, and we, the other Christian kings and princes, shall be its members. The said college shall also have voluntary and contentious jurisdiction with pure and mixed authority

When looking at the influence and impact of the ideas for European co-operation put forward by leaders and representatives of the Church in the fifteenth century – and they were too numerous to review in any detail in this book – it is essential to remember that Europe throughout this century was living under the shadow of the capture of Constantinople by the Turks in 1453 – a blow that horrified Europeans of that age in a way that is difficult for us today to comprehend; perhaps the closest analogy in our own times was the attack on Pearl Harbour by the Japanese in 1941. For a few years the fall of Constantinople reinforced the unity of European rulers but within a few years internal differences among the Turkish rulers and the reviving territorial ambitions of Western rulers brought about a return to the old intrigues and combinations. Louis XIV of France was not the only European ruler to contemplate an alliance with the Grand Turk in order to fulfil his own political ambitions.

The fifteenth century was, however, not destined to be the only period in history when the Turkish menace acted as a sharp stimulus to European co-operation. By the beginning of the sixteenth century the Turks made another lurch forward to the West and in 1523 at the bloody battle of Mohacs routed the Magyars who for several decades had stood between them and the appetizing plains of Central Europe. On several occasions during the next hundred years the Turks came to within sight of the walls of Vienna. Their last and most dangerous onslaught came nearly 150 years after the battle of Mohacs and was only frustrated by a composite army drawn from all the countries of Europe and the military genius of the legendary Polish prince Jan Sobieski who commanded them.

Another proposal for European co-operation that has found its way into most of our textbooks was the Grand Design conceived by the French Protestant Duc de Sully – sometimes also attributed to King Henri IV of France. Sully looked back nostalgically – as many more were to do after him – to the days of Charlemagne when France and Germany had been united under one ruler. Sully's Grand

over all of us and our subjects as well as those who voluntarily submit thereto, as the present assembly or its majority may decide and decree. Finally, it shall have its own coat-of-arms, seal and common treasury as well as public archives, a syndic, clerks, and all the other rights allowed and appertaining to a proper corporation.'

Article 18: 'Finally, so that our assembly does not lack funds to meet the expenses and costs necessary and useful for the maintenance of peace, the administration of justice, the designation and dispatch of envoys and messengers to all parties as well as for other needs, we pledge and undertake that every one of us shall without further delay send and transfer to the public archives through the hands of the collectors and the council of the said assembly a tenth part of all the monies which are to be collected by him or in his name . . . at a time decided on by the assembly or its majority.'

For an analysis of the 'Treaty on the Establishment of Peace throughout Christendom, see *The universal peace organization of King George of Bohemia: a fifteenth century plan for world peace, 1462/1464.* Publishing House of the Czechoslovak Academy of Sciences, Prague, 1964.

Design, published in 1638, envisaged the organization of Europe into 15 states, including six hereditary monarchies, five states whose rulers were elected, and four republics. This so-called political equilibrium between these states was to be balanced by a religious equilibrium as five of the 15 states were Roman Catholic, five Lutheran and five Calvinistic. The confederation was to have had at its head a General Council whose main function was to decide on the measures required to achieve its political objectives. These were twofold. First, the expulsion of the Turks from Europe; second, the establishment of a perpetual peace among all European peoples.[2] Towards the end of the century, in 1691, the German philosopher Leibnitz wrote hopefully of the day 'when union will be achieved, catholicity will be restored, Germany and the Latin world will recover their spiritual communion, the United Provinces and England will in their turn re-enter a Church at once Roman and reformed, and believers, all believers, will oppose the forces of disintegration that threaten our faith'.[3]

There was also, about this time, a famous British contribution to the ranks of those who advanced the cause of European unity. This was in 1693 when William Penn, the founder of Pennsylvania, published a short tract entitled *Towards the present and future Peace of Europe*. Penn advocated the creation of an international parliament with powers to settle disputes, regulate armaments and enforce its decisions against recalcitrant members, if necessary by the use of force. Penn suggested that his European parliament might have a total of 90 members, including 12 from the German Empire, 10 each from Spain, France, Turkey and the Muscovite Kingdom, six from England and three from Venice. Among the benefits that would arise from such a European settlement, Penn listed the prevention of bloodshed; the enhancement of the glories of the Christian religion; the saving of wasteful expenditure in war; greater ease of travel and communication; the possibility of developing a common front against the Turks; the promotion of friendly relations between rulers and peoples; and (rather quaintly) the possibility this would create for princes 'that hereby they may chuse Wives from themselves, such as they Love, and not by Proxy merely to gratify Interest'.

Better known than the work of Penn or Sully is the treatise by the French churchman and diplomat the Abbe de St Pierre. The Abbe was a professional diplomat and was present at the Peace of Utrecht, which marked the end of the war of the Spanish Succession, as secre-

---

[2] Sully borrowed extensively from his lesser-known contemporary, Emeric Cruce, who, in 1622, published a book under the title of *Le Nouveau Cynee ou Discours d'Estat representant les occasions et moyens d'establir une paix generale, et la liberte du commerce par tout le monde*. The book was dedicated 'Aux Monarques et Princes souverains de ce temps'.

[3] Quoted in Mayne, R., *The Community of Europe*, London, 1962, p. 37.

tary to the Prince de Polignac who led the French plenipotentiaries. From what he saw and heard during the peace negotiations St Pierre drew the firm conclusion that there was no possibility of any permanent reconciliation between absolute national sovereignties. Conflicting economic interests, military and strategic differences over frontier lines and colonial rivalries would, it seemed to him, offer virtually permanent subjects of dispute; so much so indeed that each peace treaty in turn was in fact little more than a pause for the combatants to draw breath before resuming the fray. The solution which he first put forward in 1713 – but upon which he brooded and elaborated for the rest of his life – was the establishment of a European society which would pledge itself to a policy of non-intervention in the affairs of its neighbours; thus, although there was to be no question of any degree of supranationality – a concept that was in any case inconceivable within a decade or two of the despotic rule of le Roi Soleil – the adherence of all states to a European compact would guarantee the security of all. The Abbe de St Pierre's project aroused little interest among the general public in his own lifetime. His treatise, published under the title of *Memoire pour rendre la Paix perpetuelle en Europe,* was badly written and, like so many works of the age, far too long and tortuous. Years later Jean-Jacques Rousseau, while commending St Pierre for his idea, commented that the plan he had drawn up stood but little chance of success as long as rulers continued to believe in the divine right of kings and had little inclination to submit their quarrels to judicial arbitration, even if the arbiters consisted of a panel of their fellow sovereigns.[4]

The eighteenth century was the century of grace and elegance, with fine and cultured living for the well-to-do and when there was a certain European cosmopolitanism of the *élite.* By the close of the century such different men as Washington, Lafayette, Gibbon and Bentham all spoke of Europe in general and excessively idealized terms. Washington spoke glowingly of a future United States of Europe although this, as he must well have known, was no more than euphoric verbal indulgence and was at that time completely unattainable. Perhaps the most apt tribute to this trend among the educated classes of Europe was Burke's famous remark that 'no citizen of Europe could be altogether an exile in any part of it'. It is questionable whether many Europeans would care to confirm such a feeling today.

Europe in the nineteenth century

The Romantics, particularly in France, made the idea of a united Europe their own. Lamartine, Hugo and many of their followers and

[4]In particular Rousseau wrote: 'Will our sovereign rulers be prepared to submit their differences for settlement by arbitration by legal means when the whole force of the law has never been able to compel their subjects to do so?'

admirers eulogized the abstract notion of a United States of Europe. Victor Hugo, in particular, devoted some of his most visionary rhetoric to it : in 1849, speaking at the opening of the Peace Congress in Paris he proclaimed that 'A day will come when men will see these two mighty assemblies, the United States of America and the United States of Europe, face to face, holding hands across the ocean, exchanging their produce, trade, industry, arts and genius, taking measures jointly to bring life to the wastelands of our planet, colonising its deserts and improving our world under the gaze of its Creator by harnessing together for the wellbeing of all men those two infinitely powerful forces : the brotherhood of men and the puissance of God.' But the visionary Arcadias of the Romantic poets found little response in the hearts of the sovereigns and rulers of post-Congress Europe. The Congress of Vienna in 1815 was in the direct tradition of the Peace of Westphalia in 1648 when the sovereigns of Europe or their accredited representatives met together to bring peace and respite to a war-torn continent. In 1815 the culprit was France which, under the impulses of, first, revolutionary fervour and, later, of Napoleonic ambition, had for more than 20 years turned Europe into a battlefield. At the end of the struggle the victorious powers, England, Austria, Prussia and Russia, were anxious to prevent any new French threat to European peace and stability. The method they chose was a succession of international conferences out of which grew, at the instigation of Czar Alexander I of Russia, the Holy Alliance; the Holy Alliance was in essence a personal alliance between sovereigns and had little or no influence, impact on, or following among, the peoples of the countries concerned. The abstention of England robbed the Holy Alliance of many of its potential teeth but it remained nonetheless an effective force in European political life until the Crimean War. Only a few years before its final dissolution it faced and overcame what was perhaps its severest test and in so doing won its greatest victory.

It had always been evident, from the day that England refused to participate, that the Holy Alliance would be used primarily as a weapon to reinforce the position of the reactionary ultra-conservative governments of Europe and to suppress any nascent liberal tendencies. So it was that in 1823 France, the feared foe of only eight years before, was authorized to send an army into Spain to assist in the suppression of a liberal insurgence. Twenty-five years later, in 1848, the *annus mirabilis* of continental liberalism, the Holy Alliance acted with decision and liberal and national movements in Germany and Austria were ruthlessly suppressed. Had they succeeded how different the course of European history might have been for, although many of the volcanic eruptions of 1848 had national undertones, liberal opinion generally was against excessive power of the central executive and inclined readily towards federalism. One

9

achievement of the liberal doctrine must, however, be recorded. In 1860, as a result of constant and strong pressure from London, Napolean III authorized his Minister for Commerce, Michel Chevalier, to sign a free trade area agreement with England. Within two years this had been extended to Belgium and Prussia. But the results were not what had been hoped for. French industry was not prepared for the challenge and protested bitterly at the influx of British goods. The result was inevitable and within a few years the treaty was abrogated. The concept of free trade lingered on only to be finally extinguished in 1892. Of much greater historical significance, of course, was the German Zollverein, whereby customs duties between the member states of the German Confederation were progressively eliminated. This was the instrument which the political genius of Bismark was to use with telling effect to bring about the unification of Germany.

But before passing on to Bismark and the nationalistic explosions of the 1860's and 1870's, out of which were to rise the modern states of Germany and Italy, it is timely to consider for a moment the emergence of recognizable socialist thinking, often in European terms. The first of these writers was the Frenchman Saint-Simon, a thinker and visionary, who attempted, together with his famous disciple Enfantin, to found at Menilmontant on the outskirts of Paris a virtual religion of socialism. Saint-Simon had witnessed and studied deeply the emerging industrial society of his time. In his opinion the technological and economic forces which had been unleashed by the industrial revolution and which were growing and multiplying their effects at a staggering rate before the very eyes of his contemporaries, could only be brought under control and channelled into the right direction, to allow their satisfactory development for the maximum benefit of all, in a peaceful international community offering large and uninhibited spaces to commerce and trade. Saint-Simon, however, was laughed off as a faintly ridiculous mystic and it was not until much later that he acquired an honoured place in French socialist thinking. His mantle was largely inherited by Proudhon who in his *Du Principe federatif,* published in 1863, looked forward to a world-wide system of federation, each one of which would group together a number of independent states.

The name of Bismark dominates continental European history and diplomacy in the nineteenth century. To the Junker who so brilliantly engineered the creation of the German Empire must also be attributed much of the responsibility for the advent of the extreme nationalism of the country that was to lead to the Hitlerean catastrophe. It was Bismark who deliberately fanned and nurtured the flames of nationalist feeling to achieve German unity under Prussian hegemony. At the same time it must be conceded that once Germany had been united Bismark's primary aim was to prevent

10

any further wars. He encouraged the French to seek expansion and compensation for the loss of Alsace-Lorraine, in Africa; he ignored French advice to develop a major naval base at Kiel and build a navy capable of challenging that of Britain; he emphasized that Germany had no more territorial ambitions in Europe. Nevertheless, the creation of a united Germany under Prussia announced the high-water mark of extreme national sentiment in Europe and effectively eliminated, until after the end of the First World War, any discussion of closer European unity or co-operation. Instead, it marked the consecration of power politics (machtpolitiek) based upon a carefully balanced system of defensive-offensive alliances.

The aftermath of the Great War of 1914–18

President Woodrow Wilson's famous 14 points and the creation of the League of Nations are often spoken of as major landmarks in the movement towards a united Europe. The truth of this assertion is, however, open to question. The Peace Conference of Versailles was again in the tradition of the great European postwar conferences to resolve the problems left over at the end of major European conflicts – with the significant change that this time the Americans were among the participants. Their very presence inevitably gave the Conference a world-wide significance and in Woodrow Wilson and his puritanical sense of mission and purpose they provided a force that the Europeans resented and yet could not ignore. Lloyd George who, as Prime Minister, led the British team at the Versailles Peace Conference, described Clemenceau's (his French opposite number) attitude to the American President as follows : '(he) followed his movements like an old watchdog keeping an eye on a strange and unwelcome dog who has visited the farmyard and of whose intentions he is more doubtful.' History often repeats itself and President de Gaulle has done nothing new in fomenting jealousy and suspicion of America's purpose and role in Europe. Nor, to be just, have the French been alone in their resentment of American intrusions into the affairs of Europe.

It is indeed highly questionable whether the triumph of the Wilsonian doctrines in 1919 was anything but a disaster for Europe. The rash dissolution of the Austro-Hungarian Empire left a vacuum in central Europe where the seeds of future conflict were and have ever since remained endemic. Nor were the numerous small states that were so abruptly called into being likely to be in any hurry to surrender their recently acquired independence. Like Caesar, the politicians in charge preferred to be top-dogs in their own farmyard than mere courtiers at the court of a bigger monarch. As to the much-vaunted League of Nations, the U.S. Senate refused even to ratify American participation, even though it had been the brainchild of their own President.

11

And yet, despite all the unfavourable circumstances of the time, there was for a brief period in the 1920s some revival of European federalism. Typical and illustrative of the ideas that circulated at this time was the book *Union Now,* written in 1930 by an American journalist based in Europe and imbued with enthusiasm for the federalist cause. Streit's personal vision extended beyond Europe and envisaged a vast federation embracing all the peoples living round the shores of the Atlantic. Streit was 30 years ahead of his time but, for a while, his ideas figured prominently in certain rather academic discussion circles. No one in official government circles seems ever to have given his theories any serious consideration. This is hardly surprising. The Great Depression of 1929 gave politicians plenty of other problems. Besides, in Germany, times had changed and in 1933 Hitler became Chancellor.

Nonetheless, the European thinking of the 1920s, even though it was to prove abortive in the short run, is important for two reasons. Firstly, to see what were the origins and causes of its sudden flowering; secondly, the precedents it created and left behind for a later generation to follow up. Let us consider first the possible reasons for this new awareness of Europe. There was undoubtedly among certain people at least a vague realization that Europe was no longer the sole centre of the universe. It was impossible to ignore the million and a half American soldiers that had stood, superbly armed and equipped, along the battle-lines of 1918. Less immediately evident but inescapable nonetheless was the massive industrial capacity of the new giant across the Atlantic. Then there was a fear of German revenge. Just as the Germans after 1871 had constantly to keep in mind the French desire for revenge after their humiliating defeat and for the recovery of the lost provinces of Alsace and Lorraine, so now the French in their turn feared for the German reaction to the Treaty of Versailles. Fourthly, there was the rising influence of big business. In this respect industrialists were well ahead of their political colleagues and had long since come to the conclusion that there was much to be gained from carefully defined and negotiated link-ups and associations across national frontiers. This period was, indeed, the age of the first big pan-European cartels, and in Paris there was established in the early 1920s a *Comite d'Action pour une Union Douaniere Europeenne,* to which bankers, economists, industrialists, politicians and even some civil servants adhered in large numbers. To a man they urged the virtues of close industrial co-operation and the carefully phased reduction of tariffs. One of the best-known members of the group was Gaston Riou who in 1928 was to write a book with the deliberately challenging title of *Europe, ma patrie.* In this way the 1920s were to see a number of suggestions for co-operation and even the union of specific industries across national frontiers. This was indeed to be the time when sectoral unification (which later was to come to fruition in the establishment of the Coal and Steel Community) first became fashionable. 1926 saw the formation of the first International Steel Cartel. Limited initially to continental powers, both the British and the American steelmasters later decided to join.

The Pan-Europa movement of Count Richard Coudenhove-Kalergi

Probably the best-known, if not the most popular, of the early postwar movements was the Pan-Europe organization founded in 1923 by Count Richard Coudenhove-Kalergi. Born in Japan, Coudenhove was himself a citizen of Europe in the broadest sense of the term. His father, of distant Dutch extraction, had been a professional diplomat in the service of the Austro-Hungarian Empire, while his mother was of Cretan origin. He was very much an aristocrat and chose at an early date to address himself not to the masses – to whom he was and has largely remained unknown – but to the economic and political leaders of Europe. Many of these, as we have already seen, were painfully aware of the process which Professor Toynbee was later to describe as 'the dwarfing of Europe'.[5] Coudenhove-Kalergi based his proposal for the need for European unity or co-operation on five main reasons : although Europe still remained in many ways the main centre of world power, important and far-reaching changes such as the emergence and rise of the United States, China and Japan, were already perceptible and could not, in the longer term, but reflect to the disadvantage of Europe; the brooding menace of Soviet Russia . . . a country of which Coudenhove-Kalergi was almost pathologically suspicious and fearful; the impact of nationalism which contained within it the seeds of dissolution of the major European empires and the consequent need to harmonize and guide into constructive channels its impetuous torrent; the failure of the League of Nations – which left wide open the question of who would guarantee the peace of Europe and how this was to be achieved; and, finally the increasingly obvious advantages of major economic groupings.

More precisely, Coudenhove-Kalergi directed his appeals to the Christian Democratic or Centre parties because he considered Communists and extreme right-wing parties as politically and emotionally unresponsive and, indeed, basically antagonistic to his ideas. Coudenhove-Kalergi believed strongly that only the unification of Europe would give continental industries the opportunity and the possibility of keeping pace with industrial development in the United States, Russia and the United Kingdom. The inclusion of the United Kingdom in this list was of course significant since it showed clearly that, at this time at least, he did not regard the United Kingdom as belonging to Europe. In this Coudenhove-Kalergi did

[5]*Cf.* Professor Arnold Toynbee, *Civilisation on trial,* New York, Oxford Univ. Press, 1948.

no more than reflect the thinking of large numbers of continentals who continued, many of them right up to the time of the Suez debacle, to think of Britain as a world rather than a strictly European power. Union of European states was to be achieved by means of a customs union in order to bring together German coal and French ore reserves so as to develop a pan-European mining industry.[6] But although Coudenhove-Kalergi made a number of converts and large numbers of people flocked to his movement, he made comparatively little impact and it was not until the advent of men like Loucheur and Aristide Briand that the federal idea hit the headlines and began to excite some public interest and support.

As we have seen, French governments of the 1920s put forward a number of proposals designed to bring about reductions in tariffs within, or linked together with, the creation of a network of international cartels. The earliest advocate of such a policy was the French Minister of Commerce, Louis Lecheur, who elaborated upon the idea at the Geneva Economic Conference of 1927. As a bold and imaginative economico-philosophical departure the idea was immediately popular at the League of Nations; but it was soon to be overshadowed by the impetuous genius of Aristide Briand and his famous memorandum on *The Organization of a Regime of European Federal Union*. Lecheur also received support from another prominent French politician of later years, Edouard Herriot who, in a book published under the title of *The United States of Europe,* called for an international cartelization policy with a view to stabilizing both production and prices and securing a high level of employment. Herriot also added, however, the important – and for the inter-war period the by no means politically popular – rider that all cartel agreements should be published and that the supervising bodies should include representatives not only from industry and government but also from consumer organizations and trade unions or workers.

Aristide Briand

Aristide Briand was one of the first of a group of brilliant and perceptive Frenchmen to grasp the importance and the opportunities for France of securing a workable Franco-German co-operation arrangement – a policy that was to increase in its attractions to French political leaders and to find a culmination in the Schumann proposals of 9 May 1950. In an address to the Assembly of the League of Nations on 8 September 1929, Briand said notably : 'I believe that among peoples who are geographically grouped together, like the peoples of Europe, there should exist a kind of federal link; such peoples should be able at any time to enter into

---

[6]*Cf.* Coudenhove-Kalergi, R. N., *Pan-Europa,* Knopf, New York, 1926.

close contact with one another, to discuss common interests, to take common decisions and to forge among themselves a bond of solidarity which would enable them to put up, at the appropriate time, a common front in the face of grave difficulties if these were to arise.' The key words were of course 'a kind of federal link'. What exactly did this mean? What was the French government's objective? A greater degree of control or supervision over German industry, whose renewed expansion was filling them with concern and foreboding? Ever since 1870, and even more especially since 1918, successive French governments have been obsessed with the spectre of a Germany rising from the ruins . . . even today.

But whatever may have been Briand's intentions, his appeal fell upon deaf ears. Briand had directed his appeal mainly at Germany and the German people, by whom it was coldly received. Stresemann, the German Minister of Foreign Affairs, welcomed it warmly enough, but he was a close personal friend of Briand and in any case died within a few weeks of his friend's speech. Without the positive backing of Stresemann, Briand's proposals stood no chance of success in a Germany torn with turbulence and seething with discontent. In Britain the response of both government and people – the latter were scarcely aware of it at all – was, if anything, even colder and more uncompromising. The ruling Labour government, at all events, would have nothing to do with it. Other more hypothetical reasons for Briand's failure were the world economic crisis following the crash of Wall Street in 1929 – which forced governments to take urgent measures to put their own houses in order and brought about an atmosphere that was uncompromisingly hostile to the establishment of any federal links; the rise of fascist nationalism in Germany and Italy; and, lastly, Briand's own lack of daring and, perhaps, conviction. There were inevitably many who doubted the sincerity of Briand's proposals and saw in them only a device to try and bolster up France's sagging industrial front. Whatever the cause, Briand was asked to explain and develop the thinking behind his initiative in a detailed memorandum. This he duly did. Drafted by the French civil servant and poet Alexis Leger (better known under his pseudonym of St John Perse) the memorandum dotted a lot of the i's and set out specific questions which antagonized many and reconciled few. It was consigned to a working party which, while it did produce a full report in 1931, was soon forgotten. Briand's own political career came to an end soon after and with it ended the last governmental European approach before the Second World War.

The Second World War

During the war there were a number of people in various countries which were occupied by the Germans who genuinely, if misguidedly, saw in Hitler's Reich a tremendous opportunity for the unification of

Europe. It led some of them down the path of collaboration with the enemy and, inevitably, the stigma of treachery to their own country and people became attached to them. Nevertheless, it is perhaps timely to record that among all the quislings, traitors and fellow-travellers there was a small minority of people who, at least for the first few years, looked to Germany and even to Hitler to provide an impulse or a lead towards a unified Europe. That Europe united in this way would be dominated by Germany was obvious, but it was their hope and belief that with the passing of time German leadership would gradually merge into a kind of pan-European nationalism in which other peoples would be permitted to play their full part. Such was, for example, the political standpoint of Laval in France. Otto Abetz, a German writer who in 1951 published an account of some 20 years of German policy towards France, gives the following account of a conversation between Hitler and Laval at the Fuhrer's headquarters: 'During the course of a discussion in the Fuhrer's headquarters Laval said to Hitler: You wish to win the war in order to make Europe – in fact you should create Europe in order to win the war. This statement by the French Premier was only too true. National Socialist Germany had a very real conception of Fortress Europe; nor was there any lack of understanding or appreciation of the advantages arising from a continental economic community. But the Third Reich chose not to develop a binding political philosophy for all the peoples of Western Europe and so failed to match the Atlantic Charter of the Anglo-Saxons with a European Charter of the Axis powers.'

On the allied side, on the other hand, the European idea won ground rapidly during the war. In 1944 a meeting of continental European resistance leaders was held in Geneva and they concluded their discussions by emphasizing the vital necessity for a European union. In the same year, in London, Professor Edward Hellett Carr published a book entitled *Conditions of Peace,* in which he described at length the kind of Europe that would have to be built up after the war. Professor Carr's book, which received widespread attention on the Continent, looked forward to the establishment of a number of European bodies dedicated to closer European co-operation. They included a European Transport Corporation, a European Reconstruction and Public Works Corporation, and a European Planning Authority. As the war drew to a close the enthusiasm for the idea of a united Europe grew rapidly and generated a tremendous sense of excitement and anticipation among a large proportion of Western European intellectuals which was to reach its climax at The Hague Conference in 1948.

In fact, in 1944, the first faltering steps along the road to European

[7]Cf. Otto Abetz, *Das offene Problem: ein Ruckblick auf zwei Jahrzehnte Deutscher Frankreichpolitik, Cologne,* Greven Verlag, 1951, p. 199.

unity had already been taken. This was the famous Benelux Union. The decision in principle to establish it was taken in 1943 by the three governments (of Belgium, Holland and Luxembourg) in exile in London and the first conventions were signed later that year and during the course of 1944. The participants were careful, however, to proceed with caution and it was accordingly agreed that the establishment of a full customs union would be delayed until such time as it had proved possible broadly to co-ordinate the economic, financial and social policies of the three countries. Thus, customs duties were not to be finally abolished between the Belgo-Luxembourg Union and the Netherlands or a common external tariff introduced until 1948; while it was not until 1949 that plans were eventually put forward for the elimination of quantitative restrictions. In view of the novel nature of the Benelux experiment it is not surprising that its authors decided to proceed with caution – moreover the economies of the two countries were fundamentally different : Belgium being essentially industrial, and the Netherlands at that time primarily agricultural. The arrangement, if we may anticipate a few years, met with surprisingly few major obstacles; on the other hand its success was never to be spectacular.

The postwar scene

The growing popularity of the European idea was reflected in an astonishing proliferation of European bodies, movements and organizations, including, *inter alia,* the United Europe Movement, the European League for Economic Co-operation, the New International Groups, the Socialist Movement for the United States of Europe, the European Union of Federalists, the European Commons' Council, the European Parliamentary Union, the European Movement, the Vigilance Committee for Europe, and many others. In many cases their influence was extremely limited and their impact negligible, but their multiplication and general activity made them impossible to ignore. Most of those already in existence in 1947 were in that year grouped together in a Comite de Co-ordination des Movements en faveur de l'Europe Unie.

Into the midst of this intellectual ferment there was thrown on 19 September 1946 the stirring impulse of the speech made by Sir Winston Churchill to the students of Zurich University where he called for deep and permanent reconciliation between France and Germany as a first step to the resurgence of Europe. Within a year the downward swish of the iron curtain was to give yet another – and this time decisive – impulse to the move towards European co-operation. The main response of course was the negotiation, with and under constant pressure from the Americans whose main concern was to keep Western Europe free from the menace of Communism, of the Organization for European Economic Co-operation

(O.E.E.C.). Another effect – although one that was to prove of comparatively little effect in the longer term – was the signature at Dunkirk on 5 March 1947 of a treaty of friendship and alliance between Britain and France. Although the text of the treaty spoke of alliance against the danger of any possible future resurgence of German militarism, it was clear that this was a pact directed not against Germany but against Russia. Although the treaty was later extended first to include the three Benelux countries and subsequently to allow the inclusion of Germany, it was largely overtaken by events and the establishment in 1949 of the North Atlantic Treaty Organization (N.A.T.O.). But before turning to the achievements and the disappointments of the O.E.E.C., we must turn for a moment to The Hague Congress of 1948 which was in many ways the high-water mark of private individual enthusiasm for the cause of European unity, and which Churchill was to describe so aptly as 'this historic gathering'.

Among other economic ideas for European unity or co-operation of this period was the proposal for a Franco-Italian customs union. Accord was in fact reached on a broad trade agreement and in 1949 a draft treaty was prepared for signature . . . only to come to nothing as it became increasingly clear that the economies of the two countries were far from complementary and that their enforced juxtaposition would result in more difficulties than advantages, with little gain for either side. For a short while interest in the idea revived as the proposal to include the Benelux Union in the new preferential customs area was mooted under the colourful name of Fritalux . . . but then in 1949 came the definite establishment of the O.E.E.C. into which came also the Federal German Republic of Dr Adenauer.

The Hague Congress opened on 8 May 1948 in the magnificent Ridderzaal – the Hall of the Knights – in The Hague. It was attended by more than 800 people drawn from the political hierarchy and intellectual elite of the whole of Western Europe, including the Federal German Republic. Unfortunately, the Labour government in Britain, absorbed in its own internal difficulties, had little time for, or interest in, the Congress and sent no official delegation. The Conservatives, on the other hand, were powerfully represented and led by Sir Winston Churchill, whose prestige made him the dominant personality at the Congress. The Congress worked diligently and with an intoxicating and personally disinterested enthusiasm that is difficult to conceive – and probably impossible to recapture – today. A detailed account of the deliberations and work of the Congress is beyond the scope of this chapter, but it gave rise to the first of the postwar European Councils : the proudly heralded but subsequently largely impotent Council of Europe. One of the tragedies in Britain's postwar relationships with Europe was the lack of interest of successive British governments in the Council of Europe and their early decision to circumscribe its range of operations and responsibilities as strictly as possible. Whereas many of those who had attended The Hague Congress hoped and expected to see the Council of Europe develop into an embryo of a steadily-growing United States of Europe, successive British governments made it plain that while they saw in the Council of Europe a useful forum for consultation and discussion on a wide range of cultural and micro-economic matters, it should restrict its activities to those matters and not seek to promote the establishment of a customs area or political integration. The 1949 official Labour Party publication, *Feet on the ground: a study of Western Union,* left its readers in no doubt of the Party's – and therefore presumably also the government's – attitude : 'To create a completely free trading area inside Europe, the 16 countries would have to agree, first, on removing in addition to tariffs all other restrictions on mutual trade, second, on a uniform system of indirect taxation, third, on a uniform commercial policy towards countries outside the area, and lastly on a fixed rate of exchange so immutable that there would be no obstacle to the establishment of a single European currency. By doing so the individual governments would lose all control of their own financial, commercial and fiscal policies. However desirable such a situation might be in theory, it could only work if the whole area were either a free-enterprise Capitalist Utopia or a planned socialist society' – an excessively facile and obviously inaccurate judgment – 'At the moment either of these two alternative would be quite unacceptable to some of the countries concerned, though socialists will certainly work for the latter. But even if the whole area can be led to accept a single economy, a concrete Customs Union is likely to be the last and not the first step in the process.' Even Churchill, hailed so rapturously at The Hague Congress, had, on the basic question of Britain's position, broadly similar views : 'We are with Europe, not of Europe.'

The decision to deprive the Council of Europe of any real power or ability to initiate European policies was a bitter disappointment to a large number of delegates who attended the first all-European parliamentary assembly in Strasbourg in 1949. Spaak, elected chairman of the Consultative Assembly (as the parliamentary organ created under the Council of Europe machinery was called), was particularly bitter and resigned at the end of the session. The closing words of his address had both a melancholy and a faintly menacing tone. Clearly putting the blame for the hamstringing of the Council onto the United Kingdom, he said notably : 'I do not say : let us make Europe by aligning ourselves on England for to align ourselves upon England, whether a Conservative England or a Socialist England, at the present time, would mean giving up our objective –

19

so I say : let us proceed with courage and with a clear mind and, while recognizing the risks, make for our goal.'

The rise and fall of the O.E.E.C.

The origins of the O.E.E.C. are to be found in the famous speech made by George Marshall, at that time United States Secretary of State, in June 1947, in which he called for a recovery programme for the whole of Europe based on American aid and active European participation. The response was rapid and by the middle of April of the following year the Organization for European Economic Co-operation had been installed in Paris. The idea was mooted initially by the Americans, with strong support from the three Benelux countries, and Italy and France, of making the O.E.E.C. a Customs union. Britain, however, and the Scandinavian countries were against the idea because it included an excessive degree of abandonment of national sovereignty. The proposal was eventually referred to a 13-nation Customs Union study group where it was quietly forgotten. Despite Britain's known attitude this was not the last effort made to expand the role and responsibilities of the Organization. In June 1950, Signor Pella, Italian Minister of the Treasury, proposed on behalf of his government the creation of a European preference zone designed to reduce tariffs as much as possible; while co-operation between the member states was the underlying theme of the Italian proposal, it explicitly recognized that some abandonment of national sovereignty might prove inevitable – and on this rock the whole scheme foundered. Another proposal, with less pronounced supranational characteristics, was that of Mr Dirk Stikker, the then Dutch Minister of Foreign Affairs and subsequently Secretary-General of N.A.T.O., who suggested 'A Plan of action for European economic integration' which, inspired in part by the O.E.E.C. mode of operations, would have gradually eliminated tariffs between member states on one product after another. In 1952 it was the turn of the French to come forward with proposals for the expansion of the role of O.E.E.C. M. Pflimlim, Minister of Agriculture, persuaded his government to propose to its O.E.E.C partners that they should set up a European Agricultural Community – both the philosophy and the mechanics were based in part on the Coal and Steel Community, grouping the Benelux countries, France, Germany and Italy, which was then in process of being set up – to bring about a gradual product by product integration of the whole European agricultural market. A preparatory conference was convened in Paris in March 1952 but ran into strong opposition from Britain and the Scandinavian countries who saw in it a French manoeuvre to expand French agricultural production at the expense of Commonwealth and other extra-European cheap food producers. A second French proposal, dealing this time with matters of health and hygiene, was put

20

forward in December 1958 at the initiative of the French Minister of Health M. Paul Ribeyre, who envisaged the co-ordination and improvement of measures throughout Europe for health protection and hospital facilities. A draft treaty was prepared but like so many other earnest endeavours was eventually relegated to the dead hand of yet another working party.

A somewhat kinder fate befell the proposal put forward by a French Socialist-Republican deputy, M. Edouard Bonnefous, to the Council of Europe for a transport community. A special committee set up to look into the problem reported back to the Council in April 1951 but ran into strong German and Scandinavian opposition. Finally, the matter was resolved by the creation in 1953 and within the framework of the O.E.E.C. of a European Conference of Transport Ministers – which has continued to the present day.

In its heyday, from its creation in 1948 to its achievement in the establishment of the European Payments Union – which enabled all member states to cancel out intra-European debts – the Organization for European Economic Co-operation performed a valuable and, indeed, essential service. Although it failed to develop into a full customs union area and was far from fulfilling the hopes which many ardent Europeans had placed in it, the achievements of the O.E.E.C. were real and must not be underestimated. The establishment of the European Payments Union has already been mentioned. Perhaps its most signal service was the liberalization of intra-European trade by means of the progressive removal of quota restrictions and other barriers to the expansion of trade, though not of course the reduction of tariffs which was left to the G.A.T.T.; and it also set in motion a number of comparative studies of economic policies and in so doing made a notable contribution towards preparing the ground for more ambitious forms of international co-operation. But useful though its work undoubtedly was, by 1954, or even before, it had become obvious to continental observers that the O.E.E.C. had performed and fulfilled its main function and that its further utility was questionable. While the Organization was to linger on in its existing form for another five or six years, without the dynamism or the sense of purpose of its earlier years, it tended to stagnate : a state of affairs that was brought to an end only by its translation into the world-wide and no longer therefore strictly European Organization for Economic Co-operation and Development with American, Canadian and Japanese participation.

The reasons for the decline of the O.E.E.C. can largely be traced back to its limited competence – due in turn to the triumph of the original British conception of its purpose and longevity. The British view in the early postwar days was that while European co-operation was essential in the shorter-term and desirable in the longer-term, these aims were more than adequately met by the establishment of

21

the O.E.E.C. Once the European economy had been put back on its feet, the need for close economic collaboration and the sharing of available essential raw materials would become less compelling. Thus, while the freeing of trade by the removal of quotas and the reduction of tariffs was a goal much to be desired, negotiations to this end should be carried on in an economic world unrestricted by firm regional groupings, lashed together by the protective adhesive of a common external tariff. This, however, was not how others saw it. France, the Benelux countries, Italy – and after 1948 Western Germany also – felt an overriding need for security – military, economic and political – that was absent from O.E.E.C. or even N.A.T.O. France, moreover, as we have already seen, had an abiding fear of a resurgence of German power that was no less vivid in the late 1940s than in the 1920s. The problem of the relationship between France and Germany and of France's political strategy – designed to keep some form of control over German industrial and economic power and to bolster up her own sadly battered international prestige – was from 1950 onwards to dominate completely the European diplomatic and political scene. To this end the proposals made within the O.E.E.C. on agriculture, health and transport – even the support given to the American idea of a customs union – were no more than preliminary skirmishes. Economically, France, by 1950, had made an astonishing industrial recovery, thanks in no small way to the genius of M. Jean Monnet and a band of devoted followers at the Commissariat du Plan, but mainly of course to the determination of successive governments to direct their main energies to the restoration and modernization of the country's industrial base and infrastructure; politically, the power and influence of Britain had declined and so created an opportunity which the French were not slow to seize upon; strategically, they judged the time was right to strike a mutually advantageous bargain with the Federal German Republic. The stage was cleared and the scene set, in other words, for the Schuman Declaration of 9 May 1950.

CHAPTER 2

The issue of supranationality

The 1939–45 war shattered the old European order. Men were made acutely aware of the fact that world hegemony had passed into the hands of two new and extra-European superpowers with world-wide interests and responsibilities. The United States, although often referred to as the 'daughter of Europe', saw in the old and ailing Continent only one – even if at first the most important – of a number of areas throughout the world that needed her help and protection; while for the Soviet Union war-stricken Europe offered above all a tempting testing-ground for Communist propaganda. But although there existed in certain countries in Western Europe a feeling of lassitude and despondency, a readiness to admit that the nation states of Europe, for so long the world's power-houses for art and scientific advance and achievement, were played out, there were also braver spirits in many of the countries that had suffered most severely from the war who, having learnt from bitter personal experience, recognized the folly of continued division and strife and concluded that Europe's only hope of survival lay in close co-operation and, above all, in integration. No longer rejected as unattainable ideals formed in the imagination of political or philosophical romanticists, thinking people began to weigh carefully not only the advantages and difficulties but also the possible solutions.

The time was ripe for a bold and imaginative proposal. The Hague Congress of 1948 and the initial enthusiasm for the Council of Europe had shown that Europeans everywhere were ready to flock to any rallying cry that offered them at least some hope of achieving their dreams and ambitions.

American capital aid, provided through the channel of the Marshall Plan on a scale of extraordinary generosity, and backed by an enthusiastic and dynamic response from Western European countries made a decisive contribution towards the economic and political recovery and subsequent orientation of postwar Europe. So successfully did American aid oil the wheels of Europe's factories that by 1950 the scars of one of the cruellest wars known to history were already beginning to fade and the economists began – although hesitantly, for the veiled menace of another world war still loomed on the horizon – to speak hopefully in terms of steadily rising productivity, permanent full employment and rising standards of living. It was an extraordinary achievement. It has, of course, been argued that making good the loss of assets, buildings, railway stock and the like caused by the war would in any case have ensured plentiful employment in Western Europe, even without American assistance. In some cases this is probably true, although the process of recovery would undoubtedly have been much more painful and protracted than was actually the case. France, and possibly Germany, might conceivably in time have risen through their own efforts alone. But it is difficult to imagine how many of the smaller countries of Western or Southern Europe could have resolved their economic and financial difficulties unaided.

But American assistance was not enough. Generous though it was, men saw in it a degree of dependence upon an outside power that was both temporary (it was in fact deliberately designed to set Europe on its feet again as quickly as possible) and – although this was seldom said openly at the time – galling to their pride. Few Europeans wished to remain indefinitely a subsidized outpost of the United States. Moreover, it was clear to all that American aid was not completely disinterested. The Americans, mindful of their own security, wanted a free Europe that would be a bulwark against any westward expansion of Communism.

The clarion call, when it came, was unmistakable; the response immediate and positive. The historic day was 9 May 1950, when M. Robert Schuman, at that time Foreign Minister of France, made his famous proposals for the pooling of the coal and steel industries of France and Germany, as well as any other European countries that might wish to join – including the United Kingdom. At this stage, it is worth pausing for a moment to consider why such a proposal should have originated from France. Psychologically, the time was ripe for a gesture of this kind, but governments seldom if ever act out of impulses for the common good of a multitude of nations. There actions are, inevitably, determined primarily by their own national requirements. France suffered greatly from the effects of the war. Occupied and fought over, humiliated by her powerful German neighbour, France seemed to many outside observers in the late 1940s to be in a perilous situation. With limited resources of coal and her heavy industries small in comparison with those of the United Kingdom and Germany, the prospects for the future seemed, to say the least, unpromising. The position had been relatively satisfactory during the immediate postwar years as Germany was to all intents and purposes governed by the Allies and the German coal and steel industries were subject to their control. By the end of

24

the decade, however, the end of Allied Military Government was in sight. With it there came to many French eyes a vision of German heavy industry, which was making an impressive comeback, once again moving into a dominant position in continental Europe. It is perhaps all too easy for us in Britain today, in an age of abundant energy supplies and with a large and newly-discovered natural gas-field on our own doorstep, to underestimate the basic economic and political importance at this time of the coal and steel industries. In 1948 these two industries still represented the major sources of power and of military potential. To the French, then, it was a matter of vital concern that they should be able to continue to retain some form of indirect control over the development of the German coal and steel industries – a function that had been performed up to that time by the International Authority for the Ruhr.

The International Authority for the Ruhr

The Allied Powers had agreed during the war that it would be essential once peace had been restored to maintain a considerable measure of control over the future development of German industry by means of some form of supervisory agency. Opinions varied, however, on the way in which this was to be done. The French, for example, were protagonists of a complete dismemberment of Germany, with the Saar, the Rhineland and the Ruhr all being detached from the remainder of the country, and with the Ruhr in particular being placed under permanent international control. The Big Three at their conference in Potsdam (in which France was not invited to participate) compromised by deciding to place a ceiling on German steelmaking capacity and drawing up a programme of industrial dismantlement. In the event, however, both the limits imposed on steelmaking capacity and the dismantling programme were several times revised and the former in particular was always well in excess of the actual levels of output. The attempt to keep postwar German industrial production – at least in terms of tonnage produced – in some form of straitjacket was finally abandoned with the establishment of the European Coal and Steel Community.

The British attitude during the immediate postwar years was broadly in favour of some form of international control over the Ruhr coupled with the hope that out of the discernible political trend in Germany there would evolve a movement favourable to public ownership of the coal and steel industries. A statement by Ernest Bevin made in October 1946 was particularly illustrative : '. . . we have also to consider the ownership of the basic German industries. These industries were previously in the hands of magnates who were closely allied to the German military machine, who financed Hitler, and who in two wars, were part and parcel of Germany's aggressive policy. We have no desire to see those gentlemen or their like return to a position which they have abused with such tragic results. As an interim measure, we have taken over the possession and control of the coal industries . . . we shall shortly take similar action in the case of the heavy chemical industry and the mechanical engineering industry. Our intention is that these industries should be owned and controlled in future by the public. The exact form of this public ownership and control is now being worked out. They should be owned and worked by the German people, but subject to such international control that they cannot again be a threat to our neighbours.' By 1948, however, thinking in both Britain and the United States had moved away from the internationalization of the Ruhr and inclined towards some form of international control – but with German participation – over the distribution of coal and the production of armaments. The definitive proposals for the establishment of an International Authority for the Ruhr were put forward in June 1948; the terms of reference agreed in April 1949; and the Authority established on 29 December 1949. Included on the representation in the I.A.R. were the three Benelux countries and France, the United Kingdom and West Germany. The main functions of the new body were described as the determination of the quantities of Ruhr coal and coke that should be made available to other countries; the drawing-up of supervisory measures to ensure the prevention of any rearmament on the part of Germany; and the prevention of discriminatory price and trading practices. The setting up of the I.A.R. was unpopular in Germany where Dr Adenauer stated in 1948 that it marked a severe derogation from German national sovereignty; he also doubted whether any similar organization would in fact be set up – as envisaged in the Ruhr Statute – in France and Belgium so as to enable the coal industries in all three countries to be merged in due course into one unified complex.

Closely interwoven with the primarily economic objective of maintaining indirect control over the development of German heavy industry was France's political conception of her own future role in Europe and the world. The history of the genesis, formation and development of the European Communities is, as we shall have occasion to see again and again in the following pages, inextricable from French postwar policy and objectives. France, no less than Europe, and probably earlier than the rest of Europe, had recognized the changed circumstances of the postwar world and sought to determine her own position. This role, she apparently decided, was one of leader of a small band of countries which, while forming a tight economic bloc, would also provide some kind of tutelage for German heavy industry and be prepared to accept French political and cultural leadership. In order, however, to achieve this objective, it was essential that any community of countries that was to be so formed should turn naturally to France. This, in turn, meant the exclusion of the United Kingdom.

The position of the United Kingdom

The task of the French government was made easier by the postwar mood in Britain. Both government and people tended to feel that Britain had played her part, more than honourably, in the 1939–45 war. Unlike the countries of the near Continent, Britain had not been defeated, nor had she been invaded. She had emerged victorious from a titanic struggle, during which in the words of her leader the British people had lived through their 'finest hour'. By her own dogged resistance, and together with her American and Russian allies, she had successfully overcome the peril of National Socialism. Now, the fighting was over and the thoughts of all could turn again to peace. European unity (in the looser sense of the phrase) constituted, it was freely said, a highly desirable objective. But a useful instrument for this had, or so it seemed, already been devised in the O.E.E.C. which, it was felt, was more than adequate to deal with any difficulties that might arise in the course of European co-operation. The French, for their part, resented the leading British role in O.E.E.C. But this was a minor consideration. As we have already seen, in their view – and indeed in that of most continental countries – the O.E.E.C. had by this time largely served its purpose of putting Europe back on its feet; nor did the O.E.E.C. provide any definite framework for supervision of German industrial resurgence. Besides, the main tasks now were the political revival of France, the formation of an acceptable European grouping under French leadership, the exclusion of Britain from any such group and the retention of some form of control or supervision over the German coal and steel industries. Important therefore though the economic issues at stake undoubtedly were, the real stakes in the French government's diplomatic game were undisguisedly political. Adenauer in his *Memoirs* makes no bones about it : 'In his personal letter to me (which came with the official memorandum which later became known as the Schuman Plan), Schuman wrote that the purpose of his proposal was not economic, but eminently political. In France there was a fear that once Germany had recovered, she would attack France. He could imagine that corresponding fears might be present in Germany. Rearmament always showed first in an increased production of coal, iron and steel. If an organization such as he was proposing were to be set up, it would enable each country to detect the first signs of rearmament, and would have an extraordinarily calming effect in France.' While speaking about the Bundestag debate on 13 June 1950 on the question of the Federal Republic's accession to the Council of Europe Adenauer declared : 'I was in full agreement with the French government that the signi-

27

ficance of the Schuman proposal was first and foremost political and not economic. A careful perusal of the declarations by the French cabinet showed that the intention of this Plan, to be the beginning of a federal structure in Europe, was mentioned in several places. The political importance had been underlined as strongly as possible and I could confirm from personal conversations with Monnet that the political element carried the most weight in the balance of French considerations.'[1]

The French government consequently let it be known, a few days after the Schuman Declaration of 9 May 1950, that they considered that all countries which agreed to take part in the discussions with a view of establishing a community for coal and steel should commit themselves, in advance, to the principle of placing these two key industries under a common supranational authority. It is over-whelmingly probable that the proposals were deliberately couched in this way because the French government considered that by so doing they would make them unacceptable to the British government which could not, at that time, envisage yielding its sovereignty over two basic national (and recently nationalized) industries.[2] This attitude was revealed with particular clarity at a meeting between Chancellor Adenauer and Mr Morrison, at that time the British Foreign Secretary, in Bonn in May 1951. Morrison apparently told Adenauer that : 'In England the people elected the parliament. From it derived the government and the government was responsible to parliament and in the final resort to the people. The position of parliament was stronger here than in other European countries.

[1]*Cf.* Adenauer, K., *Memoirs 1945–53*, London, Weidenfeld and Nicolson, 1966, pp. 257 and 265.

[2]*Cf.* Huizinga, J. H., *Confessions of a European in England*, London, Heinemann, 1958, p. 177: 'But what did Britain do? Challenged to put her European cards on the table at last, she attempted to hide them by refusing to say either yes or no, by hedging and quibbling and indulging in every kind of equivocation and prevarication. . . . And so we got the sorry spectacle, soon becoming little less than farcical, of British statesmen and diplomats, dutifully echoed by even the best organs of the British Press, endlessly and plaintively repeating that they were full of sympathy for M. Schuman's bold plan, but that they really had to have more details before they could decide, and that they should not be asked to "take a leap in the dark" or "to sign on the dotted line" or to "commit themselves in advance to surrender certain fundamental rights".

'As if anyone had asked them to do so; as if there were any details, and as if there were any plan even, beyond the proposal to try and see whether those of us who accepted the federal principle could work out a first instalment of a federal organization. Was one really to believe that the clever men who worked in Whitehall and Fleet Street didn't know all that perfectly well? Was it not transparently clear that these men, who ceaselessly and pathetically pleaded their "lack of information" for their inability to accept or reject the French proposal, knew only too well what it meant and for that reason would not touch it with a barge-pole? Could one possibly escape the conclusion that their refusal to take a "leap in the dark" was in reality due to the fact that they knew it to be a leap into the light of dawn, the dawn of a new federal Europe which they felt in their bones they could never join?'

Morrison said that it was very hard for the British to think of transferring the prerogatives of parliament which are superior to everything else – and that is the decisive thing in Great Britain – to a kind of supranational organization. That was a lump the British would find it very hard to swallow. They would always be ready to offer their co-operation *ad hoc*. This was not only a possibility, it was something on which one could count. Nonetheless, Europe must remember – and this was no argument, it was simply a fact – that Britain was not prepared and in the future would find it very difficult to be prepared to subordinate herself to a supranational organization that might in some way be above the British government and give it some kind of orders. He mentioned the Schuman Plan which would be studied quite fairly and open-mindedly and without prejudice. The British would, if it was necessary or justified, gladly give their help in some way. They were always prepared to do this, but it was very difficult to allow the supremacy of parliament to be depleted in any way.'[3]

The Schuman Plan

The Schuman Declaration was a political master-stroke of genius. At one stroke it paved the way for all the major French objectives in Europe. At the same time its superficially ready acceptance of the notion of supranationality enabled it to catch the favourable winds of European idealism and romanticism. So successful indeed was it that the basic underlying aims of French policy, well camouflaged beneath many layers of carefully-worded, high-sounding and stirring objectives, largely escaped comment or discussion. The reasons for this were no doubt many and varied. There was, first and foremost, the exceptionally skilful French presentation; there was also a readiness on the part of many people to believe in the European ideals of the French government; more likely perhaps, however, was the belief that the French were not powerful enough to play a permanently dominant role or that their proposal would soon run into difficulties so that their whole initiative would grind to a halt as the whole thing was quite impracticable anyway. In fact, those holding the latter view were almost proved right. By February 1951, the Schuman Plan negotiations (which had begun in Paris in June 1950) were in danger of becoming completely bogged down, and it was only as a result of the strenuous efforts made by the Americans, who were determined to try and make the negotiations succeed for political reasons, that a possible collapse was averted. Agreement was finally reached on 19 March 1951, when the leaders of the six national delegations concerned in the negotiations (Belgium, France, Germany, Holland, Italy and Luxembourg) initialled the treaty establishing a Coal and Steel Community on behalf of their respec-

[3]Adenauer, *op. cit.*, p. 389.

tive governments and left only a number of political and institutional points to be settled at a subsequent meeting of the six Ministers of Foreign Affairs. The Ministers actually met some weeks later and the treaty was formally signed in Paris on 18 March 1951.

It remains only, before turning to an examination of the first of the European treaties – the signature of which marked no less significant a date in postwar European history than the Schuman Declaration itself – to consider why the five other countries besides France should have consented to join with her in a venture that was largely French inspired and that was also largely conditioned to French thinking and French influence. It is, for instance, sometimes stated that the other Five too often allow themselves to be dominated by the French. This is an extremely dangerous and misleading argument. The Six are in the Community because every single one of them expects to derive some benefit from their union. It is true that in the early days of the European Communities much more was taken on trust and risks were more readily accepted, by some of the participants at least, for the sake of achieving the overriding purpose of common views and common ideals. Today much of the idealism has gone and hard national bargaining has become the order of the day. But this development has been largely inevitable as the conflict of national interests has shifted progressively to more and more delicate fields.

For Germany, the most populous and, economically, by far the country with the most formidable potential among the Six, the treaty represented a particularly satisfactory deal. Germany, in 1950, was still very far from having recovered full national sovereignty. The war had ended only five years before; the International Authority for the Ruhr was in full swing and discussions about the permanent tutelage of German heavy industry were by no means purely academic. In his *Memoirs,* Adenauer said of the Schuman Plan that while it was of very great economic importance, 'its underlying ideals were of even greater significance. A community of European countries was to be created on the basis of complete equality, the only basis of a genuine community. This fundamental idea was of the greatest consequence for the political life of Germany, for France, Europe and the world.

'I was convinced that the signing of the Schuman Plan would have effects in the most diverse political fields. On the last day of the negotiations the underlying ideal of the Schuman Plan had made possible a joint decision of the six participating countries which was of the greatest political importance. In a joint resolution signed by all six countries it was agreed that the idea underlying the Schuman Plan was to be promoted by these countries with all their strength in other fields as well, by frequent consultations and personal contact. The word "consultations" was very important. It means something

30

quite specific in international law and in diplomatic language. For us Germans this promise of more frequent consultations among the Schuman Plan countries on important political matters was a great political achievement.'[4]

Coming as it did six years after the end of World War Two, this was no idle boast. One of the earliest political results was the termination on 19 October 1951 of the International Authority for the Ruhr and agreement by Britain, France and the United States to release the Federal Republic from all limitations on steel production. While these concessions were made to ensure that the bill setting up the European Coal and Steel Community would get through the German Bundestag (where Dr Schumacher, Chairman of the German opposition Social Democratic Party, in a powerful attack upon Chancellor Adenauer's pro-French policies had stated that : 'the Schuman Plan was putting the economic strength of Germany . . . in the service of French diplomacy'),[5] it is also a tribute to the skill and tenacity with which Adenauer succeeded in securing exceptionally favourable terms for his country. Illustrative of his skill in the deployment of arguments is his account in his *Memoirs* on the decartelization of German industry : 'Germany had assumed that with the signature of the Treaty of Paris Law No. 27 (relating to the deconcentration of German industry) of the Allied High Commission would, as in fact had been agreed, not be executed as rigidly as originally conceived.' Yet now execution was being described as one of the prerequisites of the creation of E.C.S.C. If in effect it was a precondition, then it looked as if the S.P.D. were right that the Schuman Plan meant the deconcentration and, *ipso facto,* the weakening of the German economy. There was further support for this interpretation as a result of an article which appeared in *Le Monde* at the end of September 1951 and which stated that 'the Schuman Plan was adequately securing the West German economic potential for France and for Western Europe. This was much more important than securing the German human potential and there was therefore no difficulty in envisaging a possible neutralization of Germany.' Adenauer's reaction was typical : 'I asked myself how this could be compatible with the higher aims of European integration?' In short, no longer simply an occupied power, Germany, as a founder member of the new European Community, could look forward with confidence to playing a major role in the comity of European nations. It is worth noting at this stage that Adenauer, conscious of the need to allay French fears about Germany, had repeatedly gone out of his way to emphasize the importance he attached to good Franco-German relations and had made it plain that he would welcome a West European grouping which would include both

[4]*Ibid*, pp. 339-40.
[5]*Ibid*, p. 375.

France and Germany. Thus, in an interview with a correspondent from *Die Zeit* on 3 September 1949 he said : 'I am resolved to make German-French relations a cardinal point of my policy . . . I think I can say that reconciliation with France is more popular today in Germany than at any moment before 1945'; while in another newspaper interview, this time with an American journalist, in March 1950, Adenauer outlined his ideas for a union between Germany and France, to which Britain, Italy and the three Benelux countries could also adhere if they so wished.

For the other countries in the Community, *i.e.,* Italy and the three Benelux countries, the immediate benefits of membership of the Coal and Steel Community were both economic and political. The Benelux countries (among whom Holland had suffered particularly severely from the effects of the war) saw in the supranational powers enshrined in the Treaty of Paris a means of entering a new community of nations without thereby becoming subject to the policies and objectives of the larger member states. For these three small countries security requirements – both militarily and economically – played a big part in their decision to support to the full the movement towards European integration. It was this same consideration which made them the most ardent champions of supranationality and for action by means of a common Community accord arrived at in the interest of all six members. In the case of Italy, a not dissimilar feeling of political isolation played an important role in the crystallization of Italian policy. Italy emerged from the war not unlike a man dazed with shock, hesitant and uncertain as to which direction he should take. It is a measure of the political achievement of Signor de Gasperi, who was Prime Minister of Italy from 1945 to 1953, that he both gave his country a political faith and pledged Italy firmly to the European cause and the concept of supranationality.

But if Italy and the Benelux countries found in the common market for coal and steel a political significance – it would not be too dramatic an exaggeration to call it a European act of faith – they derived from it also some solid economic benefits. Thus, the Belgians secured substantial assistance from their fellow member states in the Community in order to modernize their coal industry and to enable it to meet the competition from the other coal-producing countries. This took the form of a special perequation or equalization fund which was financed by a levy on the (at that time) low cost German and Dutch coalfields. Direct government assistance in the forms of subsidies was also authorized. Furthermore, it was agreed that Belgian coal production should not be permitted to fall by more than 3 per cent annually in comparison with the output of the Community as a whole. Special measures were also agreed to help the small and very high cost Italian coalmining industry. But special measures of this kind were not confined to the smaller countries of the Community. The French – who feared the competition from the cheaper German coalmines – secured the inclusion among the special provisions annexed to the treaty of a complicated clause stating that French coal production would not be allowed to fall by more than one million tons beyond a reduction proportionate to a general fall in coal output in the Community. Broadly speaking, however, all countries envisaged at that time a rapidly rising demand for coal and steel and saw therefore in the provisions of the treaty a valuable guarantee of permanent access to German production of both these basic materials.

The European Coal and Steel Community

We must now turn to the Treaty of Paris itself – in many ways the testing-bench for the Treaties of Rome which were to establish, some years later, the European Economic Community and the European Atomic Energy Community, the former now generally and more popularly known as the General Common Market.

Economically, the Treaty of Paris was designed to create a single common market for coal and steel, within which coal and steel produced in the Community would be able to circulate freely. In this way coal and steel were to be made cheaper to consumers generally in the Community with beneficial consequences for the economy as a whole.

The fundamental aims and philosophy of the Treaty of Paris are set out in Articles 2 to 4 of the treaty and of these Articles 2 and 3 spell out more succinctly than any commentary the objectives which the six governments set themselves when they shaped the Treaty of Paris :

ARTICLE 2

The mission of the European Coal and Steel Community is to contribute to the expansion of the economy, the development of employment and the improvement in the standard of living in the participating countries through the creation, in harmony with the general economy of the member states, of a common market as defined in Article 4.

The Community must progressively establish conditions which will in themselves assure the most rational distribution of production and the highest possible level of productivity, while safeguarding the continuity of employment and avoiding the creation of fundamental and persistent disturbances in the economies of the member states.

ARTICLE 3

Within the framework of their respective powers and responsibilities and in the common interest, the institutions of the Community shall :

33

(a) ensure that the common market is regularly supplied, while taking into account the needs of third countries;

(b) ensure to all consumers in comparable positions within the common market equal access to the sources of production;

(c) seek the establishment of the lowest possible prices without involving any compensating rise either in the prices charged by the same enterprises in other transactions or in the price-level as a whole in another period, while at the same time permitting necessary amortization and providing the possibility of normal returns on invested capital;

(d) ensure that conditions are maintained which will encourage enterprises to expand and improve their ability to produce and promote a policy of rational development of natural resources, while avoiding undue exhaustion of such resources;

(e) promote the improvement of the living and working conditions of the labour force in each of the industries under its jurisdiction so as to harmonize those conditions in an upward direction;

(f) foster the development of international trade and ensure that equitable limits are observed in prices charged in foreign markets;

(g) promote the regular expansion and the modernization of production as well as the improvement of quality, under conditions which preclude any protection against competing industries except where justified by illegitimate action on the part of such industries in their favour.

The provisions of the Treaty of Paris can be divided into six main sections :

(i) the objectives of the Treaty (Articles 1 to 6);

(ii) the institutions of the Community and the division of power between them (Articles 7 to 45);

(iii) economic and social provisions (Articles 46 to 49);

(iv) transport (Article 70);

(v) commercial policy (Articles 71 to 75);

(vi) general provisions (Articles 76 to 100) and the Convention containing the transitional provisions.

The treaty, which was concluded for a period of 50 years, gave the Community a full juridical personality. Although based on the conception of a single market in coal and steel, it provided for a transitional period of five to seven years in order to allow for its gradual progressive establishment and to avoid any serious economic or social disturbances. Its signature and acceptance by all six governments committed them to the abolition of tariff barriers, subsidies and other special arrangements; and the elimination of discrimination in transport and general quantitative restrictions. For the coal and steel producers, it meant the compulsory abolition within the Community of discriminatory or dual pricing practices, restrictive practices, cartel agreements and associations, and unfair competition generally. Both governments and producers remained free, however, to determine their own policies towards third countries (although in steel the Community later moved towards a harmonized common external tariff).

1448233

The Treaty cartel provisions

The treaty therefore gave the High Authority (the executive body created to administer the provisions of the treaty) important and, on paper, far-reaching powers to prevent monopolistic practices in the coal and steel industries. Any combined action by firms or associations which tended, directly or indirectly, to hamper, restrain or falsify the normal play of competition and, in particular, to fix prices and to limit or control production, or share markets, was prohibited. Subject to this comprehensive interdict, the High Authority could approve particular arrangements provided it is satisfied that these arrangements would be consistent with the objectives of the treaty. Similarly, the High Authority was empowered to authorize the amalgamation of firms under any conditions it considered suitable, so long as these amalgamations did not produce entities so large that they could control production, hamper effective competition, or secure for the amalgamated companies or organizations a privileged position in the market. In practice, as we shall see later, Community thinking on cartels or, more particularly, the size and extent of industrial mergers and structure, has undergone a major transformation since the early postwar days.

The E.C.S.C. Treaty and wages

The Treaty of Paris did not give the High Authority the right to interfere with methods of fixing wages and social benefits in the member states, but the High Authority was and remains empowered to combat competitive wage cutting or the payment of abnormally low wages in relation to the general wage level in the relevant area of the Community. Nevertheless, although the High Authority's powers in connection with wages are limited, it can undertake studies and investigations which have on occasions had the effect of improving wage conditions in the Community. For example, in October 1955 the High Authority published the first results of a comparison of real wages among the Community workers. Further comparative studies of this nature have been made and published since at regular intervals. The High Authority has freely stated that the purpose of these examinations is to help in achieving the main labour objective of the treaty which is 'to promote the improvement of the living and working conditions of the labour force in each of the industries within the Community so as to harmonize these conditions in an upward direction.'

It might be useful at this stage to consider for a moment one or two practical results of the application of the rules and regulations of the Treaty of Paris.

Prices: Before 1952 most producers quoted one or more prices for a given quantity of coal or steel to consumers in their own country and higher or lower prices to consumers in other countries according to whether their products were in short or plentiful supply. Broadly the same pattern, in fact, as was followed by coal and steel producers in other countries. After the signature of the Treaty of Paris this was no longer permissible. Community producers were bound to quote the same price to all consumers for comparable transactions throughout the entire Community area. It is only fair to comment, however, that while the treaty rules in this respect were closely adhered to as long as business and trade remained good, in today's difficult market conditions Community producers' price-lists are often little more than notional; the non-discrimination rule is being flagrantly disregarded and widespread rebating is practised in order to obtain business.

Transport: Another interesting example of the Community in action is provided by the transport rules. Prior to the signature of the Treaty of Paris, a French steel producer buying German coal paid the German rail rate per ton for the transportation of his coal from the German mine to the French border and the French rate per ton for that part of the journey which took place in France. After the treaty came into force national frontiers disappeared and a single through Community rate applied. Since the cost per kilometre in both countries decreased with the distance over which the coal or steel was transported, the application of a single through rate greatly reduced transport costs to the consumer. Here again, however, it is worth pointing out that whereas the treaty rules specifically require the publication of transport rates and conditions, there was a prolonged period of controversy between the High Authority and some of the member governments about the degree of publication required by this Article, which was not finally resolved until a ruling on this issue was given by the Court of Justice of the European Communities in July 1962. This called for the full publication of all transport rates. In fact, even today although rail rates are now published in all six countries, road haulage rates in the Benelux countries are only published on an *a posteriori* basis and no measures have yet been taken in France or Germany. Moreover, there is as yet no publication whatsoever in any one of the Community countries of inland waterway or sea freight rates.

The Institutions of the Coal and Steel Community

In order to ensure that the rules of the treaty are correctly applied and that its objectives should be attained, the Founding Fathers of the Treaty of Paris envisaged the creation of four Institutions : a High Authority, a Council of Ministers, a Common Parliamentary Assembly and a Court of Justice.

The High Authority is the executive organ, the intended power-house of the Coal and Steel Community. It consists of nine members, drawn from the six states of the Community, originally two each from France, Germany and Italy, and one each from the three Benelux countries. Each member was appointed for a term of six years. Being in theory at least a body with supranational powers the High Authority has the right to bypass governments and to deal directly with the various national coal and steel enterprises of the Community. As originally conceived, it was in many ways intended to be like a Ministry of Heavy Industry for the whole of the Community. Within its field of competence the High Authority was empowered to make decisions, which are binding on governments and producers in all respects; recommendations, which are also binding but leave the ways in which the objectives in question are to be achieved to the discretion of the governments or producers; and opinions, which are of a purely advisory nature. The High Authority also has the right – which it has occasionally exercised – to fine enterprises contravening the provisions of the treaty. Attached to the High Authority – and providing a permanent forum for the coal and steel enterprises – is a Consultative Committee, consisting of 51 representatives of producers, trade unions and consumers in equal numbers. The Consultative Committee's main function is to consider and to give its opinion on matters in which the High Authority has consulted it. Such consultation is, in a number of cases, obligatory.

The first President of the High Authority, M. Jean Monnet, was appointed together with his colleagues on 7 August 1952. The High Authority took up its functions in Luxembourg three days later.

The treaty also provided for a Council of Ministers, consisting of Ministers from the six member states of the Community whose function, according to the treaty, was to assist the High Authority in carrying out its task. It was, of course, clear right from the start that it was here that the seeds of potential conflict had been well and truly sown. The men who sat in the Council of Ministers could not escape the fact that they remained also national Ministers, responsible to national parliaments and national electorates. As long as national and Community policies ran comfortably in harness together, the High Authority continued to act as the dynamic charioteer of the young European team. But once the conflicting interests of the Six began to emerge more clearly and the six horses began to pull in directions that were sometimes widely divergent, the High Authority's lack of power and experience became only too clear. But this was not yet evident in the confident champagne days of 1952 when the ink of the treaty was scarcely dry and supranationality – in the sense that it was the High Authority and no longer the national governments who were responsible for matters relating to coal and steel – was writ in letters of gold across the European sky.

INSTITUTIONS OF THE EUROPEAN COAL AND STEEL COMMUNITY
in 1952

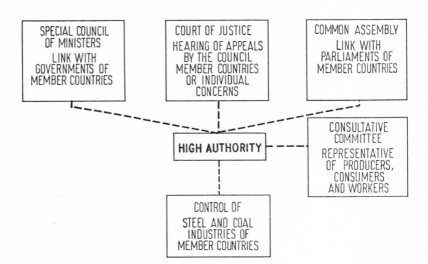

There remain the other Institutions. The Common Parliamentary Assembly was envisaged as a kind of embryo European Parliament – a name which it subsequently adopted – and consisted of 78 delegates from the Parliaments of six countries. They were not, therefore, elected directly by voters in the six countries to a central parliament. The Common Assembly's main function was originally to receive and debate the High Authority's annual reports and to hold extraordinary sessions if any special problems arose. Its only really effective power, however, lay in its right to pass a vote of censure on the members of the High Authority and, by so doing, compelling them to resign in a body. In fact this power has never been exercised. It has often been said, rather disparagingly, that the European Parliament is little better than an old women's talking shop. But this, while admittedly based to some extent on the hard factual evidence of the European Parliament's performance, would be to disregard completely the influence it can and does command throughout the Community, where its debates are widely and attentively reported and examined. The last of the four Institutions, the Court of Justice, was given the function of adjudicating on issues arising out of the application and interpretation of the Treaty of Paris – in which matters its judgments have the force of law in all six countries.

Although the purpose of the four Institutions was, and remains, to administer the Treaty of Paris they were envisaged, and indeed represent, something far more vital and dynamic. Together they constituted in the minds of the Founding Fathers a first framework of the United States of Europe with its embryo executive, legislative and judicial organs (see diagram on page 38). Five years later, in 1957, during the negotiations which preceded the establishment of the General Common Market, two new executive bodies similar in many ways to the High Authority, as well as two further Councils of Ministers parallel to that established to 'assist' and advise the High Authority, were set up, while the functions of the European Parliament and the Court of Justice were extended to enable them to cover equally matters arising from the application of the Treaties of Rome.

Accession of new members

In view of later developments it is worth recording that Article 98 of the treaty provided for the accession of new members: 'Any European state may request to accede to this treaty. It shall address its request to the Council, which shall act by unanimous vote after obtaining the opinion of the High Authority. Also by a unanimous vote the Council may fix the terms of accession, which shall become effective on the day the instrument of accession is received by the government acting as depository of the treaty.'

The issue of supranationality

Many of the points we have considered in these pages marked new and vital departures in European affairs, but the whole of the European edifice so carefully and often so lovingly erected under the framework of the Treaty of Paris was basically dedicated to one overriding objective – the acceptance by all six member states of the principle of supranationality. Supranationality was intended to be the real pulsating blood-stream of the Community and was most vividly and dramatically portrayed in Articles 58, 59 and 74 of the treaty, which laid fairly and squarely upon the High Authority the responsibility of formulating and putting before the Council of Ministers for their approval proposals designed to deal with any severe surpluses and shortages of coal or steel. In other words, instead of independent action being taken by the six governments, it became the responsibility of the High Authority to determine the most suitable means of dealing with a dangerous or potentially critical situation. This clearly was the fated and crucial testing-ground, just as the High Authority and the Council of Ministers were the predestined protagonists.

While the stage was set and the actors chosen for their parts as early as 1952, the play opened gently with generally favourable economic conditions and the great climax to the supranational drama came to a head only in 1959.

The halcyon years of the Coal and Steel Community

Between 1952 and the end of 1957 the Community enjoyed a long period of boom conditions. At a time of rapid expansion and high demand, and when there was little to fear from external competition, the Community's industries were in a strong position. In this way the conditions with which the Community had to deal lent themselves without insuperable difficulty to the introduction of the new mechanisms and rules. These circumstances, and the political will of the member states in these early years to make the Community work, were favourable to the establishment of the common market for coal and steel, which was thus brought into force relatively smoothly and without recourse even to some of the transitional safeguard measures that had been provided in order to mitigate the immediate impact of the liberalization of trade. Indeed, by 1956, the Community felt that it could justifiably claim that it had fulfilled one of the major objectives which had been assigned to it by the six governments by showing that European economic integration on a new basis of common interest and common institutions was a practical proposition, thereby opening the way politically for the negotiations which resulted in the following year in the signature of the Treaties of Rome and the establishment of the General Common Market and Euratom.

By the late fifties, however, there had come about a combination of a large number of factors which profoundly influenced the nature and operation of the Community. Prime among these was the resurgence of a more militant French nationalism, fanned by the accession to power of General de Gaulle, and manifesting itself by strong criticism of supranationality and the principle (enshrined in the General Common Market Treaty) of the majority vote. The 1958–59 Community coal crisis, brought about by a slackening in the rate of economic activity, the greatly increased availability of oil and the massive coal import programmes, principally from the United States, coincided with these political developments.

The Community coal crisis

The slackening in the rate of industrial activity in Western Europe which began in 1957 and continued until 1959, together with a succession of mild winters and the growing popularity and availability of oil, brought about a complete change in the position of the European coal-mining industry. During the early postwar years, the coal industries had been working under instructions to produce every available ton of coal in order to enable the rapidly mounting energy requirements of Western Europe to be met. From 1958 onwards there was a significant change in emphasis from maximum production to a level of output which would facilitate the production of those types of coal most suited to the changed market conditions.

But the disequilibrium in the energy market of Western Europe and the rise in pithead stocks that resulted from it cannot be entirely attributed to the fall in demand for coal and its replacement by other fuels. The problem had been vastly aggravated by the rise in coal imports from outside Western Europe, notably from the United States. The trend towards increased coal imports from outside the European area dated back to the spring of 1956, when the level of economic activity was particularly high and European coal production was insufficient to meet the demands placed upon it. At that time consumers in many countries increased their import orders from the United States in order to cover their requirements for current consumption and to build up their stocks. At the end of 1956 the political uncertainties associated with the Suez crisis led to a further sharp increase in purchases of American coal. The dearth of shipping on transatlantic traffic caused a spectacular rise of over 100% in freight rates, with the result that importers, anxious to ensure steady and regular supplies, decided in many cases to conclude long-term contracts for purchases of American coal and sought to make charter arrangements considered to be favourable at the time. Once the Suez crisis had passed there was a radical change in the freight markets with freights calling to well below their pre-Suez levels. This in turn led to a further round of speculative buying of American coal. As a result, by the end of 1959, pithead stocks of coal in Western Europe had reached the unprecedented total of some 70 million tons (equal to about one-third of the United Kingdom's total annual production at that time), and miners in all four Community countries were put on short-time working.

Supranationality put to the test

The High Authority at first attempted to deal with the worsening coal market situation by negotiating with the governments, producers and other interested parties in order to try to secure satisfactory remedial measures. It soon found, however, that its proposals were being consistently whittled down, obstructed or even flatly rejected by the Council of Ministers. Thus the Council failed to reach agreement on a Community system of financing stocks and on Community control of imports, and plainly stated that there could be no question

41

of limiting the sovereignty of member states in matters of commercial policy towards third countries. These were already ominous signs. The High Authority, however, decided to stick to its guns and to bring the question of supranational powers into the open for a decision one way or the other.

The High Authority's proposals, which were based on Articles 58 and 74 of the Treaty of Paris, provided for the declaration of a 'manifest state of crisis' in the coal industry and for the adoption of a Community plan to deal with it by the establishment under Community supervision of production quotas and import restrictions for the Community as a whole. After much discussion and negotiation with the governments, during which the High Authority twice agreed to modify its plan to meet the objections and stated requirements of individual member states but still could not gain acceptance of its proposals, the High Authority insisted on a vote. The result was the formal rejection by the Council of Ministers of the High Authority's proposals. France, Germany and Italy voted against, while the three Benelux countries voted in favour of the High Authority's proposals. The date was 14 May 1959 – almost nine years to the day since the Schuman Declaration.

Tactically, the High Authority's decision was probably the wrong one. The 1959 Community coal crisis was essentially a Belgian problem. The situation in the other coal-producing countries of the Community, although extremely difficult, could scarcely be described as critical. Above all, the attitude adopted by the Council of Ministers during earlier discussions had made it abundantly clear that they were not in a mood to accept supranational decisions or measures from the High Authority. At the same time it must be conceded that the High Authority's tame acceptance of the views of some of the Ministers – without even putting the principle of supranationality to the test – would have greatly injured its prestige. The fact remains, however, that the ground chosen by the High Authority for the first, last and decisive battle over supranationality – within the context of the Treaty of Paris – was insufficiently reconnoitred and was ill-chosen.

The High Authority's defeat marked a formal turning-point in the Community's development. Although France and Germany were acting within their treaty rights, their rejection of the High Authority's proposals was motivated mainly by political considerations and clearly constituted a refusal to accept the principle of supranational powers written into the E.C.S.C. Treaty. In opposing the proposals of the French Minister, supported by his German colleague, bluntly stated that he could not approve a scheme which would give the High Authority powers of control over the Community's coal industries; individual national governments would be responsible for the political and social consequences of the High

Authority's measures and they could not therefore allow control to pass out of their hands.

It was therefore the economic problems of the coal crisis that raised for the first time in an inescapable form the political issue between the concept of supranational action and the interests of individual member states. In this contest supranationality suffered a decisive defeat. The effect of the setback to supranationality was not to deprive the High Authority of its powers but to underline its dependence in exercising them on the co-operation and goodwill of member states. But the blow to the High Authority's prestige was a shattering one from which it never really recovered.

There is of course a certain parallel between the 1959 battle over supranationality and the Community crisis of 1965 when the real issue was the principle of majority voting and the effective power of initiative of the European Commission (the Treaty of Rome, as we shall see in greater detail in later chapters, provides for the gradual transition from a system of unanimous voting to qualified majority voting on many of the issues affecting the General Common Market). In both cases it was France which, fearful of finding herself compelled to adopt policies or actions that ran in any way contrary to her own national interests, opposed any diminution of national sovereignty. It is significant that while in 1959 France was able to impose her will comparatively easily and found willing support from Germany and Italy, the 1965 crisis found her isolated. Even so, such is the weight of France in Community affairs and the prestige of her President that it is more than doubtful whether the European Commission will again risk putting forward major proposals affecting the application of the provisions of the Treaty of Rome unless it has first carefully tested the ground and has been assured of a favourable response on the part of all six governments. But this is to anticipate. The real lesson of the 1959 coal crisis was that supranationality, as conceived and embodied in the Treaty of Paris – the theoretical power given to the High Authority to draw up and introduce measures in the event of a Community crisis – had been tried and had been flatly rejected.

The European Defence Community and initial hopes for a Political Community

While it was left until 1959 to administer the *coup de grace* to the concept of supranationality, in fact its death agonies were protracted. As early as the summer of 1954 the rejection by the French National Assembly of the proposed European Defence Community was a first if indirect indication of the way things were moving. The original plan to set up a European army was outlined by M. Pleven, at that time Prime Minister of France, in June 1950 and was designed to bring about the rearmament of Germany without re-creating an independent German army : this was to be done by creating a European army consisting of national units of about brigade strength but with a European senior line of command. The preamble to the draft treaty which was eventually drawn up stated that the signatory countries were 'anxious to preserve the spiritual and moral values which are the common heritage of their peoples, and convinced that within the common force formed without discrimination between the member states, national patriotism, far from being weakened, will be consolidated and harmonized in a broader framework' . . . and recognized 'that this is a new and essential step towards the creation of a united Europe'. Writing in his *Memoirs* about the European Defence Community, Dr Adenauer goes straight to the heart of the matter : 'The E.D.C. envisaged the renunciation by the participating countries of their most important sovereign right, namely the raising of their own armed forces, and the transfer of this right to a supranational authority. This would be of the most far-reaching importance for the creation of a united Europe. It was to lead almost automatically to a mutual collaboration of participating countries in economic and foreign policy questions, and hence, together with the Schuman Plan and other projects under discussion, was to lead very soon to a European Confederation. This treaty was an act unique in the long history of Europe which again and again, convulsed by wars and brought to the brink of the abyss by the last two wars, was to be given permanent peace and a new life.' As it was envisaged the creation of the European army would not, for example, have resulted in the establishment of a German general staff.

Soon after M. Pleven's proposal was made, the six countries that had already agreed to form the European Coal and Steel Community met in Paris to draft a further treaty establishing the European Defence Community. Despite opposition, sometimes fiercely expressed as by Dr Schumacher and Pastor Niemoller – although for very different reasons – the draft treaty received parliamentary endorsement in Germany, Italy – although here again not before some heated discussion – and the Benelux countries. In the meanwhile, however, the French had had second thoughts. The Soviet attitude which in 1950 had looked so menacing had, since the death of Stalin, become much more conciliatory; the national humiliation in Indo-China and the beginning of the final phase of the struggle in Algeria had given rise to a xenophobic unwillingness to relinquish any control over French forces. At the same time French attempts to secure greater military commitments on the European continent by the United States and the United Kingdom had proved fruitless. Above all, however, the sense of urgency had evaporated with the easing of the international situation. The whole façade of the E.D.C., it must not be forgotten, had been hastily conceived in order to enable the West to make use of German military manpower in its defensive preparations against the contingency of an attack from the east. Other reasons put forward were a growing French confidence in France's own national military strength – even though the war in Indo-China had done little to raise French military prestige and had left a feeling of bitterness in French military circles that was to survive well into the present decade. Probably the most reasonable explanation is that the supranationalists had had their day and that what France was prepared to concede, on paper, on coal and steel, she was not prepared to surrender in the field of national security.

Before leaving the subject of the E.D.C., it is worth looking for a moment at an official Note by the British government of 11 March 1953 expressing the government's willingness to take a direct part in the work of the E.D.C. by the establishment of a special mission and participation by a British Minister in the Council of Ministers, with a view to promoting co-operation and consultation on all matters of interest. It is tempting, even if futile, to speculate on what this might have led to had the E.D.C. not been stillborn.

The French Assembly's rejection of the European Defence Community marked the end also of yet another potentially far-reaching and influential agency : namely, the proposal to set up a European Political Community. At first, things had moved quickly. In September 1952 the Foreign Ministers of the Six had invited the Common Assembly of the E.C.S.C. to draft a treaty constituting a European Political Authority, covering at the same time both the E.C.S.C. and the proposed E.D.C. By March 1953 a draft had been prepared. This provided for a bicameral parliament : the lower house was to be directly elected by the people of all six countries on the basis of universal suffrage; the upper house by members elected from among the six national parliaments. Provision was also made for the establishment of a common market based upon the free movement of goods, capital and persons. The draft treaty had a lukewarm reception from the Foreign Ministers and was quietly referred to the archives. Further attempts were made in the autumn of 1953 to establish some form of common political organization but they met with equally little success and were finally abandoned upon the French Assembly's rejection of E.D.C.

CHAPTER 3

The birth of the Common Market

The revolt against the doctrine of supranationality and its final rejection did not, however, mean that the governments of the Six had abandoned their aim of creating a viable and highly centralized European community. Many observers, particularly in Britain, looked upon the French Assembly's rejection of E.D.C. and the waning prestige of the High Authority as valid indications that the postwar fervour for supranationalism had spent its force and that the member states of the Coal and Steel Community would be content to fall back upon O.E.E.C. for matters affecting trade and commerce and N.A.T.O. and W.E.U.[1] for matters of defence. This, however, was to gravely misjudge the current political and economic trends on the Continent.

Throughout the early 1950s leading Europeans like M. Spaak and M. Monnet – of whose genuine dedication to the European idea there could be no doubt – had continually discussed and occasionally put forward new ideas or initiatives designed to increase European integration. M. Monnet who, in November 1954, had announced his intention to resign as President of the High Authority in order to concentrate all his energies on 'building Europe', founded his influential Comité d'Action pour les Etats-Unis d'Europe – into which were admitted only representatives of corporate bodies (*i.e.*, political parties, trade unions and employers organizations) who were in a position both to speak for and commit those they represented to specific courses of action. Monnet himself at this time was apparently in favour of the extension of the powers of the E.C.S.C. to cover other forms of energy. An alternative proposal was to establish a new body, similar in structure to the E.C.S.C., for atomic energy in order to

[1]W.E.U. – Western European Union was hastily negotiated in the autumn of 1954 between the United States, the United Kingdom, Canada, Italy, France and the three Benelux countries and the Federal German Republic. The agreements reached provided for the admission of the Federal Republic to N.A.T.O., termination of the postwar occupation regime in West Germany and the transformation of the Brussels Treaty Organization into a new organ to be known as Western European Union.

promote the development of this new source of energy and so lessen Europe's growing dependence upon energy imports from other parts of the world. The idea of a general customs union, to embrace all forms of industrial and agricultural production, also had its adherents but was considered to be too ambitious and to pose too many difficulties to be realizable at that time. Another important factor at this stage was the growing bilateral co-operation between France and Germany, evident in the agreement reached over the Saar (where a free vote was allowed to determine whether the people of the Saar wanted to return to Germany or stay with France), the decision to go ahead with the canalization of the Moselle river so as to facilitate the transport of German coal and coke to the French steel industry in Lorraine and the promotion of economic and cultural ties between the two countries. This tended to strengthen Benelux fears of attempts to impose a Franco-German diarchy, fears which were to be revived in a more acute form in the early 1960s when the Franco-German Treaty of friendship was signed by Chancellor Adenauer and President de Gaulle. The upshot of it all was that in April 1955 it was announced by the Dutch government that the three Benelux countries would shortly propose the convening of a conference of West European governments – not limited therefore to the governments of the member states of the existing Coal and Steel Community – to consider the next steps to be taken in the field of European integration.

The three Benelux governments formally presented a memorandum to the other member governments of the E.C.S.C. in the following month. This memorandum contained suggestions both for a general common market and for action in certain specific fields such as energy and social matters, as well as proposing that a conference should be convened to study ways in which these objectives might be achieved and to draw up a draft treaty to give effect to them. The Benelux memorandum was considered at a meeting of the six Foreign Ministers at Messina in Sicily on 1 and 2 June 1955 and was broadly accepted by the other three Community countries. It was agreed that a select committee of government representatives and advisers should be set up under the chairmanship of M. Spaak and that it should report back to the Council of Foreign Ministers in the following October.

The Messina Resolution

The resolution adopted at Messina[2] by the Foreign Ministers of the member states of the E.C.S.C. opened with the words 'that the governments of the Federal Republic, Belgium, France, Italy, Luxembourg and the Netherlands believe that the time has come to make a fresh advance towards the building of Europe. They are of

[2]*Cf. White Paper* Cmnd. 9525, July 1955, H.M.S.O.

47

the opinion that this must be achieved, first of all, in the economic field', and fell into two parts. The first of these set out the fields – four in number – in which closer integration was desirable; they were atomic energy, the establishment of a general common market, the creation of a European Investment Fund, and the harmonization of conditions of work and pay.

The first of these, atomic energy, contained the seeds of the future European Atomic Energy Community and owes its pride of place to French support for and, indeed, insistence on the overriding importance of co-operation in the development of atomic energy in Europe. The resolution stated notably that 'the six signatory states consider that it is necessary to study the creation of a common organization to be entrusted with the responsibility and the means for ensuring the peaceful development of atomic energy, while taking into account the special arrangements made by certain governments with third countries.' The means by which these objectives were to be achieved were listed as follows :

(a) The establishment of a common fund derived from contributions from each of the participating countries, from which provision could be made for financing the installations and research work already in progress or planned.

(b) Free and sufficient access to the raw materials, and the free exchange of expertise and technicians, by-products and specialized equipment.

(c) The pooling of the results obtained and the grant of financial assistance for their exploitation.

(d) Co-operation with non-member states.

Next followed the section setting out the proposal for the establishment of a 'European market, free from all customs duties and all quantitative restrictions', which was described as the 'objective of their action in the field of economic policy'. The resolution stated specifically at this stage that the common market would have to be achieved by stages; this clearly was because of the magnitude of the problems involved in the creation of a market covering the entire range of industrial and agricultural production over so vast an area. It reflected also the anxieties of several countries, but notably of France, about too rapid an opening of their national frontiers to unrestricted imports from other European countries. The resolution made further stipulations that before a common market of this nature could be established, the following questions would have to be closely studied :

(a) The appropriate procedure and pace for the progressive suppression of obstacles to trade in the relations between the participating countries, as well as the appropriate measures for moving towards a progressive unification of their tariffs against third countries.

(b) The measures to be taken for harmonizing the general policy of the participating countries in the financial, economic and social fields.

(c) The adoption of methods designed to make possible an adequate co-ordination of the monetary policies of the member countries so as to permit the creation and development of a common market.

(d) A system of escape clauses.

(e) The creation and operation of a re-adaptation fund.

(f) The gradual introduction of the free movement of manpower.

(g) The elaboration of rules which would ensure the play of competition within the common market so as to exclude, in particular, all discriminations on a national basis.

(h) The institutional arrangements appropriate for introducing and operating the common market.

In fact these eight questions represented the highest common denominator of the reservations formulated by the six countries. The guaranteed inclusion of a system of escape clauses was a *sine qua non* for the French delegation and had for this very reason been included in the original Benelux memorandum. The clause dealing with the institutional arrangements was another concession to the French as the wording about, and the powers to be attributed to, the common authority had been very much stronger in the original memorandum. The creation of a European Investment Bank – the third of the fields of action listed in this part of the resolution – on the other hand represented a major advantage for the Italians, who hoped that one of the main benefits for them of membership of the common market would be a comprehensive policy of regional development, particularly for the economically backward areas of southern Italy, Sicily and Sardinia. The last point, harmonization of conditions of pay and work, was again included at the insistence of the French who feared that their shorter working week and consequently high overtime payments, as well as the legal obligation on French employers to pay equal wages to men and women doing the same work, would put them at a disadvantage.

Part Two of the Messina resolution set out the procedure to be adopted :

(1) Conferences will be called to work out treaties or other arrangements concerning the questions under consideration.

(2) The preparatory work will be the responsibility of a Committee of governmental representatives, assisted by experts, under the chairmanship of a political personality responsible for co-ordinating the work in the different fields.

(3) The Committee will invite the High Authority of the E.C.S.C. and the Secretariats of O.E.E.C., the Council of

Europe and the European Conferences of Ministers of Transport, to give the necessary assistance.

(4) The report of the Committee, covering the whole field, will be submitted to the Ministers of Foreign Affairs by not later than the 1st of October, 1955.

(5) The Ministers for Foreign Affairs will meet before that date to take note of the interim reports prepared by the Committee and to give it the necessary directives.

(6) The government of the United Kingdom, as a power which is a member of W.E.U. and is also associated with the E.C.S.C., will be invited to take part in this work.

(7) The Ministers for Foreign Affairs will decide in due course whether other states should subsequently be invited to take part in the conference or conferences referred to in paragraph (1) above.

The Spaak Report

The Spaak Committee – as it soon came to be known – held its first meeting in Brussels on 9 July 1955 and set up four committees of experts to deal respectively with the general common market, investment and social problems, conventional energy and atomic energy, and transport. A British representative attended the meeting. Shortly after the Messina meeting the Dutch Minister of Foreign Affairs, Mr Beyen, came to London on behalf of the Six to discuss British association or participation in the work of the intergovernmental committee. This was followed by a formal letter from the six inviting Her Majesty's Government to participate in the work of the committee. The British reply was guarded in the extreme; it expressed anxiety lest there should be any unnecessary duplication of the work already being performed by the O.E.E.C. and referred to the desirability of hearing the views of other affected countries. On the delicate point of Britain's possible participation in a European common market, the British government's reply stated that there were 'special difficulties for this country'; they would, however, 'be happy to examine, without prior commitment and on their merits, the many problems which are likely to emerge from the studies and in so doing will be guided by the hope of reaching solutions which are in the best interests of all parties concerned'.[3] The British representative continued to attend the meetings of the intergovernmental committee until November. By that time the work of the experts was largely completed and the committee was about to pass on to the next stage of preparing its report to the Ministers of Foreign Affairs as required under the Messina resolution and which,

[3]Cmnd. 9525, July 1955, H.M.S.O. Correspondence arising out of the meeting of the Foreign Ministers of the governments of Belgium, France, the Federal Republic of Germany, Italy, Luxembourg and the Netherlands held at Messina on 1–2 June 1955.

according to M. Spaak, required practical evidence of the political will of all the participants to proceed on the basis of the Messina resolution. Such a political will did not exist in the case of the United Kingdom.

Before passing on to a detailed examination of the Spaak Report, it is worth pausing for a moment to consider the reasons that led to the withdrawal of the British representative and the decision of Her Majesty's Government not to join with the Six in the final negotiations that led up to the signature of the Treaties of Rome.

First and foremost there was a general reluctance to take the new proposals seriously. The memory of the E.D.C. fiasco was still uppermost in the minds of many British observers of the European scene and they found it difficult to believe that what the French Assembly had refused to accept in the military field, they would now endorse in the even more vital and sensitive matter of atomic energy development – despite the fact that the French in the early stages of the 'relance europeenne' appeared to be much more interested in the proposals for an atomic energy community than in those for the establishment of a general common market. As Miriam Camps stated in *Britain and the European Community 1955–63*,[4] 'there had never been much real understanding in the United Kingdom of the depth of the drive towards real unity, as distinct from intergovernmental co-operation, on the Continent. Except for a handful of people, no one really accepted or believed in the feasibility or desirability of the "Monnet approach" to a united Europe. The *Financial Times* probably put it quite accurately when it said that the unsympathetic in the United Kingdom had regarded the Coal and Steel Community as "a cross between a frustrated cartel and a pipe-dream". In contrast to the situation on the Continent, there was at this time little or no feeling in the United Kingdom that the war had created a new situation and that only by coming together could the nation states of Western Europe hope to exert influence and to regain "great power status".' The British were perhaps too ready to interpret the hard and ruthless bargaining of the French negotiators for an unwillingness to go any farther along the path of experimental integration. If so, they were sadly mistaken, for the basic underlying objectives of French policy in 1956 were no different – if anything, indeed, they had probably been reinforced – from those of 1951 : the desire to create a small European nucleus under French leadership and the maintenance of some form of supervision (however indirect) over the industrial growth of Germany.

Besides a natural preference for European co-operation in the framework of the O.E.E.C., which we have already noted, other factors contributing to the British government's decision to withdraw

---

[4]*Cf.* M. Camps: *Britain and the European Community 1955–63,* London, Oxford University Press, 1964.

their representative from the Spaak Committee may have been an excessively rigid interpretation of the degree of supranationality inherent in the proposed arrangements for a general common market and a European atomic energy authority. This was certainly the case in 1951 when the much more obviously and intentionally supranational Treaty of Paris was being negotiated. On the other hand, there was in 1956 an imposing and rapidly mounting accumulation of evidence that the supranational giant had feet of clay and that when and where it proved necessary loopholes could be found in the hitherto imposing structure of the Treaty of Paris. On the more specific question of Euratom there was undoubtedly a feeling that Britain had a great deal more to lose than to gain. Britain already had an assured source of supply of uranium in Canada (it must be remembered that at this time natural uranium was still thought to be in short supply) and close relations with the United States. This, conversely, was the reason why several of the member countries of E.C.S.C. would have welcomed the participation of Great Britain in the proposed European Atomic Energy Community.

The objectives of the Common Market

The preamble to the Spaak report stated unequivocally that the purpose behind the European common market must be the creation of a vast zone having a common economic policy, constituting a powerful production unit and ensuring, by virtue of its size and uninhibited trading relationships, continuous expansion, increased stability, a rising rate of improvement in standards of living and the promotion of friendly relations between the member states. For these worthy objectives to be attained, a complete fusion of the separate national markets was an absolute necessity. The report went on to say that the establishment of a common market required simultaneous and co-ordinated actions in three major directions. These were, first, the establishment of normal (*i.e.,* fair) conditions of competition and the harmonious development of all the national economies concerned so as to be able to envisage the abolition, in successive stages, of all the barriers hindering the development of trade and dividing the European economy; second, the need to establish fair conditions of competition required the drawing up of rules and procedures in order to compensate for the effect of State interventions or State monopolies, as well as common actions to overcome any balance of payments difficulties that might arise and obstruct further expansion; third, the establishment of the common market called for the creation of new resources by means of the development of backward or under-developed areas and the elimination of under-employment and the provision of financial aid, where necessary, for the productive re-orientation of both enterprises and workers; and, finally, the free circulation of capital and manpower.[5]

Obstacles to trade were not of course restricted to quotas, tariffs and the operations of official government monopolies. The Spaak Report referred to restrictions in the availability of foreign currency, discrimination in transport rates according to the country of origin or destination of the goods in question and various domestic regulations, such as for example the allocation of licences. Clearly, it would serve little purpose to abolish one set of trade restrictions only to replace them by others, however sophisticated their method of application. Similarly in the field of competition, the report warned against double pricing practices which if manipulated in one way could have the same effect as tariff barriers and in another (*i.e.*, dumping) cause grave market disturbances. Another potential danger in this respect might be the temptation for governments to intervene in the market in order to assist their national industries. On the question of the free circulation of goods, the report commented that the first necessity would be to make it easier for workers to move and change their employment. But this condition applied to enterprises no less than to the workers and means would have to be devised to assist any programmes of reconversion that might be found necessary. Lastly, it was obvious that where there were major regional differences in the degree of economic development attained the sudden elimination of trade restrictions could do grave harm : in these cases the necessary safeguard measures would have to be taken and a regional development policy agreed. The sum of these proposals would inevitably add up to a fundamental transformation of the economies of the member states of the common market and it was plain that this could only be brought about gradually over a period of time. While it was possible that the generally favourable economic conjuncture in one or more countries might enable them to proceed more rapidly with, say, tariff disarmament, there would equally be other states which would find themselves compelled to have recourse to safety clauses to overcome temporary difficulties. It was, however, essential to ensure that any derogations of this kind from the agreed general line of policy should be of a strictly temporary nature.

The transitional period

It followed that there would have to be a transitional period which would lead gradually to the establishment of the full common market. But the transitional period would in itself consist of three stages, each one of which could last up to four years, with a further

[5]See Comité Intergouvernemental créé par la Conférence de Messine, Rapport des Chefs de Délégation aux Ministres des Affaires Etrangères, Brussels, 21 April 1956 (The Spaak Report), pp. 15–19.

additional period of four years which, however, would only be called upon in case of absolute economic or political necessity. While the rate of progress to be achieved and the measures to be taken in each of the three stages remained a matter for future consideration and decision, there could be no question of going back during the second or third stage on measures or policies that had already been agreed.

Turning to the obligation on the part of the six countries which were coming together in the common market to respect the provisions of the General Agreement on Tariffs and Trade (G.A.T.T.), the Spaak Report commented that Article XXIV of the G.A.T.T. specifically provides for countries joining together in a customs union or a free trade area and authorizes them to apply the most favoured nation rule only to the participating states, but added that the establishment of a free trade area among countries with largely common or contiguous frontiers as is the case in Western Europe would give rise to almost insuperable practical difficulties.[6] The only possible solution would have been the adoption of a certificate of origin procedure and the restriction of the right of free circulation to Community produce; this, however, would have necessitated the maintenance of frontier controls and customs posts which the Six were particularly anxious to abolish.

Three G.A.T.T. conditions would have to be met; first, that the elimination of tariffs should affect the vast bulk of the trade between the countries in question – since it was proposed that the common market should cover all forms of economic activity, this point was clearly covered. Second, that the customs union should be established in the course of a reasonable period of time – here the report argued that to propose ten or even 15 years for such a profound transformation as was being envisaged could not be regarded as excessive. And third, that the common external tariff should not have the effect of raising tariffs beyond the arithmetical average of the national tariffs of the states joining together in the proposed customs union.

The proposed institutional arrangements

The Spaak Report then went on to describe the institutional arrangements that would be necessary to ensure that all these objectives should be attained. The nature and powers of the institutions would be of particular importance in this instance since in most cases the actual rules and regulations that would apply to the operation of the common market would be worked out during the course of the transitional period. For example, it would not be possible to specify in the treaty setting up the common market the exact rules that would have to be followed in order to achieve a common agricultural

[6]The difference between a free trade area and a customs union is of course that in the first case all the participating states maintain their own national tariffs for imports from third countries, whereas in a customs union there is one common external tariff for all the member states.

policy or the free movement of capital. The text of the treaty would provide a framework of objectives, the detailed achievement of which would be left to the competent institutions to work out. The report stated that this meant the acceptance of four basic principles : first, pending closer integration of national fiscal, budgetary and social policies, it would be necessary to distinguish between matters of general economic policy which remained entirely in the hands of member governments and those which were indissolubly connected with the operation of the common market. Second, the need to supervise the application of the treaty rules on competition. This could only be done by a body with powers of decision. Third, the operation of the common market might require that for a certain number of specified cases and after the lapse of an agreed period of time the Community should be able to operate on a qualified majority rather than a unanimous vote basis – this obviously raised once again, although in a very much more attenuated form, the question of national sovereignty. In the event the Treaty of Rome as finally drafted contained only a limited number of instances where a qualified majority vote applied in matters of major economic or political significance (though nonetheless extending to agriculture, trade policy and social matters). Fourth, that there should be a court of appeal and some form of parliamentary control. To these four principles corresponded four separate but inter-related institutions. The first of these was the Council of Ministers which was the lynch-pin of the institutional framework as the instrument for consultation among the member governments and the co-ordination of their policies. The Council would generally take decisions and act on the basis of a unanimous vote although with a gradually increasing number of exceptions where voting would be on a qualified or occasionally even a simple majority basis. There would also be a European Commission, the members of which would be nominated by the governments, charged with the task of administering the treaty and watching over the development of the common market as a whole. It would be up to the Commission to prepare and submit to the Council of Ministers proposals for the progressive implementa-tion of the treaty's rules and the elaboration of Community policies in the various fields laid down in the treaty. There would be a Court of Justice – which would in effect be that of the E.C.S.C. but with its powers and area of competence extended to cover all common market matters. Parliamentary control was to be assumed by the Common Assembly of the E.C.S.C., but suitably enlarged. A diagram showing the inter-relationships of the three Community Executive bodies, the Councils of Ministers of the E.C.S.C., E.E.C. and E.A.E.C., and other Community Institutions is shown on page 56.

INSTITUTIONS OF THE EUROPEAN COMMUNITIES
in 1958

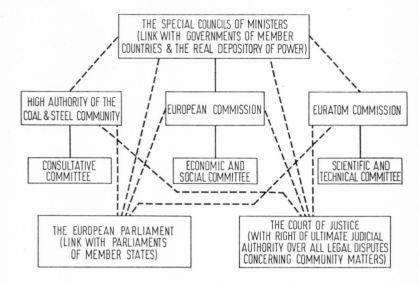

The elimination of quotas

The Spaak Report suggested that quota restrictions should be removed by means of regular annual increases. If this procedure were adopted and strictly applied quotas would within a very few years have become so enlarged as to lose any purpose and could then be completely abolished. The report suggested that a reasonable annual rate of increase would be 20%; the only exceptions to this rule being products for which existing quotas were fixed at a nil or extremely low level. In such cases it was proposed that quotas should be granted equal to 1% of national production. At the same time all bilateral quotas between certain individual member states of the Community should be turned into global quotas. In order, however, to ensure continued progress, a time limit was necessary and the report suggested that this should be limited to four years.

The report recognized that the existence of state monopolies or national purchasing agencies created special problems but insisted that these should either be abolished during the course of the transitional period or, at least, replaced by a common Community organization.

Agriculture

The Spaak Report stated that there were major differences in agricultural policy and structure among the six member states; this

56

was not simply a question of the nature of agricultural production in each country but of various and varying governmental support measures and special buying and selling arrangements. Other factors influencing national markets included internal regulations on prices, sowing times, levels of output, stocking arrangements and the subsidization of exports. These national measures had been taken to deal with pressing national problems which would not be resolved simply by the creation of a common market. From this it followed that it would not be possible to secure the free circulation of agricultural produce simply by means of the abolition of tariffs and quotas, and that for a number of products common Community solutions, in the interests of all six member states, would have to be found. While making no attempt to minimize the size of the problems involved, the report did comment that many of the problems that had seemed so formidable when looked at from a purely national point of view might well turn out to be much easier to overcome once action could be taken on a Community scale.

It was clear that in view of the special circumstances of agriculture and in order to have sufficient time to narrow the very big price differences that existed for some forms of agricultural produce without causing major market disturbances there would have to be a considerable period of transition. The report expressed the hope that during this period much could be done to reduce the cost differences between farmers in different parts of the Community by promoting the use of advanced modern farming techniques and appliances. The development of the general industrial common market was also likely to result in certain indirect (and unspecified) advantages to the agricultural sector. In a further effort to soothe the fears of farmers in some of the less favoured Community countries, the report added that despite the tremendous improvements that had been made in the field of food transportation, geographical protection was still, and seemed likely to remain, a vital factor for perishable foodstuffs. There was also the fact that for certain types of produce the Community as a whole was a net importer, while for others consumption patterns and levels varied enormously from one member country to another. Lastly, the Community was already a big exporter of some agricultural products and there was no reason to suppose that, while there might well be some increase in trade with other Community countries, supplies to traditional markets would be seriously affected or diverted.

Having thus reviewed some of the possible problems arising from the establishment of the common market in agriculture, the report then went straight to the heart of the matter and openly posed the question of what the common agricultural policy of the Community should be. There were five major questions that had to be answered :

(i) Given the importance of security of supply should the Community seek to expand its own agricultural production in such a way as to become self-sufficient in all major foodstuffs or, bearing in mind the interests and exposed production of other, essentially purely food-exporting countries, should the Community follow a policy of specialization and so balance her imports of say, meat, with exports of, say, wheat – production of which could be increased substantially provided the necessary protective measures were taken against imports from third countries.

(ii) In view of the fact that the structure of agricultural production in the Community was based and seemed likely to remain based on medium-sized family holdings rather than on exploitation on a vast scale as in the United States or Australia, what measures could or should be taken to promote the use of the most modern production methods and techniques.

(iii) What measures, if any, should be taken to stem the drift of farm-workers away from the land to the towns. What is or might be the effect of the continuation of such a trend upon agricultural production.

(iv) Given the big fluctuations in price that can occur for certain agricultural products according to whether harvests have been good or bad, what kind of market or price stabilization should the Community seek to establish. In which way, furthermore, and for which products should this be attempted.

(v) Which were the agricultural products which farmers should be encouraged to grow in larger quantities.[7]

The questions posed by the Spaak Report were formidable, but they were also fundamental to any decision on the nature of the Community's common agricultural policy – the Spaak Report did not attempt to spell out the answers, this could be left till the transitional period – but emphasized the necessity to define the general broad framework for a common agricultural policy for the Community as a whole. Obviously, it would not be sufficient merely to try and juxtapose six different and sometimes conflicting national agricultural policies. The report recalled that the basic objectives of a common policy were market stabilization, security of supply, a guaranteed reasonable level of income for normally productive farms and the gradual adjustment of the agricultural industry and community to the new situation brought about by the establishment of the general common market.

The fundamental rule was that by the end of the transitional

<hr>

[7]Cf. Spaak Report on Agriculture, *op. cit.*, pp. 44–52.

period all national arrangements and regulations would have had to have given way to, and been replaced by, common arrangements. This clearly meant that by the end of the transitional period and the beginning of the general regime for agriculture, all obstacles to intra-Community trade would have been eliminated and the establishment of a common agricultural policy or, for certain products, common market organizations, finally accomplished. It is also clear that right from the very start, therefore, the Six did not envisage a similar type of common market organization for all agricultural products. The Spaak Report specified that during the transitional period it would be the responsibility of the competent Community organs to draw up and agree a list of a limited number of products whose special importance would justify common market organizations. For all other products, the aim should be to bring about a free market throughout the Community together with some form of protection against imports from third countries by means of tariffs and anti-dumping measures.

It is interesting to note that at the time of the negotiations for the Treaties of Rome the main conflict in the agricultural discussions occurred between the Dutch and the French and not, as one might reasonably have supposed, between the Germans and the French. While the concern expressed by the Dutch, who were themselves important agricultural producers and who were anxious not to find their markets flooded by French products largely financed by Community subsidies, was understandable enough, it is difficult to understand why the Germans treated the question with such apparent nonchalance. It is true that the French had not yet devalued the franc – they were to do so twice in quick succession, first in 1957 and then again in 1958, nor had the Deutschmark yet been revalued. But even allowing for this financial realignment in favour of the competitive power of the French franc, it was a fact that was obvious for all to see that, because of the nature of her soil and the vast expanses of uncultivated land, France, with an assured, virtually captive, Community market at her feet, would strive with might and main to increase and, indeed, maximize her own agricultural production. This in turn could only mean one of two things : either a tremendous increase in exports to other Community countries and notably to Western Germany; or, increased exports outside the Community. But since French prices generally are well above world market prices, any such exports would have to be heavily subsidized – with Community and not solely French funds. One can only assume that the Germans had done their sums but had concluded that the advantages they expected to derive from free access to the French industrial market would compensate them for their increased imports of agricultural produce from France and the financial contributions they would have to make to subsidize 'Community' food exports to third countries. It may be argued that as long as it was a case of replacing expensively-produced German farm produce by somewhat less expensive imports from France the German government stood in any case to gain. There were also even some other marginal advantages – German farms were on the whole small, in the hands of peasant farmers and not really economic in the new European structure; these smallholdings would now in time be replaced, where possible, by larger farms while the smaller displaced farmers would provide much-needed extra manpower in the factories. This is no doubt true enough as far as it goes; but the new system for which the Spaak Report provided the blueprint meant that the Community countries in general, and Germany in particular, would have to reduce very substantially their imports of, on the whole, cheap agricultural products from outside the Community and replace them by more expensive Community and essentially French-produced foods.

State aids

The Spaak Report stated that all forms of State aid would have to be examined critically in the light of the general rule that all aids would be incompatible with the common market organization – whatever the form in which they were given – and especially if they had the effect of distorting competition by creating favourable conditions for certain enterprises or certain types of production. The only exceptions that could be permitted to this rule were subsidies paid to certain individual consumers or for social reasons, such as grants to hospitals, schools, charitable institutions and the like. The position was less clear with regard to aid designed to promote regional development, especially in relatively underdeveloped parts of the Community such as Calabria, Sicily, Brittany and certain extreme parts of Germany. While it was to be one of the cardinal features of the Treaty of Rome that the economically backward areas should be assisted so as to improve the standards of living of the people living there, it was equally clear that this was to be achieved within a Community policy and framework. State aids were also to be permitted to continue during the transitional period in order to assist firms hard hit by the establishment of the common market to adapt themselves to the new conditions of competition.

Elimination of distortions

The Spaak Report stated that besides open discrimination practised by enterprises or, in certain cases, by governments, and official interventions designed to assist certain enterprises or industries, there were also a number of legally enforceable measures which could have a vital bearing on the cost-price or structure of companies and industries in some Community countries and thereby distort the conditions of competition in part or the whole of the common market. The Spaak Report listed in particular distortions arising from direct or indirect fiscal measures, from social security financing arrangements, price-fixing edicts, differences in working conditions (such as unequal pay for men and women workers, differences in the number of normal working hours per week and in the rate and level of overtime payments, and the number of paid holidays), and different national policies with regard to credit payments.

In order to remove these possible causes of distortion in the operation of the common market, the Spaak Report made the following suggestions : first, that the European Commission, acting in conjunction with the industries and governments concerned, should make a detailed study of any distortions existing in the common market; second, that if the Commission found that distortions did exist and that they were seriously affecting the normal operation of conditions of competition in the common market, then it (the Commission) should be given the responsibility of preparing and drafting proposals designed to remove any such distortions; third, that during the first stage of four years, any such proposals would require the unanimous approval of the Council before becoming effective. Once the first stage had been completed, however, a qualified majority in the Council would enable the Commission to proceed. Fourth, if the correction of distortions depended primarily on changes in freely negotiated working agreements or changes to statutory instruments, then the member governments should undertake to put in hand any appropriate action; fifth, that in the event of its proposals being rejected, the Commission would have the right to accord a safeguard clause to any industry or enterprise in the Community that might be adversely affected by the continued distortion of the market. Such a safeguard clause might, for example, authorize the payment of subsidies to the enterprises concerned so as to enable them to maintain their position in the common market.

Transport

The Spaak Report stated that there were already many international bodies for transport which had contributed much towards the co-ordination of national transport policies. These achievements would automatically continue to apply in the common market area and the Community should therefore concentrate its efforts on additional means designed to secure a fully integrated transport system. These would include modifications in tariffs and conditions of transport in international (*i.e.*, intra-Community) traffic that would be necessary in order to achieve the proper working of the common market : the elaboration of a common transport policy, and the promotion of financial investment to secure developments in the field of transport in the interest of the Community as a whole.

61

With regard to freight rates, the Spaak Report stated that on all intra-Community traffic it would be necessary to abolish all payments of customs duties, discriminatory payments and arrangements, and subsidies. The transport policy of the general common market would be based on the principles already set out in Article 70 of the Treaty of Paris. There were accordingly three main objectives to be attained : first, the abolition of any form of discrimination consisting of the application by a transport enterprise, in respect of similar goods transported in similar circumstances, of rates and conditions which differed on the grounds of the country of origin or destination of the goods carried; second, the elimination of frontier dues or charges; and third, the application of through tariff rates : that is to say that tariffs would be applied on the basis of the total distance over which the goods were carried and no longer up to and from national frontiers.

Commenting on the timetable for the application of these measures, the Spaak Report recommended that all discriminations should be abolished within a period of four years. The problem of special support tariffs could, where necessary or appropriate, be examined in conjunction with the social and regional problems to which they were related. Finally, the report expressed the hope that there would be a gradual trend towards the harmonization of the level of freight rates charged by transporters in all six countries both for national and international traffic.

The Spaak Report was emphatic that a common transport policy was absolutely essential if the Community was to achieve the maximum utilization of its available resources and plan its transport network to the best advantage within the framework of the overall general common market. This would require, *inter alia,* an exact and detailed knowledge of the costs of different forms of transport. As a first step in this direction, the Spaak Report suggested the preparation of national transport accounts which would show not only the costs incurred by the transporters themselves but also the cost of the existing transport network to the Community.

Re-adaptation

The purpose of the re-adaptation provisions was to facilitate the changes that would be made necessary by the establishment of the common market, such as the redeployment of labour, closures of some enterprises and the switch-over in production lines and activities by others. It was designed in other words to ensure at the same time both stability of employment and a certain degree of mobility of labour. The re-adaptation provisions were therefore of very considerable importance as a means designed to assist in the dual process of increasing productivity and raising the general standard of living.

The Spaak Report stated that the casual link between the establishment of a common market and the enforced closure of certain enterprises made uneconomic by the changed circumstances was often difficult enough to discern clearly in the Coal and Steel Community – where only two industries were concerned – and that it would almost certainly become infinitely more difficult still in a general common market, covering as it did the whole range of industrial production. Moreover, since in a general common market Community intervention could no longer be made subject to the condition that any aid given should have a purely supplementary character in relation to the general regime or system of aid to unemployed workers, the Spaak Report suggested that the principles underlying the payment of re-adaptation funds should be progressively integrated with national systems for unemployment benefit payments and that these in turn should be progressively harmonized among the six member states. These proposals were of course of very great importance within the general social policy context of the proposed common market treaty and were closely scrutinized by the trade unions, by whom they were largely welcomed.

The actual details of the system proposed were as follows : it was suggested that there should be a re-adaptation fund fed by financial contribution from each of the member states in relation to total salaries, wages and social benefit contributions paid. The fund would provide financial assistance without insisting upon formal proof that an enterprise had got into difficulties as a result of the establishment of the common market. The principle determining the payment of aid would be based on the understanding that since the entire Community would be concerned in and gain by all increases in productivity, improvements in industrial standards, higher standards of living and rationalization processes generally, then it would be only fair for all those participating in the Community to contribute, according to the scale already described, to the re-adaptation fund and the payments it would make. The fund, it was suggested, should offer to pay 50% of the total costs involved in the following cases : the complete closure of an enterprise or plant; partial closures (*i.e.,* of certain lines or types of products within an enterprise); a reduction in employment in an enterprise of 10% of those previously employed – provided this amounted to not less than ten workers – towards the cost of removal and installation of workers if they had to move or the cost of retraining if they had to change their jobs.

Similarly, if an enterprise in the process of reconversion of its activities or production reduced or temporarily suspended part of its labour force, the fund would grant financial assistance to enable that enterprise to maintain the former level of wages for its full labour force pending completion of the reconversion arrangements. In such cases, however, it would be necessary for the government of the country concerned to make out and submit a reasoned case for assistance and for the Commission to consider and approve it.

There might also be some cases where social considerations would require the slowing down of closure or reconversion programmes. In such cases also the fund would be authorized to contribute financially subject to the submission by the government of the country concerned of detailed plans for the integration of workers thrown out of work into new industries. In such cases it would be up to the European Commission to make the necessary proposals which would then require a qualified majority in the Council.

Euratom

The Spaak Report was exceptionally circumspect in its proposals relating to the establishment of a European Atomic Energy Community. The Messina resolution, as we have seen, was specific enough in its objectives, but difficulties soon arose during the course of the discussions in the Spaak Committee, with the French once more being the niggers in the woodpile. The other Five wanted the Euratom Treaty to contain a clause saying that all the member states would agree to give up the manufacture of nuclear weapons. While there was some support for this in France also, a majority of the French National Assembly (and the Gaullist faction in particular) savagely contested the authority of any French government to surrender this right. A majority of officials and members of the Assembly seemed to see in the proposed Euratom treaty not a graceful way out of the nuclear rat-race, but an opportunity to husband and harness the resources of Europe to the French nuclear bandwagon. It is worth repeating that throughout the early stages of the negotiations both in the Spaak Committee and thereafter the French looked upon the Euratom treaty as the more important of the two and suggested that the general common market treaty, because of the complexity of the issues it raised, would probably in the end fail to materialize. For the other Five it was exactly the reverse : they were interested primarily in the general common market and regarded atomic energy as a 'sweetener' designed to secure French agreement to the more important of the two draft treaties.

But within France the big issue was the maintenance or abandonment of the right to manufacture nuclear weapons. Eventually, prodded by the Gaullists and themselves basically in favour of an independent French nuclear deterrent, the French government informed its partners in the negotiations that it saw no prospect of the draft treaties being ratified if they insisted upon a clause specifically stating that all the members of the new Community had agreed to give up the right to manufacture nuclear weapons. Instead they put forward a typically French compromise proposal : France would agree not to explode an atomic bomb before 1 January 1961, but in the meanwhile there would be no obligation to stop work on research and development of the atomic bomb. In fact, it was common knowledge that, in view of the state of French atomic technology and know-how at the time, it was materially impossible for them to attempt to explode an atomic bomb before that date. Rather, however, than run the risk of another E.D.C. debacle, the other Five accepted the French 'compromise' proposal. This marked the end of any hopes that may have existed in certain quarters of a denuclearized Western Europe.

The Spaak Report in the section dealing with Euratom stated simply that there were a number of difficult problems including, first, the power of decision over fissile materials and the question of supervision; second, commercial activities in the field of supply; third, the control to be exercised over Community installations; and fourth, the carrying out of studies and the preparation of papers on investment projects and forward demand estimates. The report was more specific with regard to the question of institutions, which it stated were essential if all the objectives foreseen in the atomic field were to be achieved. It accordingly suggested the creation of an independent commission, responsible for the operation and running of the European Atomic Energy Community, with its own distinct authority, field of competence and mandate. Like its fellow-executives (the High Authority of the E.C.S.C. and the European Commission of the general common market) the Euratom Commission would be responsible to the Parliamentary Assembly at Strasbourg and would act in conjunction with a specially established Council of Ministers who were to participate in all matters of policy. It was clearly evident, right from the start, that the member governments – and particularly the French government – had every intention of keeping a very tight rein on the activities of Euratom.

The signature of the Treaties of Rome

The Spaak Report was a document of compromise, but it was also a remarkable achievement which laid the basis for the final texts of the treaties establishing the European Economic and Atomic Energy Communities. The report was submitted to the heads of the six national negotiating delegations in April 1956 and was unanimously recommended by them to their respective governments as a basis for the negotiation of the actual treaties. Many of the suggestions contained in the Spaak Report went in fact almost unchanged or with only very minor amendments into the Treaties of Rome.

The Foreign Ministers of the six countries formally considered the Spaak Report at a meeting in Venice in May 1956. The bargaining was hard. While all six countries were keenly concerned at this stage not to let anything happen that might undo everything that had been achieved during months of hard and taxing work, the French posed a number of last-minute conditions on the grounds that unless these were met ratification of the draft treaties by the National Assembly remained conjectural. There were four main sticking points, on all of which the other Five eventually made concessions : first, the length of the transitional period. Most of the other Five would have settled for ten years, or even five. The French, however, insisted on a longer period and agreement was eventually reached on 12 to 15 years (the decision to divide the transitional period into stages was also the result of French pressure and insistence). Second, a number of special French export subsidies were to be allowed to continue subject, however, to an annual review by the Council and the European Commission. It was laid down, specifically, moreover, that the Commission could decide that these subsidies should be abolished once the balance of payments of the franc area had been in equilibrium, and the monetary reserves at a satisfactory level, for one year or more. Third, the French insisted that there should be harmonization of pay for men and women, length of paid holidays and value of overtime payments. Eventually, a compromise agreement was reached whereby the other Five undertook to ensure that on all these three points the situation in their countries would at least be equal by the end of the first stage to that which had prevailed in France in 1956. In the event of their failing to do so, it was agreed that the European Commission would be authorized, in certain cases at least, to grant safeguards. Fourth, the French pressed strongly for the need to have a unanimous decision or vote before moving from the first to the second stage of the transitional period. The other Five, suspecting French intentions to prolong the first stage as long as possible, presented a solid front and stood firm. Once again a compromise solution was found whereby the vote at the end of the first stage (of four years) to pass on to the second would have to be unanimous; if it were not, the question would be postponed for a further 12 months. The same procedure was to be adopted at the end of the fifth year. Thereafter, however, any further decisions were to be taken on the basis of a qualified majority vote.

At this stage of the negotiations the French also posed one wholly new condition : the free entry into the Community of all imports from their overseas associated territories. The French allowed free and unrestricted entry into France of all the produce from their former colonies and enjoyed in return a highly privileged position in their markets – a system not unlike that of the Commonwealth. In order therefore to maintain their links with their overseas associates, the French now proposed that all goods imported from countries associated with member states of the Community should get the same full benefit of the removal of tariffs, quotas and other trade barriers as the member states themselves. In return all of the Six would enjoy the same rights as the original European associate country in the overseas territories – while this did not mean that all restrictions on imports into, say, an associated African state from the Community would be lifted, it did mean that a German or French firm, seeking to export to it, would, in theory at least, be treated in exactly the same way. The other Five were both unenthusiastic about, and suspicious of, the French proposal and discussions continued up to within a month of the signature of the treaties. Despite the French threat that this question likewise represented a *sine qua non* for the National Assembly when it came to ratifying the treaties, the other Five refused to yield completely and a compromise was eventually reached whereby a Convention on the Overseas Territories was contracted and included with the Protocols to the Treaties of Rome, but for an initial period of five years only (the French would have preferred a more permanent and organic link), at the end of which the Council of Ministers, by means of a unanimous vote, would determine what arrangements should be made for a further period. The French also had to be content with a much smaller financial contribution for the economic development of the associated states than they originally asked for. Even so, out of some 580 million dollars to be paid into the Development Fund set up under the Convention during the initial five-year period (and to which France and Germany contributed 200 million dollars each), no less than 511 million dollars were earmarked for the French associated territories.

The six Foreign Ministers held a further meeting in February 1957 to try to reach agreement on the remaining outstanding questions which had not yet been settled. In the event, most of these questions were simply postponed till a later date, *i.e.*, till after the actual opening of the common market. This was particularly the case in agriculture, where the agricultural regulations and the common market organizations were left *in toto* till after the establishment of the European Economic Community and only the outline framework and a number of objectives had been agreed. The position was only partly less confused on the tariffs issue : virtually all the really difficult and controversial rates to be applied in the common external tariff – that is to say towards third countries – were simply put on a special list (list G) and left to be resolved during the course of the transitional period.

In this way, with some problems resolved but most of them just postponed for a solution at a later date, the scene was set for the signature of the treaties establishing the European Economic and Atomic Energy Communities in Rome on 25 March 1957.

Ratification of the Treaties of Rome

The ratification debate in the German Bundestag followed soon after the signature of the Treaties of Rome and resulted in an overwhelming vote in favour. Even so, however, the Bundestag made its approval conditional upon similar positive action by the other five countries concerned. Memories of the E.D.C. debate in the French National Assembly had by no means been completely obliterated. But this time there were to be no shocks. The debate in Paris took place in July and passed off without incident and with a substantial majority in favour. Given the concessions the French had been able to extract from their partners, it would have been extraordinary had it gone otherwise. Ratification in Italy, Holland, Belgium and Luxembourg followed in that order and on 1 January 1958 the Common Market came into being.

The 'Common Market' Treaty

The treaty establishing the European Economic Community consists of 240 Articles. The main sections are as follows:

PART ONE:
Principles. Articles 1 to 8.

PART TWO:
Bases of the Community, including Free Movement of Goods, Agriculture, the Free Movement of Persons, Services, and Capital; and Transport. Articles 9 to 84.

PART THREE:
Policy of the Community, including Common Policy, Economic Policy and the establishment of the European Investment Bank. Articles 85 to 130.

PART FOUR:
The Association of Overseas Countries and Territories. Articles 131 to 136.

PART FIVE:
Institutions of the Community, including Provisions governing Institutions and Financial Provisions. Articles 137 to 209.

PART SIX:
General and Final Provisions. Articles 210 to 240.

In addition, there were attached to the treaty a number of Protocols – designed, as we have seen, to take care of particularly sensitive or delicate questions – as well as the Implementing Convention on Overseas Territories:

Protocols
Protocol on the Statute of the European Investment Bank.
Protocol relating to German internal trade and connected problems.
Protocol relating to certain provisions of concern to France.
Protocol concerning Italy.

Protocol concerning the Grand Duchy of Luxembourg.

Protocol relating to goods originating in and coming from certain countries and enjoying special treatment on importation into one of the member states.

Protocol relating to the treatment to be applied to products within the competence of the European Coal and Steel Community in respect of Algeria and the Overseas Departments of the French Republic.

Protocol concerning mineral oils and certain of their derivatives.

Protocol relating to the application of the treaty establishing the European Economic Community to the non-European Parts of the Kingdom of the Netherlands.

Convention

Implementing Convention relating to the Association with the Community of the Overseas Countries and Territories.

Protocol concerning the tariff quota for imports of bananas.

Protocol concerning the tariff quota for imports of unroasted coffee.

These protocols are of some significance for they constitute the most obvious form of evidence of the extent to which the Six sought to protect their own particular interests when establishing the common market. Clearly, much of the treaty setting up the Economic Community is one big compromise in which the interests of all are inextricably mingled; it is for that reason that it is difficult for the outside observer to recognize easily and at once the main beneficiary of one or other provision of the treaty. In the case of the Protocols and the Implementing Convention the gains are plain for all to see.

As we have seen the treaty establishing the Economic Community is based essentially upon the Spaak Report and it would therefore be both repetitive and tedious to go through the text of the treaty on an article by article basis. We shall in any case be looking closely at the key articles in the course of the later chapters in this book. Our next task must be an examination of the common market in action.

CHAPTER 4

The Glorious Years

The Treaty of Rome which established the European Economic Community created a single market of 165 million people. A further 63 million people lived in the overseas associated countries and territories. Between the six countries which together constituted the common market there were of course enormous differences. Three of them, France, Germany and Italy, had populations of between 44 and 51 million people; two more, Belgium and Holland, had around 10 million while the sixth and last state, Luxembourg, had only 300,000 inhabitants. Nevertheless, while there were inevitably, given the wide differences in population, big variations in Gross National Product (ranging from $400 million in the case of Luxembourg to $57,000 million for the Federal Republic of Germany), the per capita production figures for five of the six states were remarkably close to one another : *i.e.*, $1,170 for Belgium, $1,080 for France, $1,120 for Germany, $980 for Holland and $1,270 for Luxembourg. The exception was Italy with only $600. All six countries had made a rapid recovery from the destruction and economic dislocation of the war : by 1950, the index of industrial production was at least 20% above the 1938 level, taken as 100, in all the member states except Germany; by 1955, the index figures ranged between 168 and 202.

TABLE 1

Indices of industrial production in the member states of the Community in 1938, 1950 and 1955.

	1938	1950	1955
Belgium	100	128	168
France	100	121	160
Germany	100	94	170
Italy	100	126	196
Luxembourg	100	137	178
Netherlands	100	145	202
Community	100	111	172

The initial rate of progress varied tremendously. Thus, while Belgium had regained her prewar level of economic activity as early as 1947, and Holland, Italy and Luxembourg by 1948, France did not fully recover until 1950 and Germany until 1951.

The economic policies of the six countries in the early postwar years were broadly similar. All aimed at achieving the fastest possible rate of economic development, keeping prices stable, ensuring full employment and maintaining a reasonable equilibrium in their balance of payments. Belgium owed her exceptionally rapid recovery partly to the industry of her people but partly also to the high price paid by the United States for the uranium deposits of the Belgian Congo. New industries flourished, particularly in the western and formerly essentially agrarian part of the couuntry. For a while too the older established industries of the south (coal and steel) boomed as they strove to meet the seemingly insatiable demand for coal and steel. By the middle 1950s, however, not only had the postwar reconstruction phase come to an end but the previous situation of overall energy shortage had begun to give way to one of energy surplus. While both coal and steel came under the aegis of the High Authority of the Coal and Steel Community, and not of the Commission of the European Economic Community, Belgium was nonetheless faced with a potentially serious overall industrial situation as she moved into the common market. In France, almost all the postwar governments had devoted their main energies to the modernization and extension of the country's industrial and agricultural infrastructure. The apparent weaknesses in the French position, such as the political instability of the Fourth Republic and the expenditure incurred by French military commitments in Indo-China and Algeria were to a large extent superficial and deflected attention from the steadily increasing underlying strength of the French economy. Germany after the war followed a generally liberal policy – with the marked exception of agriculture – which was in striking contrast with the autarkic and protectionist policy of the Third Reich. The vast German reconstruction programme ensured a high level of economic activity until well into the 1950s; this, together with a large and continuing influx of American capital and the proverbial industriousness of the German worker, combined to make the German economy by 1958 one of the strongest in Europe. In industrial terms Italy – in relation to the size of her area and population – was, immediately after the war, the weakest among the six countries. The main emphasis of all postwar governments was accordingly placed on promoting the economic development of the country. The Vanoni plan was drawn up for the development of the economically backward southern part of the country by means of an impressive programme of public works, the construction of new factories and the introduction of measures designed to rationalize agricultural production.

On the eve of the establishment of the general common market the breakdown of the gross domestic national product in the six countries was as follows :

	Agriculture	Industry	Services	Total
Belgium				
(a) In Fr. B. thousand million	34.7	228.5	219.8	483.0
(b) In %	7.2	47.3	45.5	100.0
France				
(a) In Fr. F. thousand million	1.900	5.100	5.100	12.391
(b) In %	16.0	42.0	42.0	100.0
Germany				
(a) In DM. million	14.053	84.136	69.043	167.232
(b) In %	8.4	50.3	41.3	100.0
Italy				
(a) In L. thousand million	2.736	5.443	4.719	12.898
(b) In %	21.2	42.2	36.6	100.0
Luxembourg				
(a) In Fr. B. million	1.735	10.602	6.951	19.288
(b) In %	9.0	55.0	36.0	100.0
Netherlands				
(a) In Fl. million	3.020	12.120	12.630	27.770
(b) In %	10.9	43.6	45.5	100.0

Industrially, the Federal Republic was by far the dominant partner. In 1957 out of a total value of industrial output of 70.6 thousand million units of account,[1] Germany accounted for 28.7 thousand million or 41%, followed by France with 28%, Italy 17%, Belgium 7.1%, Holland 6.8% and Luxembourg 0.3%. Agriculturally, France had by far the largest level of output and accounted for nearly 35% of the total Community production. Italy and Germany accounted for about 25% each, Holland for 8% and the Belgo-Luxembourg Union for about 6%. The share of the services sector at about 45% was broadly similar in Belgium, France, Germany and Holland; the lower figures for Italy and Luxembourg being explained by the more rural and agrarian structures of these two countries. It was this heterogeneous assembly of nations, with on the one hand some striking and important similarities but on the other hand some infinitely more striking and vital disparities – particularly in the economic field – that the common market sought to weld indissolubly together.

[1]The Community's unit of account was equivalent to one American dollar.

The impact of the Treaty of Rome

One of the first acts of the European Commission upon taking up its duties was to commission a small select working group of government experts to prepare a general review of the overall economic structure and the main current economic trends in the six member states. The final report of the working group was long and detailed and dealt with the position in each individual country in turn. The report admitted freely that the establishment of a common market involved a great number of risks but affirmed the view – as a matter of faith – that the likely and potential benefits would far outweigh any possible disadvantages :

The point of the Common Market is to make possible the maintenance of a higher rate of expansion when in individual states the rate might fall off. An immediate example of this possibility of injecting new vigour is provided by the smallest countries, which are directly dependent on external markets. We can see the Netherlands fighting against the contraction of the markets for their agricultural products caused by the competition of distant producers and the rise in production costs. In Belgium the economy is affected by fluctuations in the world economic situation. Luxembourg is finding that the mineral resources on which its extraordinary expansion has been founded are running out. A larger interior market is opening up for advances in production and for the broadening of the economic basis.

The prospect of competition increases the incentive to invest in order to modernize the means of production and to retain or expand markets. The combined Community can base the development of its production on an active population larger than that of its individual states added together, not only by helping to absorb the unemployment which is prevalent in certain areas only, and by thus turning what is a burden for one state into an asset for the Community, but also by offering a chance of work to women who, on too narrow markets, were inclined to give up from the start their attempt to find work.

The fusion of economies does not require this rhythm of development to be parallel everywhere. It is on the contrary one of the major tasks of the Community to ensure that the speed be higher in those areas which are least advanced. This is one of the tasks incumbent on the European Investment Bank; it is also a task for the overall economic policy, especially for those who manage the assistance which, not being as a rule available to the other regions, will have all the more effect in the areas which are to be given differential treatment. If help from outside is to be provided, it will be primarily in support of areas such as these, for whose development such help means both material resources and technical assistance.

These prospects suggest that two sorts of structural change are going on concurrently : those due to expansion and those caused by the progressive fusion of the economies. In order that these shall produce as few difficulties and shocks as possible, there must be greater efforts to understand, to foresee and to inform. Those concerned must know what is going on elsewhere and what markets are opening. The light thrown on short- and medium-term trends and the overall picture of the changes occurring in the Community will make it easier for both governments and business to take the necessary steps to adapt themselves along the right lines.[2]

The free movement of goods

The most spectacular and immediately effective action taken by the European Commission were the measures to reduce tariffs and remove quota restrictions on trade between the member states of the Community. As we saw in Chapter Three, the elimination of tariff and quota barriers to trade was to be accomplished over a period of up to 12, and possibly even 15 years. The first of these steps were taken, in accordance with the timetable laid down in the treaty, on 1 January 1959 when all tariffs on industrial products flowing between the six countries were reduced by 10%, while all existing quotas were enlarged by 20%. As a result, however, of the highly favourable economic situation prevailing throughout the Community in 1958 and 1959 the Commission felt the situation to be sufficiently favourable, and itself sufficiently strong in the summer of 1959, to prepare a detailed memorandum to the Council of Ministers on the desirability and the appropriateness of accelerating the implementation of the Treaty of Rome – insofar as the elimination of tariff and quota barriers were concerned – with the consequent likelihood of a shortening of the transitional period. Before finally deciding its own position on this issue the Commission gave careful consideration to the possible consequences to the economies of the six member states of such a decision, to the extent to which 'the timetable and momentum of the treaty could be substantially modified without endangering its balance', and to any possible repercussions of such a step on Community trade with third countries. On the first two of these points the Commission concluded that the Community would on balance benefit from a decision to accelerate the elimination of trade barriers, while on the third point it expressed the opinion that 'the sooner

[2]*Cf. Report on the Economic Situation in the Countries of the Community,* Brussels, September 1958, pp. 165–6.

economic integration is a fact, the more the commercial policy of the Common Market will of necessity be dynamic, open and liberal'. The Commission accordingly made the following recommendations which were submitted to the Council in February 1960 : first, that all industrial quotas still in force between member states should be abolished by the end of 1961. Special consideration was also to be given to the question of State monopolies with a view to drawing up as soon as possible a precise programme of action designed to eliminate any discrimination in respect of sources of supply and market arrangements; second, that measures should be agreed in order to ensure that there would be a parallel advance towards the implementation of a common agricultural policy; third, that customs duties should be reduced by a total of 50% during the first stage of the establishment of the common market – instead of the 30% originally envisaged : this was to be achieved by increasing the reductions planned for July 1960 and December 1961 from 10% to 20%; fourth, that the introduction of the common external tariff should begin in July 1960 instead of December 1961 as previously intended. These proposals were debated by the European Parliament in March. The Parliament strongly supported the Commission's proposals and passed a resolution which stated, *inter alia,* that 'the Commission, the Council and the Governments should accelerate simultaneous and harmonious measures to apply an economic, agricultural and financial policy and a common transport policy'. The Council of Ministers met to take a decision on the Commission's proposals in May 1960. They decided first, to reduce the customs duties in force among themselves on 1 January 1957 by not less than 30% before December 1960 by means of a reduction of 10% in July 1960 and a further 10% by December 1960. Yet a fourth reduction of 10% was to be applied before December 1961, and the Council agreed to consider and decide upon the possibility of a fifth reduction to be applied by the end of 1961 – thus bringing the total reduction to 50% – before June 1961; second, that the member states would undertake the first approximation to the common external tariff before the end of December 1960; third, that quantitative restrictions on the import of industrial goods would be abolished as soon as possible; and fourth, that the measures with regard to agriculture which were provided for in the treaty (but which had not yet been implemented) would definitely be put into effect before the end of December 1960 and that a timetable for work on the common agricultural policy would be laid down. In this connection the Council decided that, for agricultural products, the additional reduction in customs duties to be made by December 1960 would be 5% (and not 10% as in the case of industrial products). On the specific problem of quotas, the Council decided that all general quotas would be increased each year up to the end of the first stage by 20%, while the global quotas opened for the former nil or negligible quotas were set for 1961 at 5.2% of national production.

In the event the Council decided in 1961 to fix the fifth reduction of 10% for industrial goods for 1 July 1962 and the date for the second step towards the introduction of a common external tariff as 1 July 1963. The overall picture showing the dates and amounts of the reductions in customs duties and the extent of quota enlargements over the period 1958–62 are shown below in table form.

Date	Internal tariff cuts		Quota enlargements	Alignment of national tariff on the common external tariff
	Total	Minimum for each product		
Stage I				
1958	—	—	—	—
1959				
Jan. 1	by 10%	by 10%	by 20%	—
1960				
Jan. 1	—	—	by 20%	—
July 1	by 10%	by 10%	—	—
Dec. 31	by 10%	by 10% for industrial goods 5% for agricultural produce	—	—
1961				
Jan. 1	—	—	by 20% (abolition of restrictions on industrial quotas and special arrangements for enlargement of agricultural quotas)	—
Dec. 31	by 10%	by 10%	—	by 30%
Stage II				
1962				
July 1	by 10%	by 10%	—	—
Total	50%	50%	—	30%

By the end of the first stage in December 1961, four years after the opening of the common market, trade between the six member countries had increased by 73%, from $6,864 million in 1958 to $11,897 million in 1961 :

TABLE 2

Percentage increase in trade between Community countries
1958–61

Exporting countries	Importing countries					
	Belgium/ Luxembourg	France	Germany	Italy	Netherlands	Total
Belguim/ Luxembourg	—	36	71	22	45	52
France	84	—	105	182	130	113
Germany	39	78	—	91	66	67
Italy	101	137	106	—	144	116
Netherlands	35	71	63	55	—	67
Community	50	73	85	107	64	73

Trade among the Six throughout this period expanded much more rapidly and vigorously than between the Six and the rest of the world. Italy and France achieved particularly impressive – if not spectacular – increases. In the case of Italy the main reasons for this were probably the lower production costs arising from the lower levels of wages paid to Italian workers. In the case of France the devaluation of the franc by 15% by the Gaullist regime on 28 December 1958 transformed the competitive position of French industry. By reducing the cost to the other member countries of French agricultural produce it also contributed to the complexity of the subsequent negotiations on price levels for individual products within the context of the common agricultural policy.

The free movement of capital and persons
Articles 48 and 49 of the Treaty of Rome laid down that 'the free movement of workers shall be ensured within the Community not later than the date of expiry of the transitional period' and that the Council, acting on the basis of proposals prepared by the Commission, would determine the measures that were necessary to achieve this objective.

Acting on this the Commission in 1960 prepared draft regulations designed to promote the free movement of workers primarily by guaranteeing certain rights to workers from any one Community country seeking employment in another member state. The regulation provided, for instance, that after one year of full employment in a particular country a worker from another member state of the Community would be automatically entitled to have his work permit renewed in the same occupation; after three years of continuous employment he would be entitled to have his permit extended to take up any other job for which he was qualified. The Commission's proposals were adopted by the Council almost without change and came into force on 1 September 1961. Steps were subsequently taken to extend the scope of these measures to seasonal workers such as professional artistes and musicians. The Commission also put forward measures designed to ensure the right of establishment and the freedom to supply services; these provided that by the end of 1963 almost the whole of industry as well as wholesale traders and reinsurance agencies would be free of restrictions on establishment. Similar arrangements were to be introduced progressively for other industries so that by 1969 only a few special cases such as ship-building, the manufacture of railway equipment and forestry would remain to be liberalized. For services, the Commission's measures provided for 'the abolition of restrictions on moving the object on which or with the aid of which the service itself is performed, or of the material required for performing the service, and the abolition of restrictions on the transfer of funds and payments; this is envisaged before the expiry of the first stage and is now being effected'.[3] Here again a progressive extension to cover all kinds of services was envisaged so that for the film industry, for example, the complete liberalization of services was not expected to be effected before the end of 1969.

The free movement of capital is specifically provided for in Article 67 of the Treaty of Rome which states that member countries 'shall, in the course of the transitional period and to the extent necessary for the proper functioning of the Common Market, progressively abolish as between themselves restrictions on the movement of capital belonging to persons resident in member states and also any discriminatory treatment based on the nationality or place of residence of the parties or on the place in which such capital is invested'. In this connection the Commission was expected to work in conjunction with the Monetary Committee provided for under Article 105 of the treaty and which was intended to advise the Commission and the Council of Ministers on monetary problems. The Commission put forward and the Council agreed the first objective for the implementation of Article 67 in May 1960; this provided, *inter alia,* for an annual review on all existing restrictions on the free movement of capital with a view to their progressive elimination. A second directive was subsequently issued in December 1962 which virtually brought about the complete liberalization of the right to deal in securities throughout the Community and also freed all transactions connected with the movement of persons from one country to another as well as the supply of services.

A special problem which the Commission inherited was the existence in almost all the countries of the Community of government-controlled import monopolies. These concerned such commodities as

[3]*Cf. Fifth General Report on the Activities of the Community,* Brussels, 1962, p. 67.

tobacco, matches, alcohol, salt and bananas. Experience soon showed that in these cases the mere enlargement of quotas or reduction of tariffs made little or no difference to the operations of the monopolies which continued to deal with suppliers of the nationality of the country in question. The Commission concentrated its initial efforts on reaching a Community arrangement for tobacco, which represented the most complicated and delicate of all the commodities subject to monopoly control. The Commission dealt with the problem on the basis of a system of mutual tariff concessions designed to create comparable conditions of competition throughout the six countries and was finally able to secure the acceptance of all six countries for its proposals. When subsequently turning its attention to the other principal monopoly activities, the Commission stated that the abolition of the following three types of discrimination was essential to the achievement of the common market : restrictions of imports calculated in relation to potential outlets on national markets; any forms of additional charges placed on imported goods; and discrimination in respect of marketing conditions, *i.e.*, advertising. In its Sixth and Seventh General Reports the Commission claimed that considerable progress had been made in this field; thus, the Italian monopoly had increased its total tobacco imports from other Community countries from a value of Lire 320 million in 1959 to Lire 3.769 million in 1962, while the French tobacco monopoly had increased its imports from a value of 2 million francs in 1959 to 10.95 million francs in 1962. Reported progress in other directions included the French government's agreement to allow imports of potash from other member states in 1962 equivalent to 5% of national production in 1960 and to be increased annually thereafter by 15% while the Italian government, for its part, had declared its intention of winding up completely its banana importing monopoly organization.

It is worth commenting at this stage that, broadly speaking, the safeguard clauses of the treaty – notably Articles 46, 115, 226 and 235 – were invoked comparatively rarely. Among cases where safeguards were authorized were imports of biscuits and waffles from Holland and Germany and imports of sweetmeats, chocolate and chocolate confectionery from other countries into France. Several governments had recourse to Article 115 which enabled them to exempt from Community treatment imports of products originating in non-member countries and put into free circulation throughout the Community area. The total number of products of this kind involved had risen to about 60 by the end of 1962. The Commission's considered view was that these problems would in time resolve themselves as trade barriers were removed and the Community progressively developed its common commercial policy.

A good example of the Community's safeguard measures in action is one quoted in the Sixth General Report as a result of a massive increase in the export of Italian refrigerators and components to France. The French government, under pressure from its own manu- facturers, in December 1962 invoked Article 226 of the treaty and requested the Commission to authorize an import duty of 12% on all refrigerators. The Commission, after examining the market situation, accepted the French government's case and in January 1963 authorized the application of a 12% import duty subject to it being reduced gradually over the next six months to 6% and to an initial validity of six months.

Harmonization of the conditions of competition

The rules governing competition in the common market are set out in Articles 85 and 86 of the treaty establishing the European Economic Community. As these Articles are crucial to the develop- ment of the whole industrial philosophy of the common market we have quoted these two articles almost in their entirety :

Article 85.

1. The following shall be deemed to be incompatible with the Common Market and shall hereby be prohibited : any agreements between enterprises, any decisions by associations of enterprises and any concerted practices which are likely to affect trade between the member states and which have as their object or result the prevention, restriction or distortion of competition within the Common Market, in particular those consisting in :

(a) the direct or indirect fixing of purchase or selling prices or of any other trading conditions;

(b) the limitation or control of production, markets, technical development or investment;

(c) market-sharing or the sharing of sources of supply;

(d) the application to parties to transactions of unequal terms in respect of equivalent supplies, thereby placing them at a competitive disadvantage;

(e) the subjecting of the conclusion of a contract to the acceptance by a party of additional supplies which, either by their nature or according to commercial usage, have no con- nection with the subject of such a contract.

Despite the formidable character of this catalogue, the Article goes on to expressly exempt – under certain conditions – from the treaty's general interdict agreements that can broadly be said to be intended to contribute to the production or distribution of goods while at the same time assuring consumers an 'equitable share in the profit resulting therefrom'.

Article 86.

To the extent to which trade between any member state may be affected thereby, action by one or more enterprises to take improper advantage of a dominant position within the Common Market or within a substantial part of it shall be deemed to be incompatible with the Common Market and shall hereby be prohibited.

Such improper practices may, in particular consist in :

(a) the direct or indirect imposition of any inequitable purchase or selling prices or of any other inequitable trading conditions;

(b) the limitation of production, markets or technical developments to the prejudice of consumers;

(c) the application to parties to transactions of unequal terms in respect of equivalent supplies, thereby placing them at a competitive disadvantage;

(d) the subjecting of the conclusion of a contract to the acceptance, by a party, of additional supplies which, either by their nature or according to commercial usage, have no connection with the subject of such contract.

It was, however, not until February 1962 – more than five years after the commencement of the common market – that the Commission issued a regulation which set out clearly the legal basis for the implementation of the provisions of Articles 85 and 86. One of the results of this regulation and the action that followed from it was the determination of a final date (1 February 1963) by which all firms had to notify the Commission of all agreements coming within the categories provided for in Articles 85 and 86 and concluded between more than two parties and existing before March 1962. The regulation provided that firms would have an opportunity of stating their case in the event of differences of view between them and the Commission. All measures involving the direct or indirect fixing of minimum, maximum or fixed prices for goods or services, the restriction of production, sales or investments, or the sharing of markets within the common market by areas or customers, were specifically made subject to compulsory registration. Arrangements covering price maintenance contracts, licence contracts and agreements for exclusive dealing on the other hand were exempted from compulsory registration, although the Commission has of course the right to carry out any investigations it considers necessary or desirable.

The uncertainty of the first four years about the exact nature of the interpretation which the Commission would eventually put on Articles 85 and 86 had little or no staying effect on the trend that was already noticeable before the signature of the Treaty of Rome towards larger production units, associations and mergers. The

81

establishment of the Coal and Steel Community had resulted in steadily increasing pressure for amalgamation of companies, particularly on the steel side; the High Authority, which had at first adopted a fairly rigid attitude towards any applications for industrial mergers was compelled, under the pressure of events and the obvious potential advantages in the creation of larger units, to revise its original industrial philosophy and gradually moved into a position where it began actively to encourage concentration in the steel industry subject only to the condition that the interests of the consumer were reasonably safeguarded. A case study of the development of Community thinking on cartels and concentration policy has been included as an annex to this chapter. The European Commission adopted from the start a much more flexible point of view and has consistently argued that European industry, if it is to compete successfully with the giants of the United States and Japan, must become accustomed to and accept the idea of industrial mergers on a large scale. Industrial concentration has in fact occurred both on a national and international scale; among the latter one of the most spectacular was the agreement between the car manufacturing firms of Renault – which is nationalized – in France and Alfa-Romeo – which is not – in Italy.

One of the most important results in this field has been the establishment of a Community confederation of European industrialists – commonly known by its French initials of U.N.I.C.E. – with a permanent staff and headquarters in Brussels. This is indeed one of the most powerful and vocal pressure groups that has so far developed in the Community and it has not been backward in expressing its views, whether favourable or unfavourable, to the Commission on a wide range of industrial problems. These have included both the question of American investment in the Community, especially with regard to certain sensitive industrial sectors, and that of the optimum size of industrial undertakings. Similar Community organizations have been established for the mechanical and electrical equipment industries, the building industry, the printing industry, and many others. A similar tendency has also developed, although at a somewhat slower pace, among the various trade union organizations.

Regional policy

As a first step towards establishing a coherent regional policy, the Commission in December 1961 organized a conference on regional economies in Brussels. The conference concerned itself particularly with the problems of frontier areas, regions whose industries were declining, problems arising in areas which were mainly dependent on agriculture, and the measures being used or tried to stimulate their development. It had always been accepted that the Community had its problem areas, particularly in the South of Italy, and one of the Commission's first actions in this field was to consider the possibility of the creation of an industrial complex (consisting mainly of steel production and processing) between Taranto and Bari. The Commission also began at about the same time a detailed enquiry into the area consisting of the southern part of the Belgian province of Luxembourg and the north of Lorraine in France with a view to treating them as a single economic area with essentially common problems. In its Sixth General Report the Commission stated that 'the studies so far have shown that the solution of a number of problems such as water supply, training of manpower, communications and frontier-crossing conditions, and the promotion of investments in the less developed areas, would be considerably facilitated by increased co-operation between the authorities on the two sides of the frontier, and the Commission intends to encourage such co-operation.'

The Community's biggest asset in this respect was, of course, the European Investment Bank, established as a result of Article 129 of the Treaty of Rome and created for the specific purpose of contributing to the balanced development of the whole of the common market area. The Bank steadily expanded its activities throughout the period under rview. In 1962 it made advances of some 94 million units of account for investments whose total value (when taking into account contributions made by governments, local authorities or enterprises) was estimated at 237 million units of account. This included loans for general development purposes in southern Italy and for railway electrification in Britanny. It brought the total loans made by the European Investment Bank since its inception to about 250 million units of account, equal to some £90 million.

Social policy

The Community's social policy during the period under review was concerned particularly with the movement of workers, social security of migrant workers (both of which we have already discussed) and the operations of the European Social Fund. In its 1962 Action Programme, in which it outlined its plans for the future, the Commission announced its intention to promote, in collaboration with the member states, a Community policy on employment and vocational training as well as the upward levelling of living and working conditions.

The European Social Fund, established under Article 123 of the Treaty, was created in order to promote 'employment facilities and the geographical and occupational mobility of workers' throughout the Community. Provision was made for grants from the Fund to cover up to 50% of the expenses incurred in resettlement allowances and the re-training of workers who lost their employment as a result of the establishment of the common market. By the end of 1962 the Fund had made grants of a total value of 11.3 million units of account – a little over £4 million.

During the course of 1962 the Commission prepared proposals setting out the general principles of a common vocational training policy – these proposals were subsequently approved by the Council in 1963 – and continued to press member governments to honour their undertaking to introduce equal pay for men and women. Although it had been agreed that the differences in pay between men and women would be reduced in stages, several countries were either dragging their feet or finding legally defensible means of avoiding their obligation. The Commission consequently announced its intention to increase the number of inquiries and on-the-spot checks with a view to ascertaining the real position.

Transport policy

Transport, like agriculture and energy, constitutes one of the fields where the Treaty of Rome lays down certain principles to be followed in establishing a common policy, but does not define this policy in any detail.

The European Commission's first step was the preparation of a memorandum setting out the lines on which it believed the Community's common transport policy should be based. This memorandum, which was submitted to the Council of Ministers in May 1960, fell into three main parts : part one set out the economic foundations of the common policy for transport; part two described the general lines proposed for the common policy – based on the conclusions reached in part one; part three outlined the measures proposed to put this policy into effect and a suggested time-table for their application.

The memorandum stated that the transport sector presented special difficulties due to government intervention for social and other reasons, to the demands placed upon a sector that was in many cases regarded as a public service and to the fact that many transport facilities were operated at a loss. The treaty on the other hand, and Articles 74 and 75 in particular, stated quite specifically that a common policy for transport should be elaborated and that this should cover transport by rail, road and inland waterway. Turning to the common policy itself, the memorandum stated that there were three basic objectives : first, the elimination of any obstacles to the establishment of the general common market arising from the nature of national transport policies or arrangements; second, the free movement of all forms of transport services throughout the area of the Community; and third, what the memorandum described as 'the general organization of the transport

84

system' throughout the Community. This wording in fact tended to disguise the Commission's real objective of bringing about a more competitive system of transport. Looked at in broad terms the Commission's proposals were clearly aiming at the abolition of all discriminatory practices and support tariffs and the application of the general rules of the treaty in the case of government transport monopolies. This in turn required the acceptance and application of the five following principles for the transport market : equality of treatment; the financial autonomy of transport enterprises – a virtually unrealizable aim; freedom of action for all carriers; the co-ordination of investments; and the free choice of transport for users.

The memorandum then went on to describe the general organization of transport in the common market as envisaged by the Commission :

In dealing with transport rates, a distinction should be drawn between passenger and goods transport. Tariffs for the regular transport of passengers, which are generally governed by strict rules, will remain fixed but open to review in the light of changing costs or other developments. For irregular services and tourist services, a system resembling that for goods transport could be adopted.

For goods transport the Commission envisages the gradual establishment of a system of price brackets along with checks and some form of publication of rates. By price brackets is meant any system under which carriers are obliged to respect maximum and minimum limits laid down beforehand. Adoption of a bracket would permit carriers to enjoy a certain liberty in fixing prices between limits chosen in such a way as to avoid excessive competition or monopoly. Only the upper and lower limits of the bracket will have to be made public in advance. The knowledge of the market thereby furnished could be widened by the issue of price-lists.

A gradual easing of quotas is provided for at national level in order to ensure greater freedom of transport.[4]

Progress, however, was slow and it was not until November 1961 that the Ministers of the Six agreed, as a first step, to refrain from any further purely national measures in the field of transport but to bring them within the context of a common transport policy. This, nearly four years after the establishment of the common market, was little enough. Some eight months later, in June 1962, the Council, on the basis of further detailed proposals proposed by the Commission covering access to markets, transport rates, harmonization of competitive conditions, co-ordination of invest-

[4]*Fourth General Report on the Activities of the Community,* Brussels, May 1961, p. 151.

ment, and the harmonization of operating conditions, agreed on a list of problems and measures which would have to be resolved and put into operation in stages over the course of the following three years, *i.e.*, 1963–65.

During this period the national airline companies of the Community countries – although falling outside the scope of the Treaty of Rome – had begun discussions among themselves with a view to considering the possibility of establishing some form of association under the name of Air-Union. Despite the fact that the Dutch withdrew at an early date, representatives from Sabena, Lufthansa, Air France and Alitalia continued their discussions and by the end of 1962 had almost completed a draft agreement. Subsequently, however, disagreement over the part each airline was to play in the proposed association caused the scheme to be pigeon-holed, at least for the time being.

Energy policy

The elaboration of a common energy policy was complicated by the fact that responsibility for the different forms of energy was divided between the three European Executives. The High Authority was responsible for coal; the Atomic Energy Commission for nuclear power; and the European Commission for oil and natural gas. In order therefore to try to co-ordinate the work of the three Executives it was decided to set up a special inter-executive energy committee which would have the responsibility of preparing measures designed to bring about a common market in energy. Here, however, as in the case of transport, there was a sharp conflict of interests between the six member states. Thus, while Germany, France and Belgium had substantial coal industries to consider, Italy and the Netherlands had since the development of the energy surplus in 1958 followed a cheap energy policy based upon imports of oil and American coal. This had resulted, *inter alia,* in a major shift in the location of industry in these two countries – and also in France – from the traditional inland areas to the coast and had given virtually the whole of general industry in Italy and the Netherlands the benefit of low energy costs. This in turn represented a significant disparity in the energy situation in the Community as a whole.

The three executives consequently submitted in June 1962 a memorandum on energy policy to the Council of Ministers, designed to gradually establish market conditions which would combine the lowest possible prices and the free movement of all forms of energy throughout the common market with a guarantee of security of supplies. The memorandum was based on the underlying assumption that the total energy requirements of the Community would rise from 460 million tons of coal equivalent in 1960 to 700 million tons in 1970, and 850 million tons in 1975. With coal production tending to stagnate, it was inevitable that a steadily-growing proportion of the Community's energy requirements would have to be met from imports. The memorandum accordingly made the following proposals. For coal, that there should be a system of Community financial assistance to indigenous producers, free movement of coal within the Community, a Community quota system in respect of coal from countries in the Communist Eastern bloc, and a relaxation of the strict pricing rules of the Treaty of Paris (relating to coal) in order to allow greater market flexibility. For oil, that there should be free movement of crude oil and petroleum products within the Community, unrestricted entry for imports from all sources except Eastern Communist countries which would be subject to quotas, nil duties on crude oil and low duties on petroleum products under the common market external tariff, harmonization of taxes payable on motor spirit and fuel oil, publication of prices charged and, finally, a common stocking programme. For nuclear energy, that the governments should support the Euratom Commission in its research and other activities, facilitate the free movement of nuclear products, plants and personnel, and seek to ensure the introduction of nil tariffs for reactors and nuclear fuels in order to give Community industries the best possible supply arrangements and to provide opportunities for the development of the various types of installations. The establishment of the common market for energy was to be achieved in stages. First, a preparatory period which was scheduled to end on 1 January 1964 – during which the measures to be applied would be elaborated; second, a transitional period which was to run from 1 January 1964 to 31 December 1969; and the final period or full common market as from 1 January 1970. The memorandum concluded by suggesting that an immediate start should be made on seeking to obtain acceptance by the six countries of :

(1) the principle of an open Common Market for energy;

(2) the principle and maximum amount of assistance to internal production;

(3) the principle of a supply policy;

(4) the principle of special measures during the transitional period (if necessary on a country-by-country basis);

(5) the timetable for the different stages, and the measures in respect of coal and oil, to dovetail with the establishment of the general Common Market, the voting procedures being based on those provided for in the Treaty of Rome.[5]

[5]*Cf.* E.C.S.C., *Eleventh General Report on the Activities of the Community*, Luxembourg, May 1963, p. 209.

Despite repeated meetings the Council of Ministers was unable to reach any agreement on the basis of these proposals and, by the end of 1962, no solution was yet in sight. It was in the field of energy more than in any other sector covered by the Community's Institutions, that the Commission found the conflicting interests of the member states a barrier to progress.

Agriculture

Before the establishment of the common market all six states protected their farmers to a greater or lesser degree, usually by giving indigenous farmers a privileged position in their own national market. Three of the Six, France, Italy and the Netherlands, also took government-sponsored and financed measures to dispose of large quantities of their own produce in external markets at the ruling (*i.e.,* lower) world price – the difference being met by government subsidies. The new agricultural stakes in the common market were high, particularly for France and Germany. In relation to the rest of the world both countries were high-cost producers. Compared with each other, German costs were some 50% higher than those of French farmers. The French had consequently as their major economic objective, in the establishment of the Community, the German agricultural market. The original discussions in the Spaak Committee and the decisions which led on from them did not, as we have seen, define or lay down precise provisions or rules for agriculture. In these provisions, nonetheless, was to lie the key to the Community's future for the elaboration of a satisfactory agricultural policy constituted a vital and absolute *sine qua non* for France.

But the drama and publicity associated with the Community's debates on agricultural policy were not immediately evident. The beginning, indeed, was fairly uneventful with an agreement reached, comparatively easily, in February 1959 between France and Germany whereby the latter undertook to import steadily increasing quantities of French wheat over the next four years. The treaty had laid down the following objectives for the common agricultural policy : first, to increase agricultural productivity in the Community by ensuring the rational development of production, the optimum use of resources and the encouragement of the use of new techniques; second, to ensure a fair standard of living for all those engaged in farming; third, to stabilize markets; fourth, to ensure regular supplies at reasonable prices to consumers in the Community. The Commission consequently based its initial proposals on the working out and implementation of the common agricultural policy – which under Article 43 of the treaty it was to submit to the Council of Ministers before the end of 1959 – on these basic objectives. There were three steps which could be introduced immediately : the co-ordination of existing national policies and measures to improve the structure of agriculture throughout the Community; recommendations by the Commission – on the basis of detailed studies – designed to further promote the improvement in the Community's agricultural structure; and the allocation of financial aid from Community funds.

The aim of the Community's common market policy was described in the Third General Report on the Activities of the Community in 1960 as being 'to establish among the agricultural markets of the member states a common market which will have the characteristics of an internal market'. This, in turn, meant the establishment of a common level of agricultural prices – at least for a number of major products. The system proposed by the Commission divided agricultural products into three groups. For the first of these, covering wheat, coarse grains, sugar and dairy produce, the Commission suggested that there should be established a European market organization with extensive powers of intervention in each individual market and of limitation and control of imports from third countries. The second group would cover beef, pigmeat, poultry and eggs where, it was argued, no overall market organization was required. There would be little or no intervention in national market operations, although some means of guaranteeing farmers' incomes and affecting protection against imports would have to be devised. The third and last group, covering fruit, wine and vegetables, would be made subject to a system of strictly quality control and – particularly in the case of wine – to measures designed to match production and demand.

Let us look for a moment at just one product – wheat – in greater detail. Here the Commission proposed that the common organization covering the entire wheat market of the Community should be based on a target price for the following year's crop, which would be determined by the competent Community authorities before the autumn sowing. This target price would then serve as a guide in a number of essential urban areas in the Community where local production was insufficient to meet local requirements. In addition, there would be 'monthly target prices comprising additions for storage costs and interest to be calculated on the basis of the target price. The monthly target prices are to remain unchanged throughout the last three months of the farming year. Regional target prices are to be published to guide producers and traders. These regional target prices are to be so calculated that they allow for the normal cost of freight to the areas concerned.'[6]

The actual market price would be kept in line with the target price – wherever and whenever necessary – by support purchases during the last three months of the crop year by the competent

[6]*Cf. Third General Report on the Activities of the Community*, Brussels, May 1960, p. 171.

Community authorities. For the grain markets this would be a body to be known as the European Grain Office. In the event of the market price falling substantially below the target price during the earlier part of the crop year, then the Grain Office would be empowered to effect support purchases at what has come to be known as the 'intervention' price between 5% and 10% below the monthly target price. In general, however, the Grain Office would attempt to meet such a situation by offering loans to farmers to encourage them to stock any surplus produce and so reduce the level of public support prices as much as possible. Community wheat producers would be protected against imports from third countries by means of a special levy charged at all ports of entry. The amount of the levy would be calculated on the difference between the minimum import price – which would in itself be a function of the target price – and the corresponding world market price. In this way the price for imported wheat would automatically be put on a level with that of Community-produced wheat, irrespective of the price level originally quoted by the third country producer. The proceeds of the levy would be used mainly in this case to subsidize Community wheat exports. Complex though these arrangements may seem, it should be borne in mind, first, that the arrangements for wheat are the most complicated of all those applying to agricultural products and, secondly, that the accepted basic philosophy underlying the Community's policy is that Community farmers must be given absolute priority throughout the common market area and that the more self-sufficient the Community can become in terms of food production, the better this will be.

Despite continuous discussions, numerous amendments, recommendations from governments and advisory bodies and resolutions by the European Parliament, little or no real progress was made in 1960 and 1961 in the great agricultural debate. The Germans in particular, and understandably enough, had little enthusiasm for the extension and application of the common market in agriculture, which could only mean the substitution of expensive Community imports for cheap third country imports, and took every opportunity of postponing the issue. The French, however, were not prepared to see the glittering prize of the German agricultural market snatched away from in front of their very noses and, as the first stage of the common market drew to a close at the end of 1961, made their agreement on passing on to the second stage conditional upon agreement by the other Five on a definite timetable for the introduction of the common market in agriculture. The result was the first of the famous marathon sessions of the Council of Ministers and the European Commission which began late in December 1961 and finally reached agreement on 14 January 1962 after adopting the colourful expedient of 'stopping the clock' at midnight on

31 December 1961 and making the terms of the agreement reached two weeks later apply retrospectively to the end of 1961 so as to enable the second stage of the establishment of the common market to come duly into operation on 1 January 1962 : a little false perhaps, but the psychological effect was undoubtedly very great throughout the Community.

The marathon session of December 1961 – January 1962 constituted a major triumph for France. The French Ministers at the meeting, Couve de Murville, Minister for Foreign Affairs, and Pisani, Minister of Agriculture, although subjected to numerous and heavy attacks, compromise proposals and suggestions for further postponements, were implacable. Eventually, as has so often happened in the Community, the other Five gave way in the face of French intransigence, although the Germans were able to secure some minor safeguard arrangements. The result was that within less than three months regulations were issued by the Commission – largely on the basis of their own original proposals, which had been very similar to French thinking on the shape of the Community's agricultural policy – on the establishment of a common market in cereals, pigmeat, poultry and eggs. Most important of all, the Council decisions of 14 January 1962 laid down that agricultural policy would pass out of national control and become an essentially Community matter by the end of a $7\frac{1}{2}$-year transitional period. But although the ministerial decisions solved many immediate problems, they did not state specifically who would finally control the financial income resulting from the Community levies on imports from third countries. This issue was to prove of crucial importance in the Community crisis of 1965. The general financial arrangements were set out in the regulation establishing the European Agricultural Guidance and Guarantee Fund. It was, however, agreed that contributions to the fund by the six member states during the first three years should not exceed 31% of total contributions in the case of Germany, 28% for France and Italy, 13% for the Netherlands, and 10.5% for the Belgo-Luxembourg Union.

Development of relations with the Associated States

Article 133 of the treaty establishing the European Economic Community provided that imports into the member states of the Community originating from associated countries or territories would enjoy the full benefit of reductions in tariffs among the six member states themselves. In return the associated countries and territories undertook to grant preferential duties on imports from member states of the Community although retaining the right to levy such customs duties as were necessary to contribute towards the cost of further industrial development. In addition, there was the European Development Fund set up for the express purpose of providing

91

financial assistance for the social and economic development of the associated territories on a Community basis. Within two years of the signature of the Treaty of Rome, however, the position in Africa had undergone a fundamental change as almost all the former French colonial possessions and the former Belgian Congo became independent states. For a short time there was controversy in the Community between the Germans and the Dutch on the one hand and the French on the other as to the future of the association. The Germans and the Dutch argued that since the African countries were now fully independent states it was up to them to seek association with the Community under Article 238 in the same way as Greece and Turkey were in the process of doing. The French, on the other hand, supported by the African states themselves – who knew only too well on which side their bread was buttered – argued that the new independent states inherited both the obligations and the rights of the former colonial territories. Feeling ran high, particularly between Germany and France. The debate was pursued vigorously by the Africans themselves at a big parliamentary gathering organized in June 1961 at Strasbourg when there was a joint session between the members of the European Parliament and some 100 delegates from the 16 African associated states. Eventually, a compromise arrangement was reached, largely on the basis of proposals made by the European Commission, which led to the signature of a new Convention on 20 July 1963 at Yaoundé between the Six and their African associates.

The Yaoundé Convention which covers the five years from 1 June 1964 to 31 May 1969 provided for the gradual formation of a free trade area between the member states of the Community and each individual associated state and for grants and loans over this period of 730 million units of account, particularly for economic diversification and industrialization.

On free trade, the Yaoundé Convention dotted the i's and crossed the t's of the earlier agreement between the Six and the Associated States. All products from the associated states will now enter the Community duty-free by 1 July 1968. For certain products, notably pineapples, coconuts, coffee, tea, pepper, vanilla, cloves, nutmeg and cocoa, free entry came into force automatically on the signature of the Yaoundé Convention. For their part the associated African states undertook to finally abolish quota restrictions by 1967 and to complete, as soon as possible and practicable, the process of reducing tariffs on imports from Community countries. They continued to retain the right to impose duties designed to protect their own nascent industries.

The Convention provided that the financial aid furnished by the European Development Fund during this second five-year period would be used primarily for basic economic and industrial purposes such as road-building, provision of water supplies, harbour construction, as well as building more schools and hospitals. Special attention was also to be given to diversifying individual countries' agricultural production and reducing production costs so as to make the associated states more competitive in world markets.

Finally, the Yaoundé Convention provided the association between the Community and the African states with a detailed institutional framework embracing a Council of Association (to meet at ministerial level), a Parliamentary Conference – consisting of an equal number of members from the European Parliament and the Parliaments or Assemblies of the associated states who would meet once a year – and a Court of Arbitration.

Monetary policy

The Treaty of Rome was nowhere more discreet than in its references to the harmonization of monetary and fiscal policies and did little more in fact than provide for the establishment of a Monetary Committee. It was consequently left to the European Commission to take the bold step of preparing and submitting to the Council of Ministers a complex of measures designed to harmonize and bring together the monetary policies of the six member countries. This it duly did within the general framework of the 1962 Action programme which proposed first, the establishment of a special committee of Governors of the national banks of the six member states – which was seen as a kind of embryo of a future federal bank; second, the institution of an agreed and defined consultation procedure at the level of Finance Ministers or of Governors of the national banks to discuss all matters of major financial concern or interest, such as variations in bank rate, decisions relating to minimum liquidity ratios, etc.; and third, the formulation of a common Community attitude in major international financial institutions and discussions (*i.e.*, the International Monetary Fund). In the event, even this on the whole rather modest programme proved to be unacceptable at this stage in the development of the Community.

The institutions of the Community

The institutional framework of the European Community consists, as we have seen, of the European Commission, the Council of Ministers, the European Parliament and the Court of Justice. The duties and responsibilities of the Commission are set out in Article 155 of the Treaty of Rome; these are to :

ensure the application of the provisions of this treaty and of the provisions enacted by the institutions of the Community in pursuance thereof;

formulate recommendations or opinions in matters which are

93

the subject of this treaty, where the latter expressly so provides or where the Commission considers it necessary;

under the conditions laid down in this treaty to dispose of a power of decision of its own and participate in the preparation of acts of the Council and of the Assembly; and

exercise the competence conferred on it by the Council for the implementation of the rules laid down by the latter.

The last clause is crucial and revealing : the main function of the Commission is to carry out the rules determined or laid down by the Council of Ministers. The Commission has, admittedly, the right to submit proposals to the Council which the Council, in theory, must accept or reject – it does not have the power of amendment. The Commission has the responsibility for carrying out Community policies – once they have been approved by the Council – and is equipped with powers to do so. But the vital all-important consideration is that it is not the Commission, but the Council of Ministers, which is the real source of power and decision. The achievements of the common market between 1958 and 1962 – and they are real and vast achievements – often appear to flow from the action of the European Commission which, in certain quarters at least, tended to be given the credit for them. In fact, the Commission then, as now, was the secular arm carrying out the behests of the Council. The fact that the Council during these years readily endorsed the proposals submitted to it by the Commission proves only that these proposals were acceptable to the six national Ministers meeting in the Council. When the Community came to the first real 'crunch' in its development in December 1962 it was, inevitably, the six member governments, and not the Commission, who determined the issue. Pierre Drouin, in his book *l'Europe du Marché Commun*,[7] called the Community a bicephalous creature with the Council and the Commission as its twin heads. In theory and according to the provisions of the treaty this is accurate enough. In practice, there is only one – the Council. Article 145, which specifies the responsibility of the Council, may be brief but its meaning is unmistakable :

the Council shall

—ensure the co-ordination of the general economic policies of the member states; and

—dispose of a power of decision.

STEEL IN THE COMMON MARKET – A CASE STUDY

In 1965 Community crude steel production reached a record total of nearly 86 million tons – double the level of 1952 when the European Coal and Steel Community came into being. The share of each member in the Community crude steel production since 1952 has evolved as follows :

[7]Drouin, P., *L'Europe du Marché Commun*, Paris, Julliard, 1963, p. 126.

94

	West Germany	France	Italy	Per cent Netherlands	Belgium	Luxembourg
1952 :	44.36	25.88	8.66	1.65	12.30	7.15
1964 :	45.07	23.87	11.82	3.21	10.53	5.50
1965 :	42.85	22.81	14.71	3.63	10.66	5.34

The growth of Community production needs to be seen, however, in the perspective of world steel production which itself has more than doubled since 1952. The Community's share in world production which in 1952 was 19.6% was second only to that of the United States (41.1%) is now (at 19.3%) in third place after the United States (27.4%) and the U.S.S.R. (20.5%).

Crude steel consumption in the Community has grown from around 33 million tons in 1952 to some 70 million tons in 1965. The Community is among the world's leading exporters of steel; exports to non-Community countries which in 1965 totalled about 14 million tons (compared with 8 million tons in 1952), represented until the early '60s as much as 19% of crude steel production and in 1965 were still around 16%. An important feature of internal trade has been the increasing interpenetration of markets : the proportion of total business represented by tonnage ordered from one Community country by another has risen to over 20% compared with 11-12% before the establishment of the common market.

Development of structure: concentrations and E.C.S.C. policy

The structure of the steel market is traditionally oligopolistic; technical production conditions and the substantial capital investment required for the installation of plant themselves make for large and comparatively few producing enterprises. During the period of expansion since the time of establishment of the E.C.S.C. and particularly since the late '50s the need to turn out larger tonnages, the growth of the optimum size of iron- and steel-making plants, the need for modernization in the light of technological developments and the pressure to reduce costs in order to meet increasing severity of competition in world steel markets have increasingly encouraged a tendency towards the concentration of enterprises in order to form larger and better balanced units. In addition to embarking on mergers (horizontal concentrations) enterprises have also been seeking to rationalize production by specialization agreements whereby particular companies concentrate on particular products and by arrangements with others for the joint construction and use of manufacturing facilities. The development of this trend in the Community has been much influenced by the fact that the same process has been going on, and sometimes faster, in countries outside the Community.

In the European Coal and Steel Community concentrations have to be seen in the context of the Treaty of Paris provisions relating to the development of the Community's industries and to conditions of competition. Under the treaty the Community's institutions must 'ensure that conditions are maintained which will encourage undertakings to expand and improve their productive capacity' and must 'promote the orderly expansion and the modernization of production as well as the improvement of quality in conditions which preclude any protection against competing industries unless it is justified by improper action or in favour of such industries'. Restrictive practices tending to the allocation and exploitation of markets are prohibited, and the Community must 'assure the establishment, maintenance and observation of normal competitive conditions'. The particular provisions of the treaty relating to agreements (cartels) and concentrations (Articles 65 and 66) prohibit cartels with the exception of certain categories of agreement (which however require express authorization by the High Authority); and permits concentrations subject to certain exceptions.

As to cartels, Article 65 forbids all agreements which tend 'directly or indirectly to prevent, restrict or distort the normal operation of competition within the common market', and in particular price-fixing and market-sharing agreements and those which restrict production, technical development and capital investment. Exempted from this prohibition, but subject to High Authority authorization on specified conditions and for a limited period, are specialization agreements and joint buying or selling agreements for specified products which contribute to a substantial improvement in the production or distribution of the products in question, are essential to achieve these results, and not more restrictive than is necessary for that purpose; and are not capable of giving the interested parties the power to fix prices, control or limit the production or selling of a substantial part of the products in question in the common market, or of protecting them from effective competition by other enterprises within the common market.

On concentrations, Article 66 requires any transaction (whether by merger, acquisition of shares or assets, loan, contract or other means) which would have the effect of bringing about a concentration within the common market and which involves enterprises of which at least one is covered by the treaty to be submitted to the High Authority for prior authorization. The High Authority must grant the authorization (although it may attach conditions to it) if it finds that the proposed transaction will not give the interested enterprises power to determine prices, to control production or distribution in a substantial part of the market, to hinder the maintenance of effective competition or to evade the rules of competition. The High Authority is also bound to exempt from the requirement of prior authorization concentrations which, because of their relatively small size and the nature of the concentration involved, should in its opinion be regarded as meeting these conditions. Implementing regulations

96

issued by the High Authority in 1954 defined what concentrations were exempted. Finally, the last section of Article 66 deals with any enterprise, private or public, which already has or acquires a dominant position which protects it from effective competition in a substantial part of the common market. If the High Authority finds that such an enterprise is using its position 'for purposes contrary to the treaty' it must address recommendations to the enterprise to prevent the abuse and, failing compliance, can decide (after consulting the government concerned) to fix prices and conditions of sale to be applied by the enterprise in operation, or draw up production or delivery programmes which it must fulfil..

The High Authority's approach to the authorization of concentrations has, broadly, come to be based on recognition of the facts of the oligopolistic character of the steel market and the technical trends towards further concentration, and determination in the light of these facts of the necessary minimum of 'effective competition' to be maintained in accordance with Article 66 of the treaty. In the policy section of its Annual Report for 1958, the High Authority was already saying :

The structure of the Community iron and steel industry has to be considered from two angles : the need to ensure a sufficient number of production units capable of competing with one another effectively, and the need to have these of optimum size. Technical studies on this latter aspect indicate that once production goes beyond a certain volume (which increases as technical progress continues), unit costs cease to fall.

This is an essential point to be borne in mind in matters of concentration and specialization.

For some time past there has been a tendency among iron and steel enterprises in all the member countries to regroup in order to form larger and better-balanced units. At its present extent – it has maintained, and indeed increased, its momentum since the introduction of the Common Market – this development can be regarded as progress. Quite a number of enterprises are producing between one and a half and two and a half million tons of steel a year – some even more – and form integrated groups covering every stage of production, from coke and pig-iron right through to the finished products.

During the same period there has been a marked trend towards vertical integration between steel and coal. A similar development was observable some time previously between steel and iron ore.

Finally, iron and steel enterprises frequently form part of complex financial link-ups with groups of banks, commercial firms or other industries.

This situation is very definitely not in line with the theoretical set-up of enterprises competing in respect of each type of product solely on the basis of their production costs and operating conditions for the product concerned. But iron and steel production, to be economic, must be on a certain scale; moreover, steel-making proper comprises a number of stages which, if the lowest possible production costs are to be obtained, have to be carefully streamlined to ensure smooth transition from one to the next. It is therefore in itself relatively concentrated and relatively integrated and any attempt to fix the exact point at which vertical integration can be said to begin and end is bound to be somewhat arbitrary. We need only take the example of a coking-plant or a tube works to see that this is so. Moreover, even if exact limits could be laid down with reference to a particular stage in technical advance, they could well be invalidated shortly afterwards by the introduction of new processes.

A different approach is thus required. Integration must be motivated by the economic and technical advantages it offers, not by any distortions operating in its favour. . . .

As regards horizontal concentration, it cannot be allowed in the Community to reach the point of market leadership or price leadership by individual enterprises. This would lead to serious difficulties. The concentrations approved by the High Authority under the treaty are those enabling a larger number of groups to compete on equal terms.

Up to the end of 1958, however, the majority of concentrations the High Authority had been called upon to authorize were 'vertical', involving mainly steel and coal (7) and steel and processing works (12), and only nine were horizontal, affecting only relatively small percentages of Community production. A new phase then began in the momentum and scale of moves for horizontal concentrations between steelmaking enterprises; this was mainly characterized by proposals in Germany for mergers which largely involved reconcentrations, *i.e.*, a reversal of the postwar deconcentration of German steel firms.

Between 1959 and 1962 the High Authority in fact authorized the take-over of the Bochumer Verein by the Krupp-controlled Hutten and Bergwerke Rheinhausen (affecting a 1956 production of over 3 million tons of crude steel or 5.5% of Community production); of Huttenwerke Siegerland by Dortmund Hörder Huttenunion (3 million tons or 7% of Community production of rolled products); of Stahlwerke Bochum by the Otto Wolff group (2.2% of Community crude steel production or 6.9% of finished rolled products). The High Authority also authorized the acquisition by August Thyssen of a 50% holding in Rasselstein (a leading member of sheet steel, the other half of whose shares were held by Otto Wolff), and the take-over by Thyssen of Handelsunion (at that time the selling company of a number of large steel producers, including Dortmund-Hörder, Siegerland and Thyssen itself). In the case of Hutten and Bergwerke Rheinhausen/Bochumer Verein, the High Authority made it clear that it was under no obligation to maintain the postwar deconcentration measures; its responsibility was to assess the criteria and apply the rules of the treaty, and in particular to examine whether the transactions in question would give the enterprises concerned the power to hamper competition or evade the rules of competition, including the possibilities which the cencentrations would offer in this respect for the future. In the case of Dortmund-Hörder Huttenunion/Siegerland, the High Authority found that notwithstanding the strong position which would accrue to the two firms in the rolled-products market as a result of the deconcentration, they would still be in competition in the Common Market with enterprises and groups of enterprises of comparable size. The Otto Wolff and August Thyssen transactions presented special problems because they, Stahlwerke Bochum and Rasselstein were makers of sheet, while Handelsunion marketed a particularly high percentage of the plate and sheet produced by Dortmund-Hörder and Siegerland. To ensure that Thyssen, through its control of Handelsunion, would not be in a position to restrict competition between itself and Dortmund, the High Authority made it a condition of authorization that Dortmund should obtain an alternative sales channel for its products, and as a further safeguard against too close a connection between Thyssen and Dortmund, required Thyssen to give up a minority holding in Siegerland. The High Authority also imposed conditions designed to ensure that the new joint control of Siergerland by Thyssen and Wolff did not conceal a merger or unduly restrict competition between them. During this period the High Authority also considered an application made by August Thyssen Hutte at the end of 1958 for authorization of its plan to secure control of Phoenix-Rheinrohr. This concentration, the biggest so far brought before the High Authority, would have affected a potential of about 6 million tons of steel. In this case the High Authority was concerned both about the market position which the new group would acquire and possibly develop, but also about the effect of the concentration on the structure of the market for rolled products over half of which was already supplied by a small group of big producers. It therefore made its authorization conditional, not only on the renunciation of certain share-holdings by Thyssen in third firms and the limitation of certain supply agreements, but also on control by the High Authority of the major investments of the new group until further notice; this latter condition was unacceptable to Thyssen, which in 1961 withdrew its application.

In 1961–2 a group of Belgian, Luxembourg and French firms

decided to launch jointly the new steel concern, 'Sidmar', to be established in Belgium and to comprise as well as berthing and unloading facilities for large ore carriers, a complete ore-preparation plant, two large capacity blast furnaces, an L/D oxygen steel works with three converters, a slabbing mill, an 80 inch continuous hot wide-strip mill and an 80 inch four-stand tardem cold mill. Production of flats would by 1965 be approximately 10% of Community production. The High Authority authorized this project (this was the first time it had been called upon to take a decision under Article 66 in respect of a joint venture) on condition that the new enterprise's production of finished products would consist exclusively of wide strip and other flats. The main conclusions as regards conformity with Article 66 criteria drew attention to the possible 'group effect' on competition of such joint ventures. In the Sidmar case, however, the High Authority concluded that concentration would not mean a concentration of the four participating groups themselves and that although the joint control of Sidmar would have restrictive effects on the promoters' competition with each other in respect of flat products, their share of Community production as a whole would not put them in a position to hinder effective competition in the market for flats. The limiting condition attached to the authorization established an important principle, namely that a fresh assessment by the High Authority may be required if a fundamental change is made in the production programme of a joint venture which might have implications for competition and for the participating enterprises' relationships to one another.

Developments since the early '60s show a strong trend of more massive concentrations and joint ventures in the Community; these have been stimulated by growing appreciation of the advantages of large-scale operation (to some extent promoted by High Authority technical studies), the bigger capacities and cost of modern plant and the example of competing producers outside the Community. The High Authority's approach to competitive policy has at the same time evolved in ways which, within limits, permit or even encourage such development. The basis of its present attitude is clearly indicated in a statement of policy issued in 1964 :

> Increasing concentration of production in large production units is not necessarily synonomous with restriction of competition in the market. Although when two enterprises form a concentration competition between them of course ceases, the stronger market position occupied by the new enterprise so constituted can serve to intensify competition with others. The larger the production units become, the more, as a rule, the market too should broaden, with competition becoming fuller and keener. Generally speaking, in the appraisal of horizontal steel concentrations the relevant market is today more and more

having to be taken as covering the whole northern industrial triangle, comprising the component segments of the Ruhr, the Netherlands, Belgium, Luxembourg, Northern France, Lorraine and the Saar. For competition among the enterprises is more and more extending throughout this area.

Furthermore, in judging conditions of competition in the steel market and assessing impending moves towards concentration, it is becoming necessary to take increasing account of factors concerning the Community's external trade relations. . . .

The specture of 'giantism' that is held up in some quarters in view of the tendency, for technical reasons, for production units to increase in size may be discounted, especially as it is the High Authority's principle in approving concentrations to ensure that a sufficient degree of competition is maintained. Hence in concentration policy the purely quantitative aspect takes second place to other considerations : these include in particular the elimination of interlocking directorates and of certain types of delivery contract, which would be liable to impair adequate competition among the large units.

Briefly, a balanced structure based on a small number of large groups in effective independent competition with each other is acceptable, but there must be no links between groups or enterprises serving to restrict such competition.

The substantial concentrations authorized since 1963 reflect this policy. In 1963 a renewed application from August Thyssen to acquire a majority interest in Phoenix-Rheinrohr was successful; this affected about 10% of Community production of steel and 7½% of production of finished rolled products. The main condition attached to the High Authority's authorization was that no inter-locking directorates were to be permitted between enterprises of the Thyssen/Phoenix group and outside enterprises engaged in the production or marketing of steel. In 1964 the High Authority authorized the formation of two French companies of a jointly controlled company, the Societe Mosellane de Siderurgie (Somosid) concentrating their crude steel production facilities (2 million tons). Conditions were attached to the authorization designed to prevent close and sustained co-operation through Somosid of other big iron and steel concerns having interests in the two holding companies. Also in 1964 the High Authority authorized on the basis of similar principles the creation by the two French groups Sidelor and de Wendel of a jointly-owned company Sacilor (Societe des Acieries de Lorraine) to build a new steel works (over 2 million tons) at Gaudrange (Moselle) on a site mostly belonging to the founding companies and close to their existing plants. The new works will produce crude steel and the corresponding semi-finished products and merchant bars from pig iron provided by the founding companies and will have them processed or sold through the companies. The authorization is limited to these products and is subject to conditions designed to control the possible group effect of links between the founding companies and other big groups.

Towards the end of 1965 the Luxembourg Arbed iron and steel group (crude steel production + 3 million tons) announced proposals for the acquisition of the 60% holding of the French Pont-a-Mousson group in the Luxembourg steel company Hadir (1.4 million tons). The concentration was presented as part of a plan to increase Arbed's industrial potential, to rationalize its operations and to widen its production range. The production and processing arrangements of the two companies were largely complementary, but in the years ahead any duplication could be systematically eliminated by co-ordinating investments. The works, which were located on ore fields and close to major consumer centres, would be able to specialize in a very small number of products; the resulting rationalization would cut production costs and improve products. In dealing with this case the High Authority authorized the concentration project in principle, after discussion with the parties concerned, soon after it had been placed before it (the object being to bring more flexibility into the application of Article 66) and issuing a full formal authorization in due course. The full authorization, which has just been given, includes in particular conditions intended to prevent the retention of links between the new Arbed-Hadir group and other steel groups, notably Pont-a-Mousson, *e.g.,* it provided that by December 1968 Hadir must no longer sell through Davum, the Pont-a-Mousson group's selling organization. The Arbed-Hadir group now produces over 6% of the Community crude steel, but if Arbed's participation in Sidmar is taken into account the proportion affected becomes 17%.

Current developments

In 1966 there were announcements of two major concentration developments which will have important effects on the structure of the Community's steel industry; the proposed merger of Hosch AG and Dortmunder-Hörder-Huttenunion, and plans for mergers in France which will amount to a structural reorganization of the French steel industry in the context of France's new five-year economic plan.

The German merger involves the absorption by Hösch (crude steel production 2.6 million tons) of Huttenunion (3.1 million tons), in which the big Dutch firm Hoogovens (2.8 million tons – to be increased to 4 million tons by 1970) has an important holding. In explaining the merger, emphasis has been placed on the strongly complementary nature of the two companies, which have been co-operating for some years in the field of iron ore sinter, pig iron, crude steel semis and hot-rolled wide strip. The intention is to extend this co-operation to finished rolled products and to sales policy as well as to investment policy. In this way and through continued co-operation also with Hoogovens on production arrangements and the co-ordination of expansion plans, the companies hope to achieve substantial reductions in their production costs and to avoid superflous investments.

An important feature of the new arrangements is the scope they are expected to give for co-ordinated specialization by the companies involved. The Ijmuiden works situated on the coast and using ore and coal obtained cheaply from abroad will develop its pig iron and crude steel production up to the stage of semis and coils; these products will then be delivered to the Dortmund works which will concentrate their activity on rolled products and processing. The merger project was officially notified to the High Authority in the middle of January 1966. First discussions have taken place and authorization by the High Authority is expected fairly soon. The production of the new Hosch group will represent nearly 7% of E.C.S.C. crude steel production and a similar proportion of rolled products production. Taking into account Hoogovens, the production of crude steel affected (about 9 million tons) will be about 10% of Community production.

In France the Boards of Usinor, the biggest French steel producer (4 million tons) and Lorraine-Escaut, the fourth biggest producer (2.3 million tons) approved in February last year a plan for a merger of the two concerns whereby Usinor will take over Lorraine-Escaut. Also planned is the merger of the two groups' parent companies, Denain-Anzin Nord-Est (which controls Usinor) and Acieries de Longwy (controlling Lorraine-Escaut). The object of this concentration is stated to be the rationalization of the two groups' activities : it is expected that one result will be the development of Usinor's new Dunkirk coastal works (the most modern in France) and a corresponding slowing down of the activity of the old Longwy works. The High Authority is expected to authorize it subject to conditions preventing links with other big groups.

The proposed Usinor/Lorraine-Escaut merger is the first definite step towards the fulfilment of new plans evolved by the French steel industry, encouraged by the prospect of further advantageous government finance for rationalization, for reorganizing the structure of the industry with the object of enabling it to meet the demands of competition and technical progress by increasing the scale of its operations. The programme envisages the merger also of de Wendel and Sidelor (with a combined production of 5.6 million tons of crude steel, or 8.3 million tons including the Gaudrange plant) and the conclusion of technical specialization agreements designed to make the French steel industry more competitive in relation to other producers in the Community or in the rest of the world. The two new groups would have a combined steel production capacity of 14 million tons compared with a total French steel production of some 19.6 million tons last year. It is thought, however, that the High Authority will be unlikely to raise fundamental objections to the programme.

What, briefly, are the conclusions to be drawn from our examination of the development of the steel market during the last 15 years in which the Community regime has applied? Obviously, a very big expansion in both production and demand; equally obvious have been the growth, modernization and rationalization of production facilities. But another vital and perhaps less immediately obvious factor has been the change in Community thinking on the whole question of cartels and concentrations. Today, the Community – which 15 years ago came into the world armed with a formidable array of anti-trust weapons – has committed itself irretrievably to a policy of promoting concentrations in the steel industry.

CHAPTER 5

Britain and the Common Market: the first round

Three weeks to the day after the High Authority opened its offices on 10 August 1952, a Permanent United Kingdom Delegation to the High Authority of the European Coal and Steel Community was set up in Luxembourg, and on 1 September 1962 the Head of the United Kingdom Delegation, Sir Cecil Weir, presented his letters of credence to the President of the High Authority.

There followed during the next two years a period of negotiations leading to the signature in London on 21 December 1954 of an Agreement of Association between the United Kingdom Government and the European Coal and Steel Community. The Agreement was subsequently approved by Parliament and approved by the appropriate bodies in the Community countries. Among the provisions of the Agreement, which like the Treaty of Paris has a duration of fifty years, was the establishment of a Council of Association, composed on the United Kingdom side of two Ministers and the Chairmen of the National Coal and Iron and Steel Boards (both Boards were signatories to the Agreement) and, for the Community, of four members of the High Authority. The object of the Council is 'to provide means for the continuous exchange of information and for consultation in regard to matters of common interest concerning coal and steel and, where appropriate, in regard to the co-ordination of action in these matters.' There is also a clause in the Agreement providing for special meetings of the E.C.S.C. Council of Ministers and the U.K. Government with the full participation of the High Authority. The Council of Association held its first meeting in Luxembourg on 17 November 1955 and decided to establish three standing committees on coal, steel and trade relations. These committees have normally met two or three times a year and, as their names imply, have dealt respectively with matters relating to the coal and steel industries and to problems affecting trade in these two commodities between the Community and the United Kingdom.

As the only organic link between the Community and the United

Kingdom, what, it may be asked, has been the value of the Council of Association and what is there to show on the credit side after twelve years of existence? Certainly, it has not led to the adoption by the United Kingdom of Community measures with regard to, say, price publication, transport arrangements or cartel policies. Conversely, British practice has had little influence over the policies pursued by the High Authority. The position today, therefore, is that while prices in the Community, for example, are published, in the United Kingdom they are not; and that whereas in the Community the High Authority is endeavouring to ensure that transport rates should be published, carriers in the United Kingdom are under no obligation to publish their rates. The difference is much less clear-cut with regard to cartels and concentrations where – as we have seen – there has been a considerable shift in the High Authority's thinking and approach to this problem. But then to hold the Council of Association responsible for failure to eliminate such differences would be to misinterpret the spirit and objectives of the original Agreement, whose essential purpose was to promote mutual understanding. It is in this respect that the Council of Association has been most successful, so that its real value is to be found in the personal relations that exist today at all levels. These, together with the regular contact maintained between the United Kingdom Delegation in Luxembourg and the High Authority, have made an undoubted contribution to greater mutual comprehension, both by promoting a deeper appreciation, on both sides, of the problems involved, and by dispelling many of the misapprehensions that might otherwise have arisen. These beneficial effects were evident during the 1962 negotiations for British membership of the three European Communities. While the greater part of the negotiations naturally took place in Brussels, those for membership of the E.C.S.C. were held in Luxembourg and, although the suspension of the negotiations in February 1963 occurred before the main issues affecting coal and steel had been resolved, it was widely accepted on both sides that none of the problems raised were insuperable and that, given the will to succeed, solutions could and would be found.

Nevertheless, however useful or desirable the work undertaken by the Council of Association may have been, it soon became very evident that the gulf between association and full membership was vastly greater than those who had signed the Association Agreement ever imagined. Where, in the Community, there existed, at least in the early years, a sense of purpose and cohesion, the association often gave the appearance of being little more than an occasional amiable get together, at which a certain amount of interesting information could be exchanged and discussion of potentially delicate problems indefinitely adjourned. If, indeed, the Association Agreement has made one thing clear, it is that association cannot conceivably be an acceptable alternative to full membership of the European Economic Community.

The Free Trade Area negotiations

The withdrawal of the British representative from the Spaak Committee and the increasingly likely prospect that the Six would bring their negotiations for the establishment of a general common market as well as an atomic pool to a successful conclusion, compelled the British government in 1956 to reconsider its overall policy *vis-a-vis* Western Europe. There were in effect three possible courses of action. The first was to take up arms against the proposed European formations and to seek to nip them in the bud; this line of action had its adherents but came up against the implacable determination of the Six to go ahead with their own scheme with or without British participation – much though some of them preferred and still hoped for the latter alternative. The second was to do nothing and to wait and see how matters would develop in the new European grouping. This, in retrospect, might well have proved the most satisfactory course from Britain's point of view since, paradoxically enough, the Free Trade Area negotiations between Britain and the Six – and the outright support given by the Americans to the common market proposals – were in fact to accelerate and harden the cohesion of the Six. At the time, however, it seemed a counsel of despair. The Government believed – with a certain amount of justification – that the majority of the Six were anxious to have Britain in their new club and – with rather less justification – that they were prepared to pay a substantial price for her inclusion. The third possibility was to propose a new wider trading arrangement which would embrace the Six – as a single unit – the United Kingdom and other member countries of O.E.E.C., many of whom, particularly Switzerland and the Scandinavian countries, were, broadly, more in sympathy with the United Kingdom approach than with the harsher economic doctrine of the Community. It was this third alternative which the British Government finally decided to adopt.

The first indication of the new British initiative came at a session of the O.E.E.C. Council of Ministers in July 1956 when the Secretary-General of the Organization proposed that a special working party should be established to study the possibility of creating a free trade area covering all the member countries of O.E.E.C., but with the six Community countries being treated as a single entity. During the next few months, British Ministers, who had enthusiastically welcomed the O.E.E.C. initiative, declared that they envisaged the proposed free trade area as relating to industrial goods and that food, drink and tobacco would be excluded. The British Government pressed very strongly at this time for some form of arrangement whereby the work on the establishment of a free trade area could be linked with that of the Six on the formation of the general common market with a view to securing the simultaneous entry into operation of both schemes. M. Spaak was accordingly invited to come to London for discussions on the dovetailing of the two schemes but he insisted that work on the drafting of the common market treaty would have to be given priority.[1] Spaak's view – which was upheld by the rest of the Ministers of the Six – was that while the free trade area proposals were potentially useful they were inevitably supplementary to the much more far-reaching common market arrangements and, as such, were best left till after the common market treaty itself had been finalized.

The working party set up as a result of the proposal made by the O.E.E.C. Secretary-General completed its report in December 1956. The report was published one month later and this was followed in February 1957 by the publication of a White Paper which set out a proposal by the British government for the creation of an industrial free trade area. The White Paper clearly spelt out the fact that there were substantial differences between the proposed common market arrangements of the Six and the preferential trading area envisaged at that time by Her Majesty's Government[2] : 'The arrangements proposed for the Customs and Economic Union (of the Six) involve far-reaching provisions for economic integration and harmonization of financial and social policies and for mutual assistance in the financing of investment. These recommendations are to be effected within an appropriate institutional framework. Her Majesty's Government envisage the Free Trade Area, on the other hand, as a concept related primarily to the removal of restrictions on trade such as tariffs and quotas. Nevertheless, Her Majesty's Government recognise that co-operation in the field of economic policy is of great and continuing importance. In practice an appreciable movement towards closer economic co-operation may be expected to take place among the members of a Free Trade Area over a period of years, either as a matter of deliberate policy or as a spontaneous development.' Both the O.E.E.C. and the British memoranda were discussed at a somewhat stormy meeting of the O.E.E.C. Council in February 1957. Not only did the British representatives find themselves in almost complete isolation on their proposal that agriculture should be excluded (even the Scandinavians, for example, were strongly opposed to its exclusion), but the Six again made it absolutely clear that they were not in any way prepared to slow down the impetus of the negotiations on the common market in order to synchronize the opening of their common market with that of the proposed free trade area. Miriam Camps in her detailed account of the free trade

[1]*Cf.* M. Camps, *op. cit.,* p. 101.
[2]*Cf.* Cmnd. 72, February 1957, H.M.S.O.

area negotiations, relates that Pierre Drouin, at that time the Common Market correspondent of *Le Monde,* who 'reflected official French views with remarkable accuracy', made it clear in his articles 'that the French feared and, even more important, rejected intellectually the British concept of a system essentially limited to the removal of barriers to trade'.[3] Although the upshot of the O.E.E.C. ministerial meeting was a decision to enter into negotiations to examine the basis on which a European Free Trade Area might be brought into being, it was on the understanding that the negotiations would not be limited to industrial products and that satisfactory arrangements for agriculture would be devised.

The next step on the British side was the appointment of Mr. Maudling as the Minister in charge of co-ordinating the work within the British Government on the negotiations for the establishment of a free trade area, with the hope that once the six Community countries had completed the process of ratification of the Rome Treaties it would prove possible to accelerate work on the free trade area. While there was now no prospect of the two trade plans coming into operation simultaneously, the British Government still hoped that the actual process of tariff-cutting (not due to begin under the Treaty of Rome until 1 January 1959) could be synchronized. During the summer the Government also discussed the free trade area proposals in detail with the leaders of the Commonwealth countries at the London Commonwealth Conference and secured a broad measure of support for its policies.

Within the Six, on the other hand, opposition to the free trade concept was hardening. The French, in particular, were economically still fearful of the likely impact of competition from German industry under the Common Market arrangements, while politically they saw little to be gained from agreeing to British wishes to set up a free trade area, particularly in view of the fact that under the proposed arrangements Britain would continue to get the full benefit of cheap food imports from the Commonwealth. The other five member states, while desiring on the one hand to establish closer links with Britain, accepted throughout this period that their first loyalty was to their own nascent Community.

This hardening of attitude on the part of the Six – and of the French in particular – was reflected in the subsequent O.E.E.C. ministerial discussions. While it was agreed to set up an Inter-governmental Committee, with Mr Maudling as chairman, the French soon made their uncompromising attitude unmistakably clear. Their position briefly was this. To be acceptable to the Six the proposed free trade area should have a common external tariff (which would therefore have operated against all other countries,

[3] *Cf.* M. Camps, *op. cit.,* p. 117. For a detailed and admirable account of the whole of the Free Trade Area negotiations see ibid, pp. 93–231.

including members of the Commonwealth) since only by this means would it be possible to avoid major distortions of trade arising from the advantageous position that would otherwise come about for countries such as Britain, which would continue to have access to cheap food and raw material supplies from outside the free trade area. If such an arrangement were unacceptable to some of the countries concerned in the negotiations, then the only alternative course of action was to so limit the scope of the free trade area negotiations as to make the resulting trade advantages a matter of doubtful value. Despite a number of British concessions, both in regard to agriculture and the extension, wherever possible, of the provisions of the Treaty of Rome to the proposed free trade area, the negotiations became from this time onwards more and more bogged down in the quagmire of Franco-British disagreement. Eventually, in February 1958 (*i.e.,* after the formal commencement of the general common market) the French circulated a memorandum to their colleagues in the Six – based on a proposal that had already been summarily discussed at an earlier stage and had then been rejected as unacceptable by the United Kingdom – suggesting the introduction of a time-lag (decalage) of three years between the reduction in tariffs within the general common market and the free trade area. Other glaringly objectionable features in the French plan – from the British point of view – were the proposals that the transitional period for the free trade area should be longer than that for the general common market, that there should be a sector by sector approach to the whole problem, and that the continental countries should in some way share in the advantages of the Commonwealth Preference System (by means of duty-free or preferential quotas on an individual country basis).[4] The darkening clouds were rapidly becoming more and more menacing and it was now evident to all that the prospects of a successful conclusion to the negotiations had become extremely remote. In October the Six drafted a common memorandum which in effect set out the conditions which the other countries involved in the negotiations would have had broadly to accept if there was to be any likelihood of a successful outcome. This was coming dangerously, if politely, close to an ultimatum. In November, the French Foreign Minister, M. Couve de Murville, came over to London for discussions with the British Government, but the talks ended in deadlock. A few days later the Maudling Committee met for what was to be its last meeting. The meeting itself proved to be inconclusive but was followed by a statement by M. Soustelle, the French Minister of Information, in which he declared that : 'It has become clear to France that the creation of a free trade area as desired by the British, that is to say by means of the establishment of free trade between the

[4]Ibid, pp. 144–45.

110

six countries of the Common Market and the eleven other member countries of the O.E.E.C., is impossible because of the absence of a single common external tariff embracing all seventeen countries and the lack of harmonization in the economic and social fields.' M. Soustelle, however, was careful not to slam the door completely. He went on : 'This does not mean that it is impossible to find a solution which will meet the requirements both of the six countries of the Common Market and the other countries of Western Europe in their mutual economic relationships. The French Government, for its part, is already actively concerned to find such a solution. The position that has arisen should not therefore be interpreted as a dead-end. If the solution put forward by the United Kingdom has not proved acceptable as it stood, then the problem should continue to be studied.' In Britain, M. Soustelle's statement to the press had the effect of a bombshell. The next meeting of the Maudling Committee was postponed (on the initiative of Mr Maudling himself) in the apparent hope that the clear risk of failure would frighten all concerned in them into making some concessions in order to avoid their final breakdown. The rot, however, had gone too far. The British had made their concessions too few at a time and too late to seriously break open the closed ranks of the Six. As it was Mr Maudling's decision to call off the next meeting of the negotiating committee left the Six comparatively unmoved. The Free Trade Area negotiations had reached the end of the road.

The Stockholm Convention and the Outer Seven

The breakdown of the Free Trade Area negotiations left the member states of O.E.E.C. that were not in the Common Market with a profound sense of economic isolation. There was, on the one hand, the prospect of a massive and powerful preferential area in the heart of Europe which, by its very nature, could not in the longer term but discriminate harshly against the rest of Europe; and, on the other hand, a fear lest the new Community, acting as a single unit of totally disproportionate strength, would eventually seek or indeed come naturally to impose trading terms upon the other members of O.E.E.C. one by one. This fear was felt not only in government departments but also – and probably more acutely – in business circles where the ill-fated free trade area proposals had on the whole been warmly welcomed. The result was a closing of ranks by a number of the remaining member states of O.E.E.C. and a series of meetings and discussions among them which led, ultimately, to a special session of Ministers from the United Kingdom, Sweden, Denmark, Norway, Switzerland, Portugal and Austria on 21–22 July 1959 at Saltsjobaden, near Stockholm, to agree the terms of a draft plan for a European Free Trade Association comprising their seven

111

countries : an agreement which has since become generally known as the Stockholm Convention.

The European Free Trade Association of the Outer Seven envisaged the abolition of tariffs on imported goods originating in the E.F.T.A. area by means of an initial reduction of 20% on 1 July 1960 (intended to bring E.F.T.A. tariff reductions into line with those of the common market countries) and subsequent successive reductions of 10% with the object of securing the complete elimination of customs duties by 1 January 1970. Provision was made for an acceleration of tariff reductions and these provisions have in fact been implemented so that the last tariffs are now due to be abolished on 1 January 1968. The Convention also included a number of escape clauses in the event of member states getting into difficulties and provided for special arrangements for agriculture :

> Members are agreed that there should be a special agreement on agriculture designed to facilitate expansion of trade between members, having regard both to the question of agricultural policies and to the need to achieve a sufficient degree of reciprocity between them.

> Upon the request of any member bilateral discussions should take place as soon as possible between members regarding trade in specific agricultural products of importance to exporting countries and report should be made to the Ministers.[5]

Providing as it did for the creation of a free trade area the Convention made no mention of a common external tariff and – unlike the Treaty of Rome – left individual member states free to maintain their own independent tariffs towards third countries.

But if the E.F.T.A. Convention was largely prompted by a desire to obviate, at least in part, the fear of isolation, there was also a strong current of hope that by practically aligning itself upon the objectives of the Treaty of Rome – in the field of tariff reductions, quota restrictions as well as the readiness shown to include special provisions for agriculture – it might pave the way for some overall arrangement with the common market countries. The draft Convention stated this quite specifically :

> Ministers decided to recommend to their governments that a European Free Trade Association among the Seven countries should be established. The object of this association would be to strengthen the economies of its members by promoting expansion of economic activity, full employment, a rising standard of living and financial stability. Ministers affirmed that in establishing a European Free Trade Association it would be their purpose to facilitate early negotiations both with the European Economic Community and also with the other mem-

[5]*Cf. Stockholm Draft Plan for a European Free Trade Association,* Cmnd. 823, H.M.S.O., July 1959, p. 14.

bers of the O.E.E.C. who have particular problems calling for solutions. These negotiations would have as their object to remove trade barriers and establish a multilateral association embracing all members of the O.E.E.C. Governments would thus be able to reinforce European economic co-operation within the O.E.E.C. and to promote the expansion of world trade.[6]

Institutionally, the arrangements were deliberately made as simple as possible, with all decisions left to a Council of Ministers. A small permanent secretariat was subsequently set up in Geneva.

The establishment of E.F.T.A. was received with a marked lack of enthusiasm by industrial and business circles in Britain. Many of the member states – particularly in Scandinavia – were already low tariff countries and the margin of preference arising for British exports was generally considered to be insufficient to secure a substantial commercial advantage. In the case of Austria it was questionable whether the tariff reductions would in some cases even compensate for the higher transport charges from Britain than from, say, Germany. This disenchantment with E.F.T.A. was reflected in the trading figures and returns of the next two or three years which showed that British exports to other E.F.T.A. countries were increasing at rates often well below those to North America or to the common market itself – despite increasing discrimination in favour of goods from other Community countries. This economic disenchantment was paralleled by persistent reports of a growing conviction among British Ministers that, since the very character of the Stockholm Convention gave it little political significance, Britain was in danger of losing ground politically to the European grouping across the Channel.

Although the British attitude to the common market and the Treaty of Rome did not change suddenly or abruptly from one day to the next, the change in emphasis and outlook occurred nevertheless in a remarkably short space of time. Of course the concessions made during the free trade area negotiations in 1958 had, already, represented an astonishing advance on the positions adopted by the British Government only three years before in the Spaak Committee. Even so, the further shift in attitude from 1959 to the formal announcement by Mr Macmillan in the House of Commons on 31 July 1961 that the British Government had decided to seek negotiations with the Community with a view to examining the possibility of British accession seems to us now, in retrospect, to have taken place with extraordinary rapidity. At the same time, it should be emphasised that no one in 1957 could have foreseen the rate and extent at which Franco-German relations and co-operation were to develop. The accession to power on 1 June 1958 of General de Gaulle was at first looked upon with suspicion by most of the leading

[6]Ibid, p. 3.

statesmen of the other five Community countries. By 1961 relations between France and Germany, due largely no doubt to the vital personal relationship between Dr Adenauer and President de Gaulle had led to what was often referred to at the time as the Paris-Bonn axis and culminated two years later in the signature in Paris in January 1963 of the Franco-German Treaty of friendship and co-operation. This trend towards political co-operation – political union was in fact the avowed aim on both sides – between France and Germany, and the weight and authority that this was tending to give to the Community in world affairs appeared to play a paramount role in the reappraisal of Britain's attitude to the Six.

The British request for negotiations was formally accepted by the Council of Ministers on 26 September 1961; the Council further invited the United Kingdom to make a comprehensive statement at a ministerial conference to be held in Paris on 10 October. The Council also decided that while the negotiations were between the six Community states and the United Kingdom, the European Commission 'should take part in the (negotiating) Conference as adviser to the Six and would have the right to speak'. The decision to have the opening meeting in Paris represented a concession by the other Five to the French, who wanted to emphasize the role of the individual member governments at the expense of the Commission. The Five, on the other hand, while yielding to French insistence on holding the initial meeting in Paris, were successful in securing French agreement to the principle that the actual detailed negotiations should take place in Brussels with the participation of the Commission.

The opening of the common market negotiations

The introductory statement made by Mr Edward Heath – who had been appointed Lord Privy Seal with special responsibility for the conduct of the negotiations for British membership of the common market – on 10 October 1961 marked the effective opening of the negotiations. Mr Heath's statement was detailed, thorough and comprehensive and set out with perfect clarity the main issues involved as they were seen by the British Government.

After some brief introductory remarks, Mr Heath came straight to the heart of the matter by saying that the British Government fully accepted the Treaty of Rome : 'Her Majesty's Government are ready to subscribe fully to the aims which you (the Six) have set yourselves. In particular, we accept without qualification the objectives laid down in Articles 2 and 3 of the Treaty of Rome, involving the diminution of internal tariffs, a common customs tariff, a common commercial policy, and a common agricultural

114

policy.'[7] Nevertheless, there were three main problems arising from the United Kingdom's application for membership of the Community : the Commonwealth, the position of British agriculture, and the question of suitable arrangements for Britain's E.F.T.A. partners.

Mr Heath then dealt at some length with each of these three problems in turn. After emphasizing the value and the importance of the Commonwealth connection not only to Britain but indeed to the whole of Europe and the world, he divided the problem into a number of separate issues. These were, first of all, the 'less-developed members of the Commonwealth', such as Nigeria and Ghana in Africa and India, Pakistan and Malaysia in Asia. For all of these countries the preferences they enjoyed in the United Kingdom market were of vital importance. For these countries Mr Heath expressed the hope that suitable arrangements could be devised analogous to those written into the Convention with the Associated Overseas Countries and Territories annexed to the Treaty of Rome. For those Commonwealth countries for whom association did not offer a possible solution, Mr Heath referred to the possibility of a special protocol as had been the case under the Treaty of Rome for Morocco's trade with France.

Mr Heath then turned to the main commodity groups. For tropical goods, for instance, there were bound to be difficulties for any Commonwealth countries not entering into association with the Community. In such cases there appeared to be two possible alternative lines of action : 'the first, which would be appropriate where not only equality of opportunity but also some measure of protection is essential, would be to grant free entry into the United Kingdom market alone for the Commonwealth country or territory which is not associated, and then to fix the common tariff of the enlarged Community at a level which would safeguard the interests both of that country and of the countries and territories associated with the Community. The second line of approach would be to fix a zero, or a very low, level for the common tariff. For a few important commodities we believe that it would be possible to do this without significant damage to the interests of the countries and territories associated with the Community. For example, tea is a commodity of great importance to India and Ceylon, and so is cocoa to Ghana. A zero common tariff would go a considerable way to meet the trade problems of those countries if they were not solved by association.'[8] For raw materials no major difficulties were anticipated

[7]*Cf. The United Kingdom and the European Economic Community :* text of the statement made by the Lord Privy Seal at the meeting with Ministers of member states of the European Economic Community at Paris on 10 October, 1961. November 1961, H.M.S.O. Cmnd. 1565, p. 5.

[8]Ibid, p. 10.

since the common Community tariff for most of them had in any case been fixed at zero. For manufactured goods, the solution put forward by Mr Heath amounted in fact to a gradual tailing-off of the right of duty-free entry for Commonwealth goods into the United Kingdom. The problem of temperate foodstuffs, on the other hand, which were imported mainly from Australia, New Zealand and Canada, did pose a very real problem and Mr Heath quoted some figures to illustrate the extent of New Zealand's dependence, in particular, on her Commonwealth trade with the United Kingdom : 'New Zealand's total exports in 1959 were valued at £290 million. Of these £170 millions' worth, or about 60 per cent, were temperate foodstuffs; £130 millions' worth, out of the total £170 million, came to the United Kingdom. The bulk of these exports consisted of mutton, lamb, butter and cheese. Over 90 per cent of total exports of these commodities came to the United Kingdom. If in the future New Zealand cannot, by one means or another, be assured of comparable outlets for them, her whole economy will be shattered. New Zealand's problem is particularly acute because of her dependence on a relatively limited range of exports. But other Commonwealth commodity problems are the same in kind if not in degree.'[9] The notion of 'comparable outlets' which Mr Heath raised here for the first time was to be a major and recurring theme of the ensuing negotiations. For the Commonwealth it was, as Mr Heath had indicated, a matter of absolutely vital importance. For the Community countries, and for France in particular, it was unacceptable – superficially, because it damaged the supposedly sacrosanct principle of a common external tariff for the whole common market area; in practice, and in terms of hard cash, because it gave Britain a privileged economic position in the Community and closed sections of the British agricultural market to Community producers. The interests at stake on both sides were fundamental and although a compromise solution was either attained or in sight for most of the products concerned by the time the negotiations came to an abrupt end, the problem of temperate foodstuffs was throughout one of dominating importance.

The second major problem was that of British agriculture. Although Britain accepted without reservation the fact that the common market covered agriculture as well as industrial goods, there were fundamental differences in structure between British agriculture and the system generally practised in the Community. Thus, in Britain, farmers were assured of a fair and reasonable price by means of a system of guaranteed payments from the government for all their principal products : 'these guarantees are provided by means of Exchequer payments which make up the difference between the average price realized by farmers on the market and the guaranteed

[9]Ibid, p. 11.

116

price determined by the government. In addition we make direct farming grants designed to encourage improved farming methods and to raise the general efficiency of the industry. The level of the guaranteed prices, and of the direct farming grants, is settled annually by the government after consultation with the producers' representatives'.[10] The British system was therefore almost the exact reverse of the agricultural policy of the Community under which imported foodstuffs were to be subject to a levy fixed in such a way as to bring the price to the consumer into line with Community-grown produce. While this is of course a slight over-simplification of the problem, it does show its magnitude. Mr Heath's proposal here was that the United Kingdom should gradually move over to the Community system but that British farmers should, where necessary, be given a transitional period of 12 to 15 years to adapt themselves to the new market conditions and circumstances.

The third and last of the major problems referred to by Mr Heath in his statement was that of E.F.T.A. Here the British government looked forward to the creation of 'an enlarged Community including ourselves and as many of our E.F.T.A. partners as may wish to become full members'. For countries in E.F.T.A. for whom full membership was not possible for political reasons Mr. Heath suggested that the enlarged Community should give them the possibility of entering into some form of association.

Mr Heath concluded his introductory statement by emphasizing the added strength which British accession would give to the common market. Such a development would restore Europe to its rightful place in the world and oblige all men 'to treat us all with new respect'.

It is not our purpose in this book to enter into a detailed account of the 1961–63 negotiations : suffice it to say that they lasted for 16 months and after more than one moment of cautious optimism finally collapsed as a result of the French veto delivered by President de Gaulle at his notorious press conference in Paris on 14 January 1963 in the course of which he described 'England' as 'insular, maritime, linked through its trade, markets, and food supply to very diverse and often distant countries. Its activities are essentially industrial and commercial, and only slightly agricultural. It has, throughout its work, very marked and original customs and traditions. In short, the nature, structure, and economic context of England differ profoundly from those of the other states of the Continent'. To the French President, the experience of the 14 months of negotiations had shown quite clearly that Britain was not yet ready to abandon her past traditions and to play her part, wholeheartedly and unreservedly, in a strictly European community; could Great Britain, he asked, 'at present place itself, with the Continent and like it, within a tariff that is truly common, give up all preference

[10]Ibid, p. 13.

with regard to the Commonwealth, cease to claim that its agriculture be privileged and, even more, consider as null and void the commitments it has made with the countries that are part of its free trade area. That question is the one at issue. One cannot say that it has now been resolved. Will it be so one day? Obviously Britain alone can answer that'. In the face of this barrage the collapse of the negotiations could not be long averted and on 29 January the negotiations were indefinitely suspended.

Although a great deal of ink has already been spilt on analyses and examinations of the reasons that led to the breakdown, the basic explanation is simply the French determination to keep Britain out of the Community because in British membership they saw, rightly or wrongly, a threat to their own position of dominance among the Six. It is important to recall that the French gave as their reason for their opposition to British entry – and for the veto finally pronounced by de Gaulle – the fact that Britain was not yet prepared to accept all the provisions of the Treaty of Rome. This statement – or accusation – rang false to many of those who had been engaged in the negotiations which had demonstrated the sincerity of Britain's intentions and her readiness to accept the treaty subject only to a number of exceptions – mostly of a transitional character – to facilitate the period of adaptation from existing conditions to those that would prevail once she was a full member of the Community. During the initial stages of the negotiations it seems likely that the French considered that in view of the probable internal repercussions at home the British government would find itself unable to meet the conditions put forward by the Six. By the end of 1962, however, the French attempt to cloak their own interests in the spotless garb of the sanctity of the Treaty of Rome had begun to look woefully threadbare, and the evident determination of the British government to do everything in its power to bring the negotiations to a successful conclusion brought home to the French, possibly for the first time, the very real possibility of British entry into what many Frenchmen had begun to consider as a French zone of influence. Other reasons advanced against United Kingdom membership were Britain's close links with the United States, illustrated with particular effect by the Nassau Agreement between President Kennedy and Mr Macmillan, under which the Americans agreed to supply the United Kingdom with Polaris missiles, and the suspicion that Britain having once penetrated inside the citadel of Europe would in some Machiavellian way act as an American 'Trojan horse'. These accusations were little more than camouflage for the fundamental reason for France's opposition to British membership; as we have seen, looked at from the French point of view British accession had little to commend it. Perhaps if Britain had indicated its willingness to allow virtually unlimited free entry of French agricultural produce and agreed to a

118

broad measure of Franco-British technical and military co-operation the outcome of the negotiations would have been very different.

Extent of the agreement reached in the 1961–63 negotiations

1. The level of the common customs tariff

In his opening statement on 10 October Mr Heath had said that the United Kingdom was ready 'to accept the structure of the present E.E.C. tariff as the basis of the tariff of the enlarged Community. In these circumstances we (*i.e.,* H.M.G.) think that the necessary lowering of tariff levels might be achieved by making a linear cut in the common tariff as it stands today. We would suggest that this might be of the order of 20%'. There were, however, some items on which the United Kingdom wished to propose reductions.

No final agreement had been reached on this issue by the time the negotiations were suspended, due mainly to the fact that discussions on the possible application of the nil tariff duties for certain products were still in progress. There was, however, no reason to suppose that agreement would not have been reached – had the negotiations been able to continue – on the general basis of a common external tariff for the enlarged Community of the old rate for the Community of the Six less 20%.

2. British requests for nil duties in the industrial sector

The United Kingdom, at the beginning of the negotiations, submitted a list of 26 industrial products for which it requested a nil duty including, *inter alia,* aluminium, sulphur, wood pulp newsprint, lead, zinc and petroleum products which between them represented 16% of the United Kingdom's imports in the industrial sector. Progress in this case proved disappointingly slow and by the time of the suspension of the negotiations agreement had been reached on only 10 of the 26 products : *i.e.,* on two of the products in question, acetylene black and rods of copper-nickel alloy, nil tariffs were agreed; in two other cases, sulphur and cobalt oxide, the United Kingdom decided to withdraw its original request; while for the other six products provisional arrangements were devised. Of the remaining 16 items there were several on which the Six themselves had not agreed a common attitude by the breakdown of the negotiations. It is, however, unlikely that they would have agreed to the United Kingdom's suggestion for a nil tariff on the more important of these items; the Six and the United Kingdom seemed in fact to be moving towards a compromise whereby the United Kingdom would have brought its tariff for some of these products into line with that of the Six in three stages.

3. Commonwealth problems

The Commonwealth problems were wide-ranging and complex. It was in an attempt to reduce them to some kind of order that the

119

European Commission proposed that they should be classified 'on the basis of the essential characteristics of their export trade and the type of problem raised in relation to the provisions of the Treaty of Rome'.

This classification contained the following categories :

   (i) Canada, Australia and New Zealand with their exports of manufactured products

  (ii) Countries whose essential problems were linked principally with the application of the common customs tariff and the common commercial policy.

 (iii) Countries whose exports were largely affected by the Association established under Part IV of the treaty (of Rome).

 (iv) Countries whose problems were mainly agricultural but might also be affected to a greater or lesser degree by the existing Association.

  (v) Others :

    (a) Bases and transit ports.

    (b) European countries with a Mediterranean type production.

    (c) Countries which posed a special problem in connection with the export of petroleum products.

    (d) Countries coming under various categories.

 (vi) Countries whose exports did not seem to raise any special problems.[11]

(A) Canada, Australia and New Zealand

On exports of manufactured goods from these countries to the United Kingdom agreement was reached in May 1962 on the basis of a proposal by the European Commission whereby the United Kingdom agreed to align its preferential Commonwealth tariff on the common external tariff in three stages : a first alignment of 30% on accession; a second alignment of 30% on 1 January 1967; a third and final alignment of 40% on 1 January 1970.

At the same time, however, the Community 'declared itself willing to examine, in 1966 and 1969, in consultation with Canada, Australia and New Zealand, the development of its trade with these countries and to take the appropriate measures in the light of all the circumstances and in conformity with the provisions of the treaty'.[12]

On processed foodstuffs the United Kingdom initially put forward a list of some eighty products for which it requested either a nil tariff (*i.e.*, for about 10 of them) or various preferential measures. Agreement was reached in October 1962 on about 40 products on the basis of a reduction in stages on the same time-scale (*i.e.*,

[11]E.E.C. : *Report to the European Parliament on the state of the negotiations with the United Kingdom*, Brussels, February 1963, pp. 31–2.

[12]Ibid, p. 34.

120

standard decalage) as for manufactured goods; while for the remainder the Six suggested a more gradual alignment (*i.e.,* soft decalage) on the common external tariff. The United Kingdom delegation subsequently indicated its readiness to agree to the Six's proposal provided special arrangements could be accepted for canned fruit (*i.e.,* peaches, pears and pineapples), canned salmon and dried grapes. There is no reason to suppose that some form of compromise proposal could not have been devised for these three products had the negotiations been allowed to run their course.

(B) *India, Pakistan, Ceylon, Hong-Kong*

The solution envisaged in the case of these countries consisted of two main parts. First, the gradual application of the common external tariff, on the soft decalage principle, on all imports from these countries into the Community – together with special arrangements for certain key products; and, second, the elaboration of a 'common policy' for the Community towards these countries which 'might go further than purely trade matters in order to maintain and even develop in reasonable fashion the growth potential of the countries concerned while at the same time it would offer the guarantees needed to safeguard Community interests'.[13] Thus, for India and Pakistan, the United Kingdom would have aligned its tariff on the common external tariff at the following rate : 15% on accession; 15% on 1 July 1965; 20% on 1 January 1967; 20% on 1 July 1968 and the final 30% on 1 January 1970 (this soft decalage would not, however, have applied to cotton goods and jute goods). Nil tariffs were agreed on tea (which represented an important concession on the part of the Six and was of course of vital importance for the economy of India and Pakistan – and Ceylon), lemon-grass oil, polo-sticks and cricket-bats; while for a number of other products such as spices, essential oils and some tropical products it was agreed that there should be a temporary or indefinite suspension of duties.

By 'common policy' it was understood by the Six and the United Kingdom that 'the enlarged Community would declare its readiness to start negotiating with India and Pakistan on comprehensive trade agreements which should be ready by the end of 1966 at the latest. The aim of these agreements would be to develop mutual trade for the purpose of maintaining and, as much as possible, increasing the level of the foreign currency receipts of these countries, and in general of facilitating the implementation of their development plans. The means to be employed could concern in particular tariff policy, quota policy, export policy (guarantees to avoid disturbing the markets of importing countries), the encouragement of private investment, and technical assistance.'[14] For cotton goods, special

[13]Ibid, p. 41.
[14]Ibid, p. 41.

arrangements were to apply to avoid any undue harm to the export of cotton goods from India and Pakistan to the enlarged Community. The Indian Government declared its general acceptance of these proposed arrangements.

In the case of Ceylon there was agreement on the 'principle of a declaration' that the enlarged Community would be prepared to enter into a comprehensive trade arrangement with Ceylon along the lines of those envisaged for India and Pakistan. In addition, Ceylon would of course have benefited from the nil tariff for tea and the decalage arrangements for certain tropical goods. In the case of Hong Kong, the Commission believed that in the longer-term a solution would have had to be found within the overall framework of the Community's commercial policy : in the short-term the Commission proposed regular consultation between the enlarged Community and Hong-Kong with a view to authorizing the British Government to take measures to safeguard exports from Hong-Kong into the United Kingdom in the event of Hong-Kong's interests being severely threatened as a result of the application of the common external tariff.

(C) Association

In his opening statement on 10 October 1961, Mr Heath had said that the British Government hoped 'to see the less developed members of the Commonwealth, and our dependent territories, given the opportunity, if they so wish, to enter into association with the Community on the same terms as those which will in future be available to the present Associated Overseas Countries and territories. . . . Association may, therefore, be a solution for the problems of many Commonwealth countries and territories.' The Six subsequently indicated that they would be prepared to consider associate status from independent Commonwealth countries 'having characteristics similar to those of the present associates. In the event, some Commonwealth countries, *i.e.*, Nigeria, Ghana and Tanganyika, declared that, because of essentially political considerations, they could not agree to the association formula. For such countries new proposals were subsequently put forward by the Commission – and were accepted by the Six and the United Kingdom delegation – on the following lines : '(i) The possibility of association would remain open to these countries on the basis of . . . the new (*i.e.*, Yaoundé) Convention of Association; (ii) Trade agreements could be concluded between the enlarged Community and these countries. These agreements would not confer the same advantages as association, and they would not go as far as the agreements to be concluded with India and Pakistan. The scope of these agreements would be considered later; (iii) Imports from these countries into the United Kingdom would benefit from the system of soft decalage in the alignment of the British tariff on the common customs tariff as agreed for manufactured goods from India, Ceylon and Pakistan.'[15] Another alternative solution suggested by the British delegation for Commonwealth countries which remained unassociated was to grant free entry into the United Kingdom market for certain tropical products and then to fix the common external tariff at a level which would take account of the interests of both the Commonwealth countries concerned and the existing Associated States of the Six. This proposal was not acceptable to the Six, who tended to regard it as a device to completely transform the existing structure of the common external tariff for tropical products. Although the Six did agree to suspend customs duties on tea and a few other minor products, the United Kingdom eventually agreed to the application of the soft decalage procedure to all other tropical exports from non-associated Commonwealth countries.

(D) Other Commonwealth countries
    For these countries and territories a variety of measures were either agreed or envisaged. Thus, in the case of Basutoland, Bechuanaland and Swaziland (which were already included in the South African Customs Union), the solution envisaged was a special Protocol permitting special treatment on importation into the United Kingdom; for Aden, association under Part IV of the Treaty of Rome; for the Federation of Malaysia, for whose main export – rubber – there was already a nil duty, the application of the decalage principle; for Malta, a transitional period pending subsequent association with the Community; for Cyprus, association; for Gibraltar, eventual association; while for the Federation of Rhodesia and Nyasaland, studies into the principle of association and arrangements for Rhodesian tobacco had not progressed beyond the initial stages when the negotiations were suspended.

(E) The general problem of Commonwealth Preference
    The Six also raised the question of Commonwealth Preference in reverse, *i.e.,* the preferences given by Commonwealth countries to the United Kingdom. Such preferences were regarded as distorting the conditions of competition among member states of the enlarged Community and, had the negotiations continued, great pressure would undoubtedly have been brought to bear either for their abolition or, at least, gradual phasing out or, alternatively, their extension to all other member states of the Community.

(F) Commonwealth agricultural exports
    The strongly expressed view of the Six was that there could be no permanent or even long-term guarantees for Commonwealth
[15]Ibid, p. 51.

exports of temperate foodstuffs – notably cereals – to the Community. While the Six were prepared to negotiate specific but limited transitional arrangements, they insisted that permanent solutions in this field could only be found within the context of world-wide agreements. The products for which they indicated their readiness to negotiate transitional arrangements were cereals, flour, dairy produce, meat and sugar. British requests for special arrangements for Commonwealth exports of beef, veal, mutton and lamb, as well as duty-free quotas for apples, pears and tobacco (from Canada and India) had not been examined in detail by the time the negotiations were suspended.

(G) The special case of New Zealand

The special and exposed position of New Zealand was generally recognised by the Six. The Commission in its report on the negotiations admitted 'that New Zealand's special situation can be recognised as regards butter, because of butter's place in that country's exports and the particularly difficult position of this product on world markets. In this connection the Commission considers that the Conference (*i.e.*, the negotiating delegations of the Six and the United Kingdom) should have sought the best practical means by which New Zealand could gradually adjust itself to the new situation that would have been created by United Kingdom membership of the Common Market.'[16] While the problem of New Zealand had not been resolved at the time of the breakdown, the positions of the two sides were not irreconcilable and there is no reason to suppose that agreement could not have been reached.

4. British Agriculture

The British delegation opened the discussions on the integration of British agriculture into the common market with a request for an arrangement which would have provided for an annual review – based on national reviews carried out by responsible government departments – with guarantees for farmers as well as for a transitional period so as to allow for a gradual change-over from existing market conditions to those applying under the Community's common agricultural policy. The proposed annual review was accepted by the Six, but on the understanding that this would be carried out not by the national governments meeting in the Council of Ministers but by the European Commission. With regard to the request for transitional arrangements for British agriculture, on the other hand, the Six were far less accommodating and insisted that the date fixed for the completion of the common agricultural policy, *i.e.*, 31 December 1969, would have to be adhered to.

As far as agricultural policy decisions which had already been

[16]Ibid, p. 66.

taken by the Six when the negotiations commenced were concerned, Mr Heath stated that these were acceptable to the British Government subject to the following adjustments :

(a) To allow for the drastic change in the supply and demand situation within the Community as a whole resulting from the accession of the United Kingdom and certain other countries;

(b) To meet the Commonwealth countries' vital needs and to enable the United Kingdom to fulfil its obligations to the Commonwealth;

(c) To enable the system in force in the United Kingdom to be harmonized smoothly and gradually within the new system to be established;

(d) To expand the regulations on certain points.[17]

The Community regulations already in force at this time were those relating to cereals, pigmeat and egg markets as well as for fruit and vegetables; while regulations on dairy produce, beef, rice and sugar were in course of preparation. On cereals, pigmeat and eggs, the United Kingdom delegation asked for the reduction of guaranteed prices – and the deficiency prices arising as a result – for the duration of the transitional period as well as for a number of specific amendments on wheat (*i.e.*, lowering of the lower limit of the target price fixed by the Community), barley, oats, pigmeat and eggs. The Six's attitude was stiff and uncompromising. Their line was that :

(a) The common agricultural policy must be applied in its entirety by the United Kingdom by the end of the transitional period;

(b) The system of deficiency payments granted on the basis of a guaranteed price must be abolished at the very beginning of the transitional period in respect of all products for which common regulations existed;

(c) A system of degressive subsidies to consumers or – if these involved major difficulties – to producers would provide a solution to any difficulties, such as a sudden and excessive rise in consumer prices, which might result from the move from one system to the other.[18]

With regard to fruit and vegetables, the United Kingdom delegation originally requested a standstill period of five years before applying the first tariff reductions for certain particularly sensitive horticultural products; thereafter duties would be progressively reduced and completely abolished by 1 January 1973. In addition, certain other measures and temporary exceptions were requested, including the provision of financial assistance to horticulturalists to

[17]Ibid, p. 70.
[18]Ibid, p. 74.

assist them in changing over to the new market conditions. Here again the Six were completely uncompromising; they took the view that conditions would be no worse for United Kingdom horticulturalists than for their counterparts in the Community, and that there was therefore no justification for the exceptional measures put forward by the United Kingdom delegation. There had been no change in the formal positions of the two sides when the negotiations were suspended.

The United Kingdom delegation also made a number of comments on the Community's proposals for the common market organization (for the Six) for dairy produce, beef, rice and sugar. Thus, on dairy produce for example, the British delegation suggested that the Community's protective system should be based on a price that 'would ensure a reasonable income to efficient and economic producers such as New Zealand' and that any quotas that might be imposed should not affect the volume of British imports from the Commonwealth; while for sugar, the United Kingdom delegation requested that the total acreage of sugar beet in the Community should be limited so as to safeguard the export trade of Commonwealth sugar producers. The Six took note of the United Kingdom's observations but no guarantee was ever given that these would be incorporated into the draft regulations.

5. The financial regulation

Part of the agricultural agreement among the Six on 14 January 1962 was the financial regulation which provided for the establishment of the Community's Agricultural Guidance and Guarantee Fund and for the use that was to be put to the income accruing from the levies imposed upon agricultural products imported from third countries. The regulation had not laid down, however, into whose hands the income from the levies should be paid, *i.e.*, the Commission or the national governments. It was in order to clarify this situation that the Commission in December 1962 transmitted a draft resolution to the six member states which firmly stated, *inter alia*, that 'after the expiry of the transitional period revenue arising from the application to imports from non-member countries of the duties in the common customs tariff and from agricultural levies shall accrue to the European Economic Community as revenue of its own'. Not all the money, however, was to be retained by the Commission. On the contrary. 'The Commission shall each year carry out in respect of each member state a comparison between the amount of the customs duties and levies charged on its territory and its share in Community expenditure borne by such member states under the terms of Article 200(1) of the treaty. Those member states for which the comparison shows that they are levying more than they are contributing to expenditure shall pay a financial contribution equal to two-thirds of the difference noted. Those member states for which the comparison shows that they are contributing more than they are levying shall receive from the Community a payment equal to two-thirds of the difference noted.'[19] These proposals were little to the liking of the French and contained the seeds of the great Community crisis of 1965. But December 1962 was hardly the most opportune moment for the French to precipitate a major conflict within the Six – particularly since postponement of the issue was a comparatively simple matter – and the whole question was simply left over for settlement at a later date.

6. *The problem of E.F.T.A.*

In his opening address in Paris Mr Heath had referred to the position of the other six member countries of E.F.T.A., and of Finland and Ireland. During the 16 months of the negotiations a number of these countries applied in their turn for membership or association with the Community. Ireland was the first to do so on 31 July 1961; after this there followed in turn Denmark, on 10 August 1961; Austria and Sweden, on 12 December 1961; Switzerland, on 15 December 1961; and Portugal, on 18 May 1962. A major problem, however, arose from the fact that the member countries of E.F.T.A. had agreed that no one country would adhere to the European Economic Community unless or until the interests of the other six countries had been reasonably safeguarded. This, as the Commission stated in its report to the European Parliament, raised two important issues : '(a) As regards the timing, Britain's accession was put off to a more uncertain date, which depended on the course of other negotiations for accession or association; (b) As regards the substance of the matter, Britain's accession itself became contingent upon the success of these other negotiations.' The Six saw, or pretended to see, the proposed accommodation of all the member states of E.F.T.A. as an issue which called into question the whole nature of the Community. Once, for instance, arrangements had been made with the E.F.T.A. countries it would have been hard to justify the exclusion of the remaining European states of the O.E.C.D. from the common market, either as full members or as associates. This would have led to a Community of some 10 or 12 member states and almost as many associated states. For a union of states which was still in an essentially formative stage and which had therefore not yet clearly found its own soul or rationale, the danger of disintegration or smothering of its original conceptions was very real. This problem, which was genuinely felt by many people in the Community of the Six to be virtually insurmountable in 1962 – if, that is, the essence and the spirit of the Community were not to be radically altered by its virtual metamorphis into a kind of cross-breed between the full-scale customs

[19]Ibid, p. 88.

union and a conventional free trade area – was clearly brought out by the European Commission in its report to the European Parliament to which we have already turned so often. 'This brings us to reflect in more general terms upon the real difficulties in the negotiations. The question was not only one of reconciling British systems and commitments with the letter of the Treaty of Rome : it was rather one of reconciling them with a Community in the full surge of development. The British application for membership involved an obligation to accept not only the treaty but the substantial advances made since the treaty was signed. It was on these advances that discussion was sometimes most difficult. But the fact that in certain fields the content of the treaty was still in a preliminary stage, and that, broadly speaking, the implementation of its various aspects was in an intermediary phase, may also be considered as having made matters more difficult for the negotiators. The problem was one of reconciling with Community arrangements the action taken to adjust the British system whilst paying due heed both to Great Britain's vital interests and to a Community system which itself lay largely in the future.'[20]

[20]Ibid, p. 111.

CHAPTER 6

The Community in trouble

The aftermath of the breakdown

The Gaullist veto of 14 January which blocked, for the time being at least, Britain's accession to the common market, marked also the first major open disenchantment between France and her five Community partners. If throughout the early 1950s the Five had broadly accepted French leadership of the Community it was because they shared many of the aspirations of France's political leaders and were themselves convinced that European economic and political integration was vital if Europe was to retain any influence or significance in the postwar world. French leadership was at this time seen as a fertile source of ideas, as a magnet capable of drawing to it the aspirations of Europeans frustrated and embittered by the collapse of the old European order. Men like Schuman, Monnet and Faure, while no doubt acting in the interests of France, were careful to pay homage to the virtues and values of European integration, in which all the participating states had an important part to play, and would have shrunk from any too obvious or flagrant attempt to impose French domination within the Community. The French tactics in these early years – when France was largely negotiating from a position of weakness – were extraordinarily successful. While, on the one hand, French aims and objectives generally prevailed, French motives on the other hand were often allowed to go unquestioned or were shrugged off on the assumption that France's longer-term objectives were in any case unattainable. It seemed to most observers, for example, to be rather foolish for a nation which had only recently suffered the humiliations of Dien-Bien-Phu and Suez to seek to embark on the development of an atomic bomb which, once completed and successfully exploded, would still be treated with derision by the two major nuclear powers. While the return to power of General de Gaulle had sown the first seeds of mistrust among the Six, France in 1958 was still toiling under the weight of the Algerian incubus and was in no position to attempt to assert herself in the Community. In the economic sphere, France compared unfavourably with Germany and was compelled to devalue her currency before attempting to meet the full challenge of the common market. Admittedly, the other Five – and Germany in particular – had been alarmed by French proposals made soon after the return of de Gaulle for a controlling triumvirate at the head of N.A.T.O. But de Gaulle's well known desire to try and restore the political prestige of France and to cut a figure on the world stage was generally regarded with a mixture of admiration and amusement. Little by little, however, admiration and amusement began to give way to concern as the policy of Gaullist France – greatly strengthened by the end of the Algerian struggle as a result of the French disengagement from North Africa and the rapidly improving internal economic situation – became more openly aggressive, assertive and decisive in its attitude towards her partners in the Community. Very soon the Five found themselves confronted with a Gaullist challenge on three fronts : relations with Britain; relations with the United States; and – although this came to a head a little later in time – the fundamental character of the Community itself.

The challenge over Britain came with the press conference on 14 January. President de Gaulle's statement that the United Kingdom was not yet ready for membership of the common market and the implication that the negotiations should therefore be discontinued, came as a bombshell not only to the United Kingdom delegation but also to the other five member states of the Community. For almost two weeks after the press conference the Five sought desperately to persuade the French to come to some form of compromise agreement which would at least have allowed the negotiations to continue. The French, however, were adamant. Stoutly and cleverly though their representatives, and Couve de Murville – their Foreign Secretary – in particular sought to make their partners accept their point of view that the progress – or rather the lack of it – during the 16 months of negotiations with the United Kingdom had demonstrated how unready Britain was to accept the obligations incumbent in membership of the common market, their arguments rang miserably hollow and it was plain for all to see that the French were imposing their will regardless not only of the opinions but of the directly conflicting views of the other Five and the European Commission.

The only real chance of rescuing the negotiations lay with Dr Adenauer who was due to make a formal visit to Paris from 20 to 23 January 1963. In the event very great pressure was brought to bear upon Dr Adenauer, both by eminent political personalities in the Six and by President Kennedy urging him to use his good offices in persuading the French President to raise his veto and continue the negotiations. Dr Adenauer, however, was unwilling to jeopardise in any way the main purpose of his visit to Paris which was the signature of the Franco-German treaty of co-operation. For Dr Adenauer, this treaty represented the culmination of the work of a lifetime and the final consecration of Germany's return to the European comity of nations. To some extent, of course, the German readiness to proceed with the signature of the treaty represented a tacit acceptance and even approval of the French veto; but Dr Adenauer himself was generally believed to entertain little enthusiasm for British membership of the Community and was in any case completely dedicated to his primary aim of eradicating Germany's war-guilt complex.

There was a good deal of speculation at the time of the press conference that President de Gaulle considered that he had been misled by Mr Macmillan at their conference at Rambouillet on 15 December 1962 on the British government's intentions with regard to the maintenance of a national nuclear deterrent. While it is indeed likely that de Gaulle regarded the Nassau Agreement, whereby the United States agreed to supply Polaris missiles to the United Kingdom, as further evidence of the continued existence of the Anglo-American special relationship which he bitterly resented, it is hard to believe – and out of line with the French attitude throughout the negotiations to British membership – that the Nassau Agreement did any more than confirm President de Gaulle's firm view that the interests of France required that Britain should be kept outside the common market for as long as possible.

Perhaps the most representative and illustrative statement of the resentment felt among the representatives of the other Five at the high-handed French action in rejecting Britain's application without prior consultation within the Community came from Mr Spaak at the last meeting on 29 January 1963 between the negotiating delegations of the Six and the United Kingdom :

. . . Great Britain has been excluded, without valid reason in the opinion of five of the delegations of the Common Market from the negotiations over its entry. . . . When we made the Rome Treaty we proclaimed without cease that the Community we were forming was an open Community. This is written into the text of the Treaty. Today, without being able to explain our attitude to Great Britain, we are forced, some of us against our wishes, against our will, against our hopes, not to respect the policy we laid down . . . what is happening today is unfortunately much bigger and more important than the question of the negotiations between the Community and Great Britain. It is the foreign policy of the Community countries which has suddenly been altered. It should be remembered that for over a year each of us, including the French delegation, has ceaselessly maintained that our aim was to receive Great Britain into the Community, and that in order to succeed we would conduct the negotiations loyally. On 14 January we

131

were faced with a spectacular reversal of French policy demanding a spectacular reversal of our own policy, without being forwarned by any of the diplomatic means at the disposal of our countries, and without even being permitted to discuss the reasons leading up to this event. . . . As soon as one member of a Community wishes to compel all the others to take decisions which are of capital importance for its life, the Community spirit ceases to exist. It will be extremely difficult, I am convinced, to continue to develop the economic Europe. As for the political Europe about which we had dreamed as a necessary consequence of economic organisation, I do not know when it will be possible to speak of this again, for there is incontestably no more confidence . . .[1].

The action of France – and even more the manner in which this action was conducted – killed the old Community spirit of ready trust and compromise and replaced it by an unfettered conflict of natural interests and even the implied use of threats. But it would be wrong to see this development as a blow to the position of France in the Community as seen through Gaullist eyes. Where the Five saw – and largely still see – the creation of Europe as their ultimate goal, to the French government the common market is essentially a valuable economic coalition – albeit a coalition that has its political potentialities – and represents therefore a springboard from which France may better survey and enhance her position in the world at large. Seen from Washington or Moscow, Peking or London, the Gallic cock may look a somewhat bedraggled fowl; seen from the Elysée Palace, it stands fair to dominate the European farmyard.

Having succeeded in his first major objective of keeping Britain out, without incurring anything more drastic than the ill-will of his partners in the Six, President de Gaulle was free to turn his attention to the infinitely more difficult and taxing task of trying to evict the American 'presence' in Europe. The difficulty of course was that the majority of Europeans realised only too well their absolute military dependence upon the United States in the face of possible attack from the East. Admittedly, the menace of a Soviet attack has receded considerably since the days of Stalin; but might not a Europe bereft of American troops and, above all, the American nuclear umbrella, prove too tempting a target? To the French President, it was intolerable that among the leading industrial enterprises of the world virtually all the top places were occupied by American companies – and of course one or two Anglo-Dutch giants. Then there was the penetration of American capital and industry in Europe itself, either by the creation of new companies or the take-over of existing established European companies.

[1]*Cf.* Agence Europe, *Documents,* quoted in Miriam Camps, *op. cit.,* pp 489–90.

132

Admittedly, the number of American-owned or controlled companies in relation to total European or Community industrial enterprises was small, but their number was nonetheless growing rapidly and was, moreover, concentrated in certain key sectors such as oil, chemicals, motors and computers. This form of American industrial colonization, as it was soon being called by the French press, came in for bitter attack, and the French Government took deliberate measures to control any further expansion of American financial interests or participation in specified sectors of the French economy. French efforts to enlist general Community support in this respect, however, met with little success.

French resentment at American economic power and expansion was paralleled by intense irritation at the American military presence in Europe. Once his initial attempt in 1958 to create a triumvirate (*i.e.*, consisting of the United States, the United Kingdom and France) at the head of N.A.T.O. had failed, de Gaulle deliberately and systematically set about reducing the French commitment to, and participation in, N.A.T.O. – culminating in the formal request to the Americans to quit all their bases on French soil and to the North Atlantic Treaty Organization itself to leave France.

While the anti-American policy of the French Government met with some response in certain quarters throughout Western Europe – and was of course welcomed with glee by the Communist world – the general reaction both in the Community and the rest of Western Europe was one of profound concern. While the French argument that excessive American financial penetration into the industrial markets of Europe was intellectually sound and received widespread support in industrial – if not in government – circles elsewhere in the Community, French policy with regard to N.A.T.O. was both dangerous and irrational. Not only was France's own nuclear deterrent incapable of providing the Community with a satisfactory means of defence, but France's insistence on the need to have the means to ensure her own national protection could hardly fail to prompt similar claims from other countries, and notably from Germany. In his press conference of 14 January 1963, President de Gaulle had said : 'But for a great people to have the right of self-determination and to possess the means to safeguard this right is a vital necessity, for there are no absolute virtues in alliances whatever the nature of the sentiments that may have forged them. A people which deliberately forgoes, even if only for a time, the right to self-determination, runs a grave risk of losing this right for ever. And then, moreover, the conditions in which we find ourselves today leave us no choice but to act in this way.' Noble words, no doubt, but words and sentiments that could apply to Germany no less forcibly than to France. Why, moreover, should the other Five place any more confidence in a French nuclear deterrent – assuming for a moment that this could afford them adequate means of security – than the French themselves seemed prepared to place in American readiness to come to Europe's assistance in the event of war. As de Gaulle himself had said, alliances are not immutable and he himself has made it abundantly clear on a number of occasions that he sees in the common market no more than an essentially economic alliance.

This last point constitutes the third of the Gaullist challenges to the Community. To the other Five the common market was an irreversible and undeniable profession of faith. But where they worked on the assumption that in the Community there would be a broad measure of equality and no attempt by any one country to impose its will or concept of the nature of the Community upon its partners, Gaullist France lost little time in staking in unmistakable and often objectionable terms its claim to leadership within the Community. In this respect, it seems probable that de Gaulle may very well have overplayed his hand. To many of the leaders of the other Five, and Dr Adenauer in particular, there seemed to be, in the prevailing circumstances of the time, good and justifiable reasons for accepting French moral and intellectual leadership in the Community of the Six – although this of course did not necessarily mean that they considered that such a situation would continue indefinitely. Dr Adenauer, as we have already seen, acquiesced readily enough with the French veto on Britain's application for membership of the Community; but even he, staunch supporter of the Franco-German rapprochement though he was, had drawn back from any form of action that might have precipitated a crisis with the Americans over the defence of Europe. When later that year Professor Erhard succeeded Dr Adenauer as Chancellor, it became evident even to the French that if confronted with a choice between the United States and France, the new German Government would not hesitate in favour of Washington.

This reluctance on the part of the Germans may well have been one of the reasons which led the French to press strongly and ruthlessly for their pound of flesh in the agricultural sphere. Thus, six months after his veto on British membership of the Community, President de Gaulle, in another of his carefully staged press conferences on 30 July 1963, openly threatened that unless further substantial progress was made by the end of that year in the construction of the Community's agricultural policy, France would withdraw from the common market : 'The Treaty of Rome was fairly specific with regard to industry, but it did little more than provide an outline for agriculture. It did not resolve the agricultural question. At the beginning of last year France secured from her partners an undertaking to find a solution to all these problems or else there would be a standstill. Since then great advances have been made, but even greater progress has still to be made before the end of this year. Why? Because the date of 31 December has been agreed, as you know, among the Six for completion of the regulations that are still in suspense . . . and, finally, we chose the date of 31 December because it is in the spring of next year that the tariff negotiations between the United States and Europe will get under way and the great buffetings that might well arise on that occasion make it vital that the Common Market should have been completed by that date or else run the risk of dissolution. The year 1963 will therefore be decisive for the future of European unity.' The message, if not altogether explicit, was clear enough. It was to be repeated – and implemented – as we shall see, in a much harsher, brutal and unmistakable tone some sixteen months later as the curtain-raiser to the great Community crisis of 1965. Before we turn to examine in more detail this major turning point in the affairs of the Community, we must glance quickly at two other developments where the conflict of interests and ambitions was at this time exacerbating relations between France and her five Community partners : the renewed attempts to promote a European Political Union and the doubtful fortunes of Euratom.

The proposals for European Political Union

The first tentative move since the E.D.C. debacle in 1954 towards a renewed attempt to set up some kind of formal European Political Authority came in November 1959 when the Foreign Ministers of the Six, at one of their periodic meetings at Strasbourg, agreed on a formula of regular consultations on international political developments. A little over a year later, in February 1961, at a meeting of the six Heads of State (or governments) a decision was taken to set up a committee of representatives with a mandate to draw up concrete proposals providing for regular meetings of the Heads of State of the member countries of the Community. A report was duly prepared and submitted to the next meeting of the Heads of State in Bonn on 18 July 1961. The final communiqué issued at the end of this meeting suggested that a further momentous step along the road towards European unity had been taken. The communiqué stated, *inter alia,* that the Six had decided :

    1. To give shape to the will for political union already implicite in the treaties establishing the European Communities, and for this purpose to organize their co-operation, to provide for its development and to secure for it the regularity which will progressively create the conditions for a common policy and will ultimately make it possible to embody in institutions the work undertaken.

    2. To hold, at regular intervals, meetings whose aim will be to compare their views, to concert their policies and to reach

common positions in order to further the political union of Europe, thereby strengthening the Atlantic alliance. The necessary practical measures will be taken to prepare these meetings. In addition, the continuation of active co-operation among the Foreign Ministers will contribute to the continuity of the action undertaken in common. The co-operation of the Six must go beyond the political field as such, and will in particular be extended to the sphere of education, of culture and of research, where it will be ensured by periodical meetings of the Ministers concerned.

3. To instruct their Committee to submit to them proposals on the means which will as soon as possible enable a statutory character to be given to the union of their peoples.

But the Committee, under the chairmanship of a French diplomat, M. Christian Fouchet, soon ran into difficulties as the conflicting conceptions of the French and the other Five on the nature and the purpose of a Political Union became more obviously and glaringly apparent. Where the French saw in the proposed Political Union an organization with a wide range of competence, covering foreign policy, cultural matters, defence and general economic matters – apparently superimposed therefore on the existing European Commission – acting as a closed unit completely distinct from N.A.T.O. and unsympathetic towards any proposal for outside participation (as, say, by the United Kingdom), the other Five saw in it a means to, first, reinforce and then to go beyond what had already been achieved by means of the formulation of common policies in the field of defence and external relations; the close association of the European Parliamentary Assembly with the work of defining such common policies (as well as the activities of the hitherto dormant provisions of Article 138 of the Treaty of Rome which provided for direct elections to the European Parliament); and the gradual application of majority voting within the ministerial council of the proposed Political Union. In the face of two such utterly opposite and irreconcilable conceptions of the functions of Political Union the prospects for an acceptable and workable compromise seemed remote. As the other Five pointed out France's all too manifest rejection of any particle of supranationality within the proposed Political Union was impossible to reconcile with her determination to exclude the United Kingdom from any such organization on the grounds that Britain was not yet ready or prepared to submit herself to Community disciplines and priorities. In these circumstances the work of the preparatory committee, despite some valiant efforts to close the gap between the positions of the French and the other Five, ground steadily to a halt. The Community's second attempt to establish some kind of formal political link had fared no better than the first.

The declining fortunes of Euratom

The European Atomic Energy Community, which was established in 1958 in order to promote the development of a European atomic energy industry, has had a confused and unhappy history. The tasks originally assigned to it were basically threefold : the co-ordination of development work in the member countries of the Community so as to avoid any wasteful or unnecessary duplication of efforts; ensuring that the initial impetus towards the development or examination of new techniques was adequately maintained and followed up; and, lastly, the development of relations and contracts, on behalf of the Community as a whole, with outside atomic powers, *i.e.*, the United States and the United Kingdom, with both of whom co-operation or association agreements were subsequently agreed.

Euratom sought to satisfy the first of its responsibilities by means of the application and supervision of the first five-year plan (1958–62) research programme – which had been laid down in Article 215 of the Euratom Treaty – together with an allocation of $215 million. Subsequently, in June 1962, the Council of Ministers approved the proposals laid before it by the Euratom Commission for a second five-year research programme, covering the years 1963–67, and providing for a total expenditure of $455 million. Of this amount $232 million was allocated for further development work on atomic reactors and associated research; $127 million on the Community's four joint research centres at Ispra (Italy), Petten (Holland), Geel (Belgium) and Karlsruhe (Germany); and the balance on radiation and thermonuclear fusion studies, training and information services. The second programme was intended essentially to continue and expand the work commenced in the first Community programme, namely the improvement of existing types of reactor, the development of new types and the promotion of research in a wide variety of subjects related to the peaceful uses of nuclear energy. Ispra, by far the largest of the Community's joint research centres, is the location of the Orgel project : this is a 'heavy water-moderated, organic liquid-cooled and natural or enriched uranium-fuelled reactor concept' selected by Euratom as especially promising for the second generation or intermediate stage of nuclear power-stations to be installed in the Community from the early 1970s onwards. At the same time, and in order to stimulate development work in the member countries, Euratom has entered into a number of association contracts, including one with the French government for the construction and operation of a sodium liquid-cooled test reactor at the Cadarache testing centre in Provence. Finally, Euratom – as already indicated – has negotiated several important agreements with the competent authorities in the United States providing for joint studies of various American reactors, including the more advanced breeder-

137

reactor types, with a view to their eventual construction and operation in the Community area.

Nevertheless, when all has been said, the credit entry on Euratom's balance-sheet makes far from impressive reading; nor, of course, does the total figure of resources allocated to Euratom of $670 million – a little under £240 million – for ten years' work suggest that it is to this body that all six Community governments are looking for the main impulse for the development of atomic energy in the Community. The situation at the time of the establishment of Euratom was, admittedly, confusing and very different from one country to another. Thus, whereas the French had already embarked upon a major programme of military expenditure with a view to building up a French nuclear striking force – with civilian or peaceful uses of nuclear energy being regarded as little more than a useful offshoot – in Germany, the government had not at that time evinced any strong interest in atomic energy, although some private firms were beginning to consider seriously the economic and financial potential of nuclear power-stations; while the other four Community countries had shown little or no enthusiasm for embarking upon expensive research programmes. The position was further complicated by the fact that while the field of atomic research and development was dominated by the Americans – and, to a much lesser extent, the British – the French, who were at that time far ahead of their nearest rivals within the Community, were obstinately insisting, for seemingly predominantly nationalistic reasons, upon concentrating the bulk of their resources on natural uranium, graphite-gas reactors, and wished to see their policy supported by the rest of the Community. The other Five, on the other hand, were concerned only with the development of the most economic types of reactor and were particularly reluctant to be reduced to the role of passive supporters of the general French line of policy.

It is obvious that in such circumstances the task of the Euratom Commission was one of exceptional difficulty. Nevertheless, under the Presidency of M. Etienne Hirsch, a former colleague of M. Jean Monnet and a fervent European, the Euratom Commission sought to give a Community character and impulse to all the work affecting the development of atomic energy throughout the Community. The attempt failed and ended in the replacement of M. Hirsch by another Frenchman, M. Chatenet, under whose direction Euratom soon abandoned any lingering 'supranational' aspirations and resigned itself to fulfilling a complementary role, *i.e.,* supplementing the work already being carried out in the six member countries. Even this far less ambitious role however soon aroused French opposition, for the other Five, while compelled to accept the fact that the French government was almost exclusively concerned with its own line of research and development, were not prepared to see Euratom reduced to the role of complementing French national research, with the result that the bulk of the credits voted for Euratom were allocated to research on American-type reactors. At one stage the disagreement became so bitter that French implications that Euratom was 'misappropriating Community funds' (*i.e.,* by encouraging interest in American-type reactors) were countered by virtual accusations of intolerance and excessively nationalistic policies on the part of France. Relations became particularly embittered when the French government, replying to Euratom's request for full information and control over fissile materials imported by Euratom from the United States and elsewhere but subsequently allocated to the individual member states of the Community, categorically refused Euratom's right to exercise any kind of supervision over its military programme or any fissile materials, whatever their source, allocated to it.

The fact that Euratom has so far survived the tragi-comic quarrels and differences of the past few years is, unfortunately, not so much a tribute to a general Community conviction or appreciation of its potential services in the future as a reluctance to commit a crime of Community lèse-majesté by proposing its dissolution or a formal far-reaching revision of the treaty which established it. There is also the fact that although France – by insisting on giving priority to her own national programme – has probably profited little by her participation in Euratom, several of the other member states, and in particular the Federal Republic of Germany, have made full use of the opportunities which the establishment of Euratom has afforded them for research and development into nuclear energy. As an exercise in European co-operation, on the other hand, the results to date, marked by the conflicting interests of several of the member states and the intransigent position adopted by France, have been extremely meagre.

The Community crisis of 1965

In its Sixth General Report, published in June 1963, *i.e.,* less than six months, therefore, after the Gaullist veto on Britain's accession, the European Commission wrote 'though the shock (the unilateral action taken by France) was severe and the crisis grave, they could not be allowed to call into question the very existence of the Community. The Treaties of Rome and Paris are not merely the expression of a policy; they have founded a new consitutional order, and it is in moments of crisis that one appreciates the value of a permanent constitution, stable institutions and immutable rules. With the full support of Parliament the Commission has therefore sought above all to ensure continuity in the work of the institutions and compliance with the rules of the treaty in all fields.' Just how permanent, stable and immutable the Community's constitution, institutions and rules were in their eyes the French government was shortly to demonstrate. It is nevertheless impossible to quarrel with the Commission's interpretation of its own role at this time. Whatever the views held about the way in which France had acted to exclude Britain from the common market, the fact remained that she had not gone beyond her formal treaty rights. The Commission's primary role was that of custodian of the Treaty of Rome and the rules and regulations that had derived from it and to prepare further proposals designed to bring about and if possible accelerate the full common market called for in the Treaty of Rome. The result was the Commission's 'Initiative 1964', a virtual package of measures covering the acceleration of the full customs union and the application of the common external tariff, monetary union and social policy.

With regard to the accelerated introduction of the full customs union the Commission proposed that :

A. On 1 January 1965 the member states should again reduce by 15% their total customs charges in conformity with Article 14(4) of the treaty. On this date the customs duties would be reduced for each product by at least 10% in relation to the basic duty. For Community products in respect of which application has been made before 1 October 1964, to have recourse to the safeguard clause, this reduction may be limited to 5%.

B. On 1 January 1966 the member states should again reduce the total customs charge by 15%. On this occasion customs duties would again be reduced for each product by at least 10% in relation to the basic duty.

C. Before the member states introduce their adapted tariffs, they and the Commission should examine case by case any problems to which the application of the above measures would give rise in certain sectors of the Community economy.

D. On 1 January 1967 the remaining customs duties should be abolished.

E. On 1 January 1966 the third and final adjustment towards the common external tariff should take place.

F. As regards the products indicated in Annex II of the treaty, including those coming under a common market organization, there should be a quicker abolition of customs duties and of the 'fixed components' provided for in the regulation pursuant to Article 43.

   The customs duties and 'fixed components' should be reduced to zero with effect from 1 January 1968.

   On this date the common external tariff and the 'fixed component' provided for under the regulations for the final stage should also be applied.

With regard to the monetary union of the six member states, the Commission stated that it would shortly be formulating definitive proposals; while in the sphere of social policy, it drew the attention of the member governments to the need to intensify the work already in progress with a view to ensuing the levelling upwards of living and working conditions throughout the Community.

Discussion on these proposals by the Council of Ministers were, however, overtaken by the submission to the Council by the Commission in May 1965 of a further detailed set of proposals covering the financing of the common agricultural policy and the method of financial control over the income arising from the agricultural levies and customs duties on agricultural produce.

The proposals submitted by the Commission stated first of all that the organization of the agricultural market of the six countries on a Community basis would inevitably require a massive increase in the financial income of the Commission since it would in future become responsible for the total volume of support price expenditure – instead of only a part as in the past. It was accordingly suggested that the income arising from the payment of the customs levies on all foodstuffs imported into the Community from third countries should be made available for this purpose. Whereas hitherto, however, these levies had been paid into the treasuries of the member states, the Commission now proposed that as from 1 July 1967 – the date envisaged at this time for the free and unrestricted circulation of all industrial and agricultural products throughout the Community – these levies should be paid directly to the European Economic Community. These funds, which if paid direct to the Commission, would of course have ensured its complete financial independence, would then be used for 'the promotion of measures compatible with the objectives of the Community'. Furthermore, in order to ensure some form of parliamentary control over the very large sums that would in this way have passed into the hands of the Commission, it was proposed that the Community's budget should be made subject to the control of the European Parliament in Strasbourg. There was also the fact that as from 1 January 1966 the treaty provided for a substantial increase in the number of fields where decisions could thenceforward be taken on a qualified majority basis and no longer by means of a unanimous vote; it followed that if on certain points five of the six member states supported a measure put before them by the Commission – with the approval of the European Parliament – the odd man out in the Community would then be obliged to accept the verdict of the majority.

The Commission's own succinct account of its objectives in formulating these proposals was set out in its Eighth General Report :
    . . . the immediate purpose of which (*i.e.,* the Commission's proposals) was to lay down the rules for financing the common

141

agricultural policy, but which would also serve the even more important purpose of re-shaping the Community's financial structure by ensuring that it should have resources of its own and by organizing parliamentary control of their use.

Under the Commission's proposal, agricultural levies and customs duties proper should be treated as Community revenue once the common tariff was introduced – in principle on 1 July 1967. The change-over would be made gradually, so that after a transitional period of five years they would be paid in full to the Community.

The logic of a customs union where duties are levied only at the external frontiers irrespective of the final destination of the goods demands that the relevant receipts be used to meet common expenditure. All earlier experience, whether with ordinary customs unions, federations or confederations, confirms this. Moreover, the treaty explicity envisages it. The Commission's proposal therefore draws the normal conclusions from what the Community has already achieved.

The Commission has frequently expressed its desire to see the powers of the European Parliament increased, particularly in budgetary matters. At the close of its discussions in December 1965, the Council itself stressed the importance it attached to a widening of the budgetary powers of the Parliament and decided to turn its attention to this matter at an early date. The Commission therefore considers its proposals for amendments to budget procedure and the strengthening of the Parliament's powers as an essential component of the new financial system which it has submitted.

If the Commission's proposals are acted upon, the influence of the Parliament in drawing up the Community budget will be considerably increased, but without upsetting the present institutional balance. On the other hand, once the Parliament is elected by universal suffrage, a more thorough revision will have to be undertaken, with a view to transferring to the Parliament a right of decision in the matter of creating Community revenue.

The Commission's position was therefore clear enough; its proposals – if accepted – would have strengthened enormously the position and influence of the European Institutions at the expense of the national governments. They were in fact audacious proposals. In particular, the proposal to make the Commission financially independent by giving it its own direct sources of revenue and, above all, by making the budget subject to the approval of the European Parliament, combined with the fact that as from the beginning of the third stage of the common market the treaty provisions would make it, theoretically at least, impossible in many

142

fields of Community policy for one member state to wield a veto and oppose the wishes of the other five, constituted a fairly massive dose of supranationality as well as a direct challenge to the nationalistic policies of the French Government. In preparing its package-deal the Commission was fully aware – and, indeed, stated publicly – that its proposals for budgetary control by the European Parliament went beyond the letter, if not the spirit, of the Treaty of Rome. The Commission also knew full well that its proposals could not but provoke a head-on clash between the supporters of a federalist Europe – with a maximum degree of Community organization and control – and the political and economic conceptions of the Europe of de Gaulle and his followers. If, despite the clear indications which de Gaulle had already given – through the veto on British membership in 1963 and his threats about the future of the common market in 1964 – both of his obduracy and his views on the political role of France in the world, the Commission nevertheless decided to go ahead with its proposals, it can only have been because it firmly believed that there was a reasonable chance of their acceptance by all six member states. The bait, it must be conceded, was cunningly and attractively presented. Was not the fundamental objective of the proposal, after all, not the completion of the arrangements for the organization of the Community's agricultural market with its inestimable advantages to French farmers? The fact that the income derived from the levy – under the proposed arrangements – was in future to pass directly into the coffers of the Commission (whereas up to that time the Community had had to depend for its funds on fixed government contributions) would not have affected the extent of the penalty imposed upon imported third country foodstuffs or the degree of financial assistance likely to be given by the Community in order to improve and rationalize French agricultural production. In this way the final irrevocable implementation of the common agricultural policy – and the removal of any remaining doubts about its completion – gave French farmers an assured and well-protected market. Moreover, the Commission felt confident that it would be supported by the other Five and – rightly or wrongly – by the vast mass of public opinion; as well as being convinced on the logic of its own case. Above all, however, the Commission calculated that the economic attractions to France of the final implementation of a Community agricultural policy largely tailor-made to her own requirements would more than offset any political doubts about the proposed financial independence of the Commission or the enhancement of the responsibilities of the European Parliament.

The Council of Ministers, which had already met once to discuss the Commission's proposals on 15 June 1965, but without reaching agreement, met again on 28 June in Brussels. For the French the

143

purpose of the meeting was simply to finalise the financing arrangements for the common agricultural policy. For the other Five, the occcasion and the matters at issue were not so simple. The Germans for their part wished to be secure as a *quid pro quo* for their acceptance of the agricultural financing arrangements French agreement to seek a favourable outcome to the Kennedy Round negotiations in the G.A.T.T.; to achieve the simultaneous progression of the industrial and the agricultural markets; and to arrive at the harmonization of fiscal policies. The Germans were especially concerned lest the French, having once secured their vital objective in the field of agriculture, would simply apply a policy of obstruction with regard to other Community issues where French interests might have been unfavourably affected. The Dutch wished to make the expansion of the powers of the European Parliament a *sine qua non* of their approval of the agricultural financing arrangements. Inevitably, at this crucial point in the development of the Community, each one of the Six sought to further his own interests at the expense of his Community partners. At the same time, it must be recognized that while the other Five were undoubtedly seeking to protect their own interests as far as possible, they were also broadly in agreement with the proposals of the Commission, thus leaving the French in a position of isolation. Even so, the Six on the fateful night of 30 June were within a measurable distance of reaching agreement : all six countries had basically accepted the proposed financing arrangements for the common agricultural policy – only the allocation of the income derived from the levies remaining to be decided at a later date. The French even accepted the principle that the income derived from the levies should be transferred to the Community as soon as 'the need for this became evident'. The breaking-points were the proposed extension of the powers of the European Parliament and the wider application of qualified majority voting once the Community passed on into its third stage. On these two issues the French would make no concessions. Discussions continued, fruitlessly, till late into the night, but at 3 a.m. on the morning 1 July the Ministers separated – without having reached agreement and without fixing a date for further discussions.

Many explanations have been put forward for the events that led to the Community crisis of 1965; but the underlying reason was clear enough. Basically, the Commission's proposals marked a second – less obvious but no less real – battle for the construction of a supranational Europe. The proposals of the Commission, while carefully couched and presented in such a way as to avoid arousing national susceptibilities, would nonetheless have given very substantial powers to the European Parliament in the running of the Community. It was a confrontation that was, sooner or later, unavoidable between two entirely different conceptions of the nature, purpose and future of the Community. Given the character and outlook of a de Gaulle, his ready acceptance of the Commission's proposals was clearly unthinkable. At the same time the Commission and the other Five may well be pardoned for believing that, given the value for France of the stakes at issue, the French government would at least have paid lip-service to the notion of greater parliamentary control over the use to which the Community's agricultural income would be put.

It has been argued in certain quarters that the 1965 crisis was deliberately provoked by the French in order to 'cut the Commission down to size' and to scotch once and for all the theoretical conception of a common market in which a large number of important international issues could be decided on the basis of a qualified majority vote. De Gaulle himself, in his *Memoires de Guerre,* has written : 'All my life I have thought of France in a certain way. This is inspired by sentiment as much as by reason. The emotional side of me tends to imagine France, like the princess in the fairy stories or the Madonna in the frescoes, as dedicated to an exalted and exceptional destiny. Instinctively I have the feeling that Providence has created her either for complete successes or for exemplary misfortunes. If, in spite of this, mediocrity shows in her acts and deeds, it strikes me as an absurd anomaly, to be imputed to the faults of Frenchmen, not to the genius of the land. But the positive side of my mind also assures me that France is not really herself unless she is in the front rank.'[2] While others may dismiss such emotional outpourings as a piece of anachronistic if sublime mystical nonsense, they are nonetheless representative of the mind and character of the man who governs France and who, as such, cannot be expected to sympathise with the truly European type of Community as conceived by Adenauer, de Gasperi or Monnet. For de Gaulle, nationalism is not only far from dying, it is the mainspring of the life of a nation. Against this background, the suggestion that the French deliberately engineered the crisis of 1 July 1965 gains in plausibility. Was it really likely that the other Five, who in 1963 had submitted so tamely to the Gaullist veto over Great Britain, would now risk the destruction of the Community over some additional powers for the European Parliament or insistence on the application of qualified majority voting? The French clearly did not think so. It is more than possible that the French were themselves taken by surprise at the failure of their virtual ultimatum, only to find that it was too late to draw back without an intolerable loss of face. Equally, the

[2]*Cf.* De Gaulle, *War Memoirs,* Vol. I, *The Call to Honour* 1940–42, p. 1. Weidenfeld and Nicolson, London, 1955.

other Five, over-convinced perhaps of the advantages France stood to gain from the common agricultural policy and its financial provisions, may well have doubted up to the last moment – and perhaps even beyond – in the sincerity of the French threat.

The French, understandably, tried to make the most of their case, pointing especially to the efforts made by some of their partners – and notably the Italians – to revise or amend some of the agricultural agreements that had already been concluded in the course of earlier negotiations. They also argued, justifiably enough, that there was no provision in the Treaty of Rome for linking the completion of the common agricultural policy with, say, the successful outcome of the Kennedy Round tariff negotiations. But the other Five were not slow in making counter accusations. There was, of course, the ill-will aroused in 1963 as a result of the Gaullist veto, and fanned by the table-thumping threats of 1964 and 1965 over the agricultural negotiations; there was the constant denigration of the Commission and, indeed, all the Community institutions. But these features, irritating though they were, could not be described as going against strict Community obligations. Where, however, France did err, legally, was first in her refusal to accept the principle of qualified majority voting as from the start of the third stage of the common market – despite the fact that a previous French government had negotiated the treaty and that it had consequently been solemnly ratified by the French National Assembly – and, above all, in the French Government's unilateral decision, after the breakdown of the discussions between the Six in Brussels on 1 July, to cease to participate in the working of the Community, even going so far as to withdraw the head of the Permanent French Delegation to the European Economic Community in Brussels.

The French boycott and the possibility it evoked of a dissolution of the common market caused widespread dismay in French industrial and agricultural circles. Both had profited enormously from the common market. Between 1959 and 1964 the sales of French motor cars, for example, had risen eightfold to Germany, by fourteenfold to Italy and sixfold to Holland. Sales of chemical products had risen tenfold to Germany and fourteenfold to Italy and Belgium. Among the Six, it was France which, with Italy, had experienced the greatest relative increase in its exports to other Community countries, i.e., whereas total French sales over the period had risen threefold – or by 300% – the corresponding figure for the other Community countries were 2.5 for Belgium and 2.4 for Germany and Holland. In the agricultural field, France stood even more to lose by a breakdown of the common market. Of the $29 million, for instance, earmarked for the support of the Community's national agricultural markets from the sums paid by the Six into the European Agricultural Guidance and Guarantee Fund

146

in the year 1962/63, France received no less than 85%; while the losses resulting for France from the dissolution of the Community market organization and the non-application of the proposed financing arrangements for agriculture, particularly with regard to wheat, barley, dairy products, sugar and wine, would have been enormous.

In these circumstances it was significant – and understandable – that the French were careful not to burn their boats completely. Although the Head of the French Permanent Delegation to the European Communities was withdrawn, his assistant remained behind and the written procedure adopted by the other Five for the duration of the French boycott – and to which the French responded – enabled progress on outstanding matters of Community policy to be continued. Thus, while relations were certainly considerably strained between the Five and the Commission on the one hand and the French on the other hand, the break was never complete. Within days of the dramatic French walk-out of 1 July, Spaak in particular was at pains to emphasize the need for Community solidarity : far from taking any action which might further antagonise the French Government, Spaak urged the Council of Ministers to invite the French to resume their place at the negotiating table and to avoid any course of action that might further exacerbate French susceptibilities. Fundamentally, none of the Six were prepared to see the common market, for the construction and expansion of which they had toiled so laboriously and which was also electorally popular throughout Western Europe, collapse in ruins. Spaak's views were readily endorsed. After a delay of only two or three months – which coincided with the traditional summer political recesss on the Continent – came the first moves towards a resumption of the negotiations among the Six and with them a clear indication that, despite the dramatic events of 1 July 1965, and the differing conceptions of the future role and nature of the Community which they had so brutally brought out into the open, there did exist a desire for compromise. A French journalist, in a graphic account of the Community crisis, wrote that Couve de Murville, confronted by the demands of his five Community colleagues on the night of 30 June, had commented that a veritable Pandora's box had appeared to open in front of him; but that Robert Marjolin (a French Vice-President of the European Commission) – clearly of a more optimistic disposition – had recalled that while, according to Greek mythology, the opening of Pandora's box led to the escape of all the good and evil of the world, one great and redeeming virtue had remained safely inside . . . hope.[3]

[3] Cf. *Le Figaro* of 17 January 1966 for an article entitled : Tout le drame de l'Europe, by Serge Bromberger and Jean Lecerf.

147

CHAPTER 7

The community compromise of 1966 — and since

The formal French boycott of the common market lasted until the end of January 1966. Tentative feelers for a meeting of Foreign Ministers of the Six to try and find a *modus vivendi* which would allow the full resumption of Community activities began in the autumn of 1965 and culminated in two sessions of the Ministers of the six countries – but without the presence of the European Commission – in Luxembourg on 17/18 and 28/29 January 1966. The two Luxembourg meetings produced a compromise which was in effect a drawn battle. The Five stuck to their viewpoint that with the entry of the Community into the third stage of the common market the provisions of the treaty for qualified and simple majority voting would automatically apply – as the signatory governments had solemnly recognized and undertaken when formally signing the treaty. The French formally registered their disagreement. But no attempt was made by either side to impose their views on the other and the matter has in effect been allowed to wait for a solution in the indefinite future. The second French objective of curtailing the powers of the Commission met with a rather less hostile attitude on the part of the other Five. Theoretically, the Commission's powers to initiate new proposals remained unaffected. In practice, it is clear that for as long ahead as one can see at the present time, the Commission will have to tread very warily and will take good care to ensure that no further proposals are submitted unless they have first been largely cleared with the individual member governments. The French agreed that the proposal originally put forward by the Dutch some few years before for the amalgamation of the three European Executives – to be followed by the fusion of the three treaties – should now be proceeded with, although they also made it clear right from the start that they would not be prepared to accept Professor Hallstein – whom they regarded as the mainspring behind the Commission's initiative in 1965 designed to promote the effective role and financial independence of the European Executive – as President of the new single Commission. On agriculture, the last of the main elements in the 1965 crisis, the Six agreed to proceed on the basis of the Commission's original proposals. This, in effect, represented an important concession to the French – who stood to gain by far the most by its adoption and implementation – since no commitment was given by them with regard to the Kennedy Round G.A.T.T. negotiations beyond a broad and rather vague understanding to work towards their successful conclusion. These compromise arrangements were set out in considerable detail in statements issued after the second ministerial meeting in Luxembourg at the end of January 1966. In view of their importance for the present and future relationship between the Commission and the Council of Ministers, we have below quoted extensively from these texts :

(*a*) *Relations between the Commission and the Council*

Close co-operation between the Council and the Commission is essential to the functioning and development of the Community.

In order to improve and strengthen this co-operation at every level, the Council considers that the following practical methods of co-operation should be applied, these methods to be adopted by joint agreement, on the basis of Article 162 of the E.E.C. Treaty, without compromising the respective competences and powers of the two institutions.

(1) Before adopting any particularly important proposal, it is desirable that the Commission should establish the appropriate contacts with the governments of the member states, through the Permanent Representatives, without this procedure compromising the right of initiative which the Commission derives from the treaty.

(2) Proposals and any other official acts which the Commission submits to the Council and to the member states are not to be made public until the recipients have had formal notice of them and are in possession of the texts.

The Official Gazette should show clearly which acts are of binding force. How those texts that must by law be made public are in fact published will be decided in the course of work now being done on the re-organization of the Official Gazette.

(3) The credentials of Heads of Missions of non-member states to the Community will be submitted jointly to the President of the Council and to the President of the Commission, meeting together for this purpose.

(4) The Council and the Commission will inform each other rapidly and fully of any approaches relating to fundamental

149

questions made to either institution by the representatives of non-member states.

(5) In accordance with Article 162, the Council and the Commission will consult together on the advisability of the procedure for, and the nature of, any links which the Commission may establish with the international organizations pursuant to Article 229 of the Treaty.

(6) Co-operation between the Council and the Commission on the Community's information policy, which was the subject of the Council's discussions on 24 September 1963, will be strengthened in such a way that the programme of the Joint Information Service will be drawn up and carried out in accordance with procedures which are to be decided upon at a later date, and which may include the establishment of an *ad hoc* body.

(7) Under the financial regulations relating to the drawing up and execution of the Community budgets, the Council and the Commission will decide on means for more effective control over the commitment and expenditure of Community funds.

(b) Majority voting

I. Where, in the case of decisions which may be taken by majority vote on a proposal of the Commission, very important interests of one or more partners are at stake, the members of the Council will endeavour, within a reasonable time, to reach solutions which can be adopted by all the members of the Council while respecting their mutual interests and those of the Community, in accordance with Article 2 of the treaty.

II. With regard to the foregoing paragraph, the French delegation considers that where very important issues are at stake the discussion must be continued until unanimous agreement is reached.

III. The six delegations note that there is a divergence of views on what should be done in the event of failure to reach complete agreement.

IV. The six delegations nevertheless consider that this divergence does not prevent the Community's work being resumed in accordance with the normal procedure.

Finally, the Council adopted the following programme of work :

A. The draft E.E.C. and Euratom budgets (which had been held up during the French boycott) will be approved . . . before 15 February 1966.

B. The E.E.C. Council will meet as soon as possible to settle as a matter of priority the problem of financing the common agricultural policy. Concurrently, discussions will be resumed on the other questions, particularly the trade negotiations in G.A.T.T. and the problems of adjusting national duties on imports from non-member countries.

C. The representatives of the member states' governments will meet on the day fixed for the next Council meeting and will begin discussions on the composition of the new single Commission and on the election of its President and Vice-Presidents.

D. They will also agree on the date – in the first half of 1966 – when instruments of ratification of the treaty on the merger of the institutions are to be deposited, on condition that the required parliamentary ratifications have been obtained and agreement has been reached on the composition and on the presidency and vice-presidency of the Commission.[1]

On the face of it, most of these arrangements seemed reasonable and natural enough. But beneath the carefully-worded phrases lay a determination that in future the Commission would be compelled to act with great circumspection. This, certainly, has been the result to date. Any new proposals under consideration or in course of preparation by the European Commission are discussed at length at the various processing stages with the six permanent national delegations in Brussels, by whom, whenever or wherever necessary, they are referred back to national capitals for further instructions. While such a procedure may have the advantage of improving harmonious relations among the Six and between the member governments and the Commission, it has, inevitably, considerably diminished the Commission's powers of initiative. In Gaullist eyes, the role of the Commission is, in essence, that of a body of highly technical experts whose main task is the carrying out of policies agreed by the six member states at ministerial or even Heads of State level. This in effect it is rapidly becoming. It should be added, however, that, according to press reports, at least one other government (*i.e.,* that of the Federal German Republic) is by no means averse to the effective limitation that has been placed on the status and powers of the Commission.

In the Community the Luxembourg compromise was generally greeted with a feeling of relief that work towards the establishment and completion of the common market could be resumed. The loss of face and power incurred by the Commission, while regarded by most of the member governments as a matter for regret, seemed a small price to pay in comparison with delays in progress towards the abolition of tariffs or the formulation of Community policies. It had been evident since the issue of supranationality was decided in 1959 that effective power to shape and co-ordinate the policies of the Community was firmly in the hands of the governments and

[1] *Cf. Ninth General Report on the Activities of the Community,* Brussels, June 1966, pp. 31–33.

that the initial enthusiasm for independent supranational agencies on the basis of the High Authority had had their day.

The issue of qualified majority voting was a very different matter. On this point the other Five were, and have since remained, firm and united in their conviction that the transition to qualified majority voting is a necessary and inevitable step in the continuing process of creating a united Europe. At the same time, it was and remains evident that there can be little hope of progress in this respect as long as de Gaulle remains President of France. Rather, however, than risk a major setback to the existing European machinery the Five compromised by accepting, in effect, a postponement of a formal Community pronouncement on this issue. The Gaullists, on the other hand, while they have gained a respite have by no means won the battle, for the day that de Gaulle steps down from the presidency and a somewhat more genuinely European-minded government comes to power in France, a positive decision on qualified majority voting by six countries will not be long delayed.

It is both paradoxical and ironic that the intensely nationalistic and chauvinistic régime in France has, by its insistence on the fundamental importance of the national will and national identities in the Community, contributed, probably decisively, to an underlying decline of French influence in the Community. By its clear and often unnecessarily brutal pursuit of French national objectives in the political, economic, industrial and financial fields, the actions of the present French Government have inevitably given rise to an attitude of resentment towards and suspicion of new French initiatives. With this development and the consequent demise of the old Community spirit of ready give-and-take, the Community has entered into a period of hard national bargaining where concessions are exchanged for counter-concessions and Community policies are based essentially on the highest common denominator of the political and economic objectives of the six countries. To a large extent such a development was, as we have seen already, unavoidable as the Six sought to establish common policies in increasingly delicate and controversial fields. The actions of the Gaullist régime in France, designed no doubt to promote the psychological as well as the political and economic recovery in France by means of a display of bombastic national self-assertion, have at least had the merit of bringing the conflicting interests of the six member states out into the open and marking clearly the values of the chips stacked by the side of each participant at the Community's gaming table. But whatever the intensity of the feelings aroused by the fate of the Commission or the attempt by any one country to utilise its participation in the Community as a means to enhance its own national political prestige in the eyes of the rest of the world, the overriding desire on the part of the vast majority of those who took part in the Luxembourg talks was to get the Community wheels back on the move. Paul-Henri Spaak probably spoke for most of his colleagues when he said soon after the compromise agreement among the Six had been reached, that 'one cannot say that all the difficulties have been overcome, by any means, but we have succeeded in what we had to do. . . . As for majority voting, we are obliged to recognize that we are not entirely in agreement. But what is essential is that we recognize that the disagreement which continues does not hinder France from coming back to Brussels, nor, therefore, the Community from resuming its activities.' The renewal of the Bonn-Paris axis since Kiesinger and Strauss replaced Erhard and Schroeder as the dominant figures in the Federal German Government, which is due to the apparent German conviction that for the time being at least a closer alliance with France offers the best prospects of a relaxation of the post-war state of tension between the Federal Republic and her Eastern European neighbours, cannot wholly conceal the deep division on the fundamental issue over the future line of development of the Community that continues to exist.

The Community today

Within three or four days of the compromise arrangements having been reached in Luxembourg on 29 January 1966, the European Commission issued a communiqué welcoming the agreement and the possibility this created for the normal resumption of its activities. It pointed to the volume of work that lay ahead (due in large part to the delay that had arisen in the dispatch of Community affairs as a result of the French boycott) and emphasized its anxiety to work in the closest possible collaboration with the Council of Ministers.

During the two years that have elapsed since the elaboration of the Luxembourg compromise the Community has made significant progress towards the establishment of a common market in industry and agriculture as well as some further advances towards the formulation of common policies in social matters, transport, energy and the harmonization of fiscal and monetary policies. The present position in each of these major fields is set out below; for ease of reference and comparison we have taken them in the same order as in Chapter Four, where we looked at the situation as it was towards the end of 1962.

The free movement of goods

By the end of the first stage, tariffs had been reduced by 40%, quota restrictions on industrial imports largely abolished, and national tariffs aligned on the common external tariff to the extent of 30%. Further steps to reduce tariffs and align national tariffs on the common external tariff were taken in 1962 and 1963 with the result

153

that by 1 July 1963 total tariff reductions had reached 60% for industrial products and 45% for agricultural products; while the degree of alignment on the common external tariff had reached 60% for industrial products and 30% for agricultural products. In 1965, following the extensive agricultural policy decisions taken by the Council of Ministers in December 1964, the European Commission submitted new proposals for the customs union to be accelerated and completed by 1 July 1967; this was to be achieved by means of a further reduction in customs duties on industrial products of 10% on 1 January 1966 and a final reduction of 20% on 1 July 1967. For agricultural products for which there was no common market organization, the Commission proposed that customs duties should be reduced to 35% of their original 1957 level on 1 January 1966, to 20% on 1 January 1967, and abolished entirely on 1 July 1967. With regard to the common customs tariff, the Commission proposed that this should be applied in full as from 1 July 1963. Consideration of these proposals by the Council of Ministers was affected by the Community crisis, and although the further 10% reduction laid down in the treaty was duly applied by all six countries, it was not until after the normal resumption of Community business in the early part of 1966 that a decision on a further acceleration of the completion of the customs union was finally taken. The Council of Ministers then agreed that there should be a small reduction of 5% in all tariffs on 1 July 1967, followed by a final reduction of 15% on 1 July 1968. It was also decided that the final alignment of national tariffs on the common external tariff, *i.e.*, of 40%, would be accomplished in one step, on 1 July 1963. In this way all customs duties and restrictions on trade in industrial goods and any remaining restrictions on the free circulation of agricultural products (for products covered by a common market organization, customs duties were replaced by Community levies) within the Community will have been abolished by the middle of 1968 – *i.e.*, $10\frac{1}{2}$ years after the opening of the common market on 1 January 1958. The complete timetable for the elimination of customs duties and the establishment of a common external tariff is shown on page 156.

During the ten years since its formation, the European Economic Community has been one of the fastest-growing economic areas in the world. Between 1958 and 1966 the industrial production of the six member states rose by 64% compared with an increase of 32% in the United Kingdom. In the steel and electricity industries the Community is now the third largest producer in the world; in the output of motor vehicles it ranks second only to the United States. Above all, trade among the Six, which in 1966 was worth $23.200 million, has since 1958 increased by nearly 350%. Average living standards in the Community have soared and are now generally regarded as having surpassed or at least caught up with British levels

154

in at least four of the six countries. To take only one example, whereas in 1958 the number of private cars in use per 1,000 inhabitants was some 50% greater in Britain than in the Community, by 1966 the overall figure for the Community was marginally greater than that for the United Kingdom.

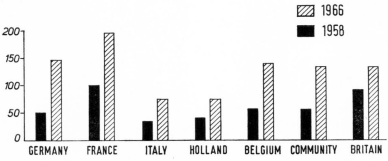

PRIVATE CARS IN USE IN THE COMMUNITY AND THE
UNITED KINGDOM (PER 1000 INHABITANTS)

Source: European Community Information Service, *The Facts,* March 1967.

Similar trends can be readily discerned in such diverse fields as the length of paid holidays, the number of electrical appliances per head of population, and the standard of housing. In all these fields progress in the Community has been impressive and rapid and has far outstripped the rate of advance in the United Kingdom.

In the case of third countries, the value of imports by Community countries rose from $16.156 million in 1958 to $26.826 million in 1964; while for exports the corresponding figures were $15.911 million and $24.158 million:

TABLE 1 (in $ million)

Year	Belgium/ Luxembourg	France	Germany	Italy	Netherlands	Community
			IMPORTS			
1958						
In $ million	1.674	4.382	5.465	2.528	2.107	16.156
In %	10	27	34	16	13	100
1964						
In $ million	2.755	6.304	9.516	4.867	3.384	26.826
In %	10	23	36	18	13	100
			EXPORTS			
1958						
In $ million	1.675	3.985	6.401	1.969	1.881	15.911
In %	11	25	40	12	12	100
1964						
In $ million	2.086	5.503	10.303	3.690	2.575	24.158
In %	9	23	43	15	11	100

THE COMMUNITY'S CUSTOMS UNION

	First Stage					Second Stage			Third Stage			
	1.1.58	1.1.59	1.1.60	1.1.61	1.1.62	1.7.62	1.7.63	1.1.65	1.1.66	1.7.67	1.7.68	1.1.70
A. Elimination of intra-Community duties:												
1. Agricultural products												
(i) Reductions made on the basis of national duties in force on 1 January 1957		10%	10%	5%	10%	5%	10%	10%	10%	10%		
(ii) Total reduction		10%	20%	25%	35%	35%	45%	55%	65%	75%		
2. Industrial products												
(i) Reductions made on the basis of national duties in force on 1 January 1957		10%	10%	10%	10%	10%	10%	10%	10%	5%	15%	
(ii) Total reduction		10%	20%	30%	40%	50%	60%	70%	80%	85%	100%	
B. Introduction of the Common External Tariff												
1. Agricultural products												
(i) Adjustments made					30%				30%		40%	
(ii) Total adjustment					30%				60%		100%	
2. Industrial products												
(i) Adjustments made				30%		30%				40%		
(ii) Total adjustment				30%		60%				100%		

Note: The remaining 25% will be abolished by 1 July 1968 but the final phasing remains to be decided.

Source: E.E.C. Commission Annual General Reports.

The Commission has kept a close watch over the final elimination of quantitative restrictions and measures with equivalent effect, and the operations of government monopolies. By the end of 1965 there were less than 60 quotas still in force in the Community (including 30 for France), concerning mainly fish, tropical products, oils and fats, wine and products of the canning industry. These have since been further reduced. The Commission has, however, admitted freely that while the number of remaining quotas is now very small, there is still a very great deal to do in the elimination of measures with equivalent effect. A Council decision has consequently been prepared under which the member states will, except in a few exceptional cases, undertake to abstain from making imports and exports from and to other Community countries subject to such formalities as licences, visas and other official forms of authorization. In its Eighth General Report the Commission stated notably that for some of these measures (*i.e.*, with equivalent effect to quotas) like, for example, 'price-fixing, general principles must be worked out. . . . Where technical specifications are concerned, this is not always easy. Harmonization of legislation, particularly, will bring about the removal of many such obstacles, but if measures with equivalent effect come to light while such harmonization is under consideration, they will nonetheless be made the subject of directives' (*i.e.*, designed to correct them). In the case of government monopolies, the measures applied so far have met with only modest success and the Commission has consequently put in hand a number of studies designed to re-examine various ways and means of resolving the problems created by the continued operation of these monopolies as well as to evaluate their compatibility or otherwise with the normal operation of the common market.

The free movement of capital and persons

Since 1962 the Commission has continued to promote the liberalization of capital movements in the Community. Specialist committees were set up to examine such questions as the actual organization of the capital market in the member states and to look into the difficulties arising from major differences in savings and investment procedures. Nevertheless, progress in this respect has been comparatively slow, particularly with regard to such matters as the admission of other Community issues on national capital markets.

The Commission has also continued to work to ensure the free movement of workers throughout the Community. New regulations which were issued in the course of 1964 included a procedure whereby the European Co-ordination Office informs all member states at the beginning of each quarter of any regions or occupations anywhere in the Community for which priority for home (*i.e.*, national) workers has been maintained or re-established. Where such cases occur the member states in question are called upon to give the reasons which have prompted this action. The Commission in a recent memorandum to the Council of Ministers has emphasized the need to secure the maximum mobility of labour throughout the Community, stating *inter alia* that 'in the search for greater efficiency, the main aim of the Commission and member states will have to be to ensure the maximum scope for jobs for the manpower available in the Community. In this connection, greater efforts will be necessary particularly with a view to improving the existing machinery for clearing employment offers and requests. Moreover, in order to overcome the qualitative imbalance between supply and demand, a common crash vocational training drive will have to be organized for those workers who may be prepared to emigrate but who are nonetheless prevented from doing so because they lack sufficient vocational skills or training.' With a view to pinpointing the main problems arising in this field the Commission's advisory committee on general social policy has recently put in hand a number of special studies into such matters as the effective application of the Community's regulations on freedom of movement, the problems of integrating foreign workers and the way in which they are generally received, the relationship between foreign workers and employers and trade union organizations, and the main reasons prompting men to emigrate. The Commission has also prepared and published a *Comparative Dictionary of trades in which migration is most frequent in the E.E.C. countries,* listing a total of 119 occupations and designed to facilitate and speed up the work of advertising job vacancies throughout the Community area.

Harmonization of the conditions of competition

In its Seventh General Report the Commission stated that 'the most urgent practical task . . . facing competition policy makers is probably the harmonization of turnover tax systems in the member states. The multi-stage systems with cumulative effect found in five countries do not allow of any exact calculation of the countervailing charge on imports of individual goods or of the refund on exports. This results in distortions of competition between states. Moreover, the cumulation effect of this system favours the integrated – mainly large – enterprises. The Commission has therefore proposed the replacement of the existing system by an added value tax system which does not affect competition. The European Parliament has welcomed, supported and improved on this proposal. The basic features of this common added value system have also been worked out. Alignment of the systems and rates would make it possible to abolish the tax frontiers which prevent the six national economies from merging into one common market.'[2]

[2]*Cf. Seventh General Report on the Activities of the Community,* Brussels, June 1964, p. 61.

158

It was however not until February 1967 that the Council of Ministers finally accepted the Commission's proposals for the adoption of a system of added value taxation for the Community. Member states then undertook to replace their present systems of turnover taxes by an added value tax system by the beginning of 1970; agreement was also reached on the abolition of tax frontiers and the co-ordination of added value taxation rates – although the dates for the application of these further measures remain to be fixed. The principle of the added value tax was set out in Article 2 of the Commission's directive :

The principle of the common tax on the added value system is the collection for goods and services of a general consumption tax exactly proportional to the price of such goods and services irrespective of the number of transactions involved in production and distribution stages prior to the collection of the tax.

At each stage of this production chain, the tax on the value added – calculated from the price of the goods or services – is payable (after deduction of the tax on the added value which the various price components have already attracted).

The common tax on the added value system includes the retail stage.

Member states shall, however, be authorized, during a transitional period which will expire when tax frontiers are abolished – and subject to the consultations envisaged (under Article 5 of the Directive), to apply this system only down to the wholesale stage and to levy an independent supplementary tax at the retail stage or at a stage previous to it.

Each one of the Six will be free to fix the level of the added value tax at whatever level it chooses. Thus, in France the tax has already been fixed at 16.5% and in Belgium at 15%. In Germany, the level is likely to be 11 or 12%, in Holland 9 or 10%, and in Italy 10%. In the case of French exports to, say, Holland, the article in question will carry the Dutch and not the French level of added value tax. The suggestion was made at one stage during the discussions by the Ministers of the Six and the Commission that tax frontiers should be abolished and the levels of added value tax equated throughout the Community by 1970. It soon became apparent, however, that such a step was regarded as excessively ambitious in the shorter term, although it was formally recognized that the harmonization of the levels of taxation in all six countries – leading eventually to the abolition of tax frontiers – constituted a long-term policy objective of the Community.

But taxation is of course only one of the many elements that can make for a distortion of the conditions of competition. State monopolies, subsidies, cartel agreements, disparities in company law, differences with regard to patent regulations, differences in standards, and legislation are all potential causes of distortion and this list is by no means exhaustive. And even then these factors are, as Mr von der Groeben put it, no more than the 'outer skin of the problem'. Inside and constituting the real meat of the problem are the 'six different economic orders with varying structures, six different legal systems, and six social systems, each with its own peculiar structure'.[3]

Competition policy, as the Commission has repeatedly stressed, is not an end in itself but a means of ensuring a viable and economically sound and prosperous Community. To achieve this the Community's competition policy has, in the view of the Commission, five basic objectives : first, to eliminate distortions; second, to establish a workable competitive system; third, to open up the national domestic markets; fourth, to do away with frontier controls; and fifth, to promote a system of international competition as free from discrimination as possible. At the same time the Commission has been at pains to stress that it is not opposed to the formation of larger economic units. It is generally recognized in Brussels that in present world trading conditions the amalgamation of companies and the development of giant European firms, capable perhaps one day of rivalling those of the United States, is in the best economic interests of the Community. In order, however, to prevent major internal market disturbances the Commission is pressing strongly for the determination of a 'European' form of company and 'European' patents.

It is indeed against agreements of the exclusive dealing type rather than against the development of major industrial or economic units that the Commission has set its face – its main objectives, it must be recalled, being the promotion of Community interests and protection of the consumer. The Commission's first decision prohibiting a restrictive agreement (concerning the German company of Grundig Verkaufs GmbH and the French Constan company) in September 1964 was very much a test case and created a notable precedent. The agreement made between these two companies made Constan the sole importer and supplier of Grundig products throughout the whole of France. The two firms had, furthermore, signed a supplementary agreement on the use in France of a special

[3]Speaking upon this theme at a lecture given at the University of Marbourg in 1965, Mr Von der Groeben, a member of the European Commission, went on to say that 'in Germany, there is a social market economy. The economic systems of the other member countries also bear the stamp of the market economy, although in some ways they differ appreciably from the German model. In France there is a market economy with a superstructure of planning and intervention. In Italy, where the outlines of a five-year economic plan including social aims have been published, there is a market economy directed mainly via the big public undertakings. In the Netherlands the market economy approach is coupled with overall analytical forecasts intended to provide the authorities, the two sides of industry, and management with guidance on the effects to be expected from any given measure.'

160

trade-mark designed to prevent other French firms importing Grundig products into France via, say, German wholesalers. The Commission concluded that these arrangements, by impairing the commercial freedom of action of both Grundig and Constan as well as other interested firms, constituted a restraint of competition. The argument put forward by the two companies that since trade between France and Germany in Grundig products had increased substantially since the introduction of their joint organization, was rejected by the Commission on the grounds that 'if a restraint of competition meant that trade between the member states developed under different conditions than they would otherwise have done, and that exchanges of goods between the member states were appreciably influenced, this constituted infringement of Article 85, especially as in this case the area reserved for Constan coincided with the frontiers of one of the member states. It was an arrangement rendering integration of the national markets in a common market more difficult. Obvious evidence for this was the difference in prices of Grundig products in Germany and in France.'[4] From the actions and decisions taken by the Commission to date in the field of competition policy a number of underlying principles or guide-lines have clearly emerged. Thus, for example, the fact that one of the parties to, say, an exclusive dealing agreement has its headquarters in a country outside the Common Market does not enable it to escape the provisions of Article 85. At the same time a distribution agreement between a manufacturer established in one of the member countries and a distributor in a non-member country would not be considered as affecting competition within the common market. On the other hand, the Commission is unlikely to take any action in a case brought to its notice unless the degree of restraint of competition is appreciable. Exclusive dealing arrangements within the Community, particularly if the area or areas concerned correspond to the geographical boundaries of one or more member states, are broadly unacceptable, even though it has been formally admitted that in certain special circumstances exclusive distribution agreements can provide a positive spur towards the improvement of production or distribution.

The Commission has also put in hand studies of certain specific markets where the increase in intra-Community trade has lagged markedly behind the general overall trend. The first of these enquiries was begun in June 1965 and concerned the margarine industry where, despite very substantial differences in price levels among the Six countries, there had been comparatively little increase in the flow of intra-Community trade. Other studies of a similar nature have been undertaken since.

The Commission has also done a great deal of work on the

[4] Cf. *Eighth General Report on the Activities of the Community*, Brussels, June 1965, pp. 68–9.

elaboration of an official Community doctrine on the question of monopolies. As we have seen, Article 86 of the treaty prohibits the abuse of a dominant position within the common market, but the term 'dominant position' may of course apply equally well to production, distribution or, indeed, financial strength. The Commission's view was that the determining factor on which it would base its judgement or opinion would be a given firm's 'position as supplier within the Common Market'. It follows from this, of course, that, in the Commission's view, it would be quite conceivable for a non-Community enterprise to enjoy a dominant position within the common market.

The Commission's conclusions were that any kind of concentration which led directly or indirectly to the creation of a monopoly was likely to attract the clauses of Article 86 relating to 'an abuse of a dominant position' and would therefore not be permissible. This was the 'only interpretation that accords with the objectives of the treaty in general and with the rules of competition in particular.' It was at all times imperative that the freedom of action and choice on the part of the enterprises and consumers should be safeguarded; to this end 'no cartel and no enterprise in a dominant position must be permitted to destroy competition and the economic freedom of others by establishing a monopoly on any market'.

In the case of state aids the Commission has recently broken these down into three main categories. These are, first, the aids which were being granted by member governments to specific industries before the opening of the common market. Aids of this kind have, according to the Commission's reports, either been abolished already or are due to disappear during the course of the next few years. Second, there are a certain number of aids arising directly from the creation of the common market and formally authorized in order to enable the industries in question to adapt themselves to the new circumstances. Aids to the shipbuilding and film industries as well as financial assistance to promote regional developments in the Community are accepted by the Commission as falling within this second category. Third, there are some remaining national aids which are officially recognized – such as, for example, government assistance for particular industries or regions in the face of 'natural calamities or other extraordinary events', *i.e.*, the disastrous floods in various parts of Italy early in 1967. Basically, the Commission is today prepared to authorize only those financial aids which are intended either to 'promote the economic development of regions where the standard of living is abnormally low or where there is serious unemployment' or to 'facilitate the development of certain activities or of certain economic regions, provided that such aids do not change trading conditions to such a degree as would be contrary to the common interest'.[5] During

[5]Ibid, p. 80.

the 12 months ending in March 1966 the Commission issued its findings concerning 45 cases of general or specific aids in the Community; among the forms of aid specifically approved, authorized or proposed by the Commission were the operations of the Cassa per il Mezzogiorno (the official Italian state agency with responsibility for promoting the economic development of southern Italy); a 10% grant towards the cost of ship construction in Community countries; the harmonization of national aids to the film industry; and finally, measures designed to promote the rationalization of the Italian and German textile industries.

Regional policy

In order to probe more deeply into the problems connected with various regional development policies, the Commission in 1963 decided to set up three specialized committees charged respectively with an examination of possible methods designed to accelerate the modernization of less-developed areas of the Community, the problem of ageing industrial regions (*i.e.,* producing coal, steel and textiles), and the effectiveness of the various forms of assistance tried out both in the Community and in third countries with a view to promoting regional development. It was on the bases of the reports prepared by these three committees that the Commission in May 1965 submitted to the Council of Ministers and the European Parliament its First Memorandum on Regional Policy in the European Economic Community, in which it advocated the preparation of a selected number of regional programmes, based on a 'detailed study of economic and demographic trends' and the co-ordination of public and private investment. Such programmes should preferably 'be on the same lines for the greatest possible number of regions . . .' but particular 'attention will have to be given . . . to the large peripheral areas which are predominantly agricultural, certain agricultural areas affected by structural weaknesses, declining industrial areas, areas lying along the frontiers between member states, and areas adjacent to the Soviet Zone. In the large peripheral areas in the Community, the first step should be to promote the growth of industrial development areas, where industrial activities and complementary services are grouped together to form a coherent whole, capable, after initial aid, of self-sustained development. In smaller less-favoured regions, which can benefit from proximity to great industrial concentrations, an effective method would be to create secondary industrial centres having the communal amenities necessary to inhibit an exodus of the rural population'.[6]

By the end of 1965 the number of loans approved by the European Investment Bank had increased to 117 totalling 614 million units of

[6]*Cf. Ninth General Report on the Activities of the Community,* Brussels, June 1966, p. 151.

account, while the total value of the schemes to which it had contributed was nearly 3.000 million units of account. Some of the most spectacular of these have been the construction of the Val d'Aosta motorway, the irrigation of the Metaponto plain in Italy and the Cediz valley in Turkey – a country which became associated with the Community in September 1963. Loans were also granted for schemes in the other member countries and in the African associated states.

We saw in Chapter Four that one of the first projects considered by the Commission was the creation of an industrial complex between Taranto and Bari in the South of Italy. This survey, which was carried out by a consultant firm, was officially handed to the Italian government in November 1965. Describing the plan, the Commission states in its *Ninth General Report* :

The aim of the scheme is not only to develop one of the least-favoured regions of the Community but also to try out a new method of industrialization suitable for large underdeveloped areas.

The centre of the development pole (area) is Bari in Apulia, and the branch of industry to be promoted there is heavy and medium mechanical engineering; there will be established simultaneously the whole complex of ancillary industries required in that sector, together with a sufficient number of other industries (industries that produce finished goods and use intermediate goods and services) to justify economically the existence of the complex of related industries. A study was made of the Mediterranean market in order to decide which industries it would be desirable to establish in Bari and the optimum size of production unit for each of them, taking into account the present state of technology and the competitive position within the Community. For each unit of production thus defined, the needs of each of the industries were then worked out; finally, the total needs per industry were calculated in such a way as to define the markets for the various units of production corresponding to them, and to make sure that these markets guarantee a minimum return on each unit of production.

The initial nucleus envisaged comprises about 30 factories; nine of these will produce finished goods, and about 20 will provide them with intermediate products and services. The whole complex should offer employment for about 10,000 workers and require industrial investment amounting to about 100,000 million lire (*i.e.*, some £58 million).

The consultant firm is going to study by agreement with the Cassa per il Mezzogiorno, which will have to effect them, what public investments are necessary for the functioning and development of the new industrial centre. The construction and opening of the factories concerned will be spread over four years, so that they should be in full production by about the end of 1970, by which time the common market will have been fully established.'[7]

Social policy

In the Community as a whole, gross hourly wages rose by about 75% between 1958 and 1965. The increases were particularly high in Italy and Germany – 90% and 80% respectively – and lowest in Luxembourg with 40%. Even allowing for monetary depreciation, average real income in the Community in 1964 was some 40% higher for workers in industry than in 1958. While these increases cannot of course be directly attributed to the activities of the European Commission, they are nonetheless the result of the tremendous increases in trade and production that have followed on from the reductions in tariff barriers between the Six. The Commission's role has been to assist in the creation or maintenance of general economic conditions that encourage full employment, to encourage the alignment of social security systems and the promotion of measures designed to bring about comparable levels of wages, holidays and conditions of work throughout the Community area, as well as to watch over the implementation of the principle of equal pay for men and women.

The social security systems of the six Community countries, while among the most advanced anywhere in the world, often operate in sharply different ways. While the Six are at one in that they do not have a uniform system for any particular risk applying to all the population groups covered, there are in each country a number of specialized schemes for specific groups of workers (*i.e.*, mineworkers, railwaymen) which can differ greatly from one member country to another. The question is further complicated by the fact that there are significant differences in organizational and general administrative arrangements, legal provisions and the nature and provisions of various optional or compulsory supplementary schemes. The original proposals on social security prepared by the Commission and embodied in the regulations of 1958 were aimed – as we saw in Chapter Four – at achieving equality of entitlement to social security benefits for all nationals of all six Community countries, irrespective of their place of employment. This was followed, in 1963, by the submission of proposals by the Commission to the Council of Ministers designed to further the process of harmonization of national social security systems and included – in the form in which they were finally adopted – studies of benefits to be paid in cases of employment injury or occupational disease; the elaboration of a common agricultural social policy; the definition of a number of

[7]Ibid, pp. 152–3.

'social-security concepts which will be the subject of alignment'; and a study of the economic effects of social security arrangements.

The Commission has also organized seminars and discussions on a Community basis on such matters as industrial health and hygiene, social services, housing policy, education, vocational training and scientific research. In the specific field of education, for example, the Commission has stressed the importance of achieving a large measure of mutual recognition of university and technical degrees or diplomas; directives were prepared to this end during the course of 1965 for degrees in architecture, engineering, economics, medicine and dispensing chemistry, while arrangements were in hand for mutual recognition of degrees for dentists, surgeons, opticians, lawyers and tax consultants – the equivalent for the liberal professions, in other words, of the free movement of workers.

Financial grants made by the European Social Fund by the end of 1965 amounted to 31.7 million units of account, including 29 million units of account for the re-training of workers made redundant as a direct result of the establishment of the common market, and nearly 3 million units of account in resettlement grants. In all, some 450,000 workers benefited from these grants. The main beneficiaries were France and Italy, with approximately 10 million units of account apiece, although in the case of Italy the assistance was spread over a very much greater number of workers (*i.e.*, 275,000 compared with 70,000 in France).

Transport policy

The European Commission, in May 1963, submitted proposals to the Council of Ministers for the promotion of a common transport policy covering, first, 'the establishment of a rate bracket system for goods transport by rail, road and inland waterway'; second, 'the introduction of a Community quota for goods transport by road within the Community'; third, 'the harmonization of certain provisions affecting competition in transport'; fourth, 'the preparation of a survey on infra-structure costs in rail, road and inland waterway transport'; fifth, 'the standardization of procedures for issuing licences for road haulage between member states'. These proposals covered the three main areas where, in the considered view of the Commission 'Community action in transport should be brought to bear : integration, organization and harmonization'.[8]

It was, however, not until June 1965 – only a month or so in fact before the beginning of the Community crisis – that the Six made their first real significant breakthrough in the field of transport. The draft agreement then reached laid down the basis of a common policy for transport, for rail, road and inland waterway, to take effect in two three-year stages, *i.e.*, 1967–70 and 1970–73. It was

[8]*Seventh General Report, op. cit.,* p. 195.

agreed that during the first of these two stages there would be a compulsory bracket-rate system for all goods transport by road and rail from one member state to another. For international traffic by inland waterway, rates would be free subject only to an obligation to publish any rates applied that were above or below agreed reference tariffs. As from the beginning of the second three-year period, this system would also be applied to all internal traffic, including transport by road and rail. In order, however, to prevent any major disturbance of the transport market, the Commission made provision in its original proposals for the following safeguard measures :

(a) A uniform 20% range for rate brackets, but with the Council retaining the possibility of reducing this for certain types of transport.

(b) The facility for member states temporarily to fix maximum or minimum rates for transport coming under the reference system in order to prevent any abuse of dominant positions or cut-throat competition.

(c) Communication to the national authorities and the Commission of the rate applied within the brackets of representative transport determined in advance; however, these rates would not have to be published.[9]

The draft agreement also provided for a large measure of harmonization of the existing conditions in the national transport markets, particularly with regard to national regulations governing access to the haulage trade and agreements of all kinds between transport enterprises, as well as proposals for a common Community solution to problems arising from non-governmental interference in competitive transport situations and the apportionment of infrastructure costs. On this last point the Council took a decision in February 1966 which provided, first, that member states should communicate to the Commission all details of actual and new investment projects, whether for rail, road or inland waterways, that could be regarded as being of Community interest; second, that the Commission would inform all six member states of any projects communicated to it; and third, that provision would be made for joint consultation on such projects at the request of the Commission or any one of the member states.

The Commission has also taken the initiative in suggesting studies for putting forward proposals on the publication of Rhine shipping rates, standardization of weights and dimensions of Community commercial vehicles, transport by pipeline, road safety, the improvement of 'frontier-crossing conditions and the co-ordination of sea and air transport'. One of the most interesting – if at the same time rather more academic – studies that has been put in hand by the

[9]*Ninth General Report, op. cit.,* pp. 214–5.

Commission in the field of transport is a survey of the likely density and flow of road traffic along the Liège-Luxembourg-Strasbourg route during the next decade or so. According to the Commission, the aim of this study, which is of a pilot nature, is to forecast traffic 'in 1970 and 1980 in an area which covers a part of the territories of four Common Market countries and in which trade flows are likely not only to develop considerably but also to follow different patterns'.

Energy Policy

Progress in the field of energy policy has continued to be painfully slow. The proposals set out in the Commission's 1962 memorandum had proved impossible to agree and it was not until April 1964 that hopes of a satisfactory Community settlement were temporarily raised when the six governments agreed on the terms of a special Protocol of Agreement relating to energy problems. The Protocol, while recognizing that the elaboration of a common energy policy would require a considerable period of time, nonetheless emphasized that this remained a vital link in the overall common market and re-affirmed the overriding importance of assuring low prices for energy, security of supply, the orderly substitution of new and cheaper sources of energy for any uneconomic indigenous coal production, stability of costs, free choice for the consumer, and fair conditions of competition between different forms of energy in the common market. The six governments also agreed on a number of basic principles for coal and oil. For coal, it was recognized that there was a 'need to provide state support for rationalization measures taken by the collieries, and invited the E.C.S.C. High Authority to propose a procedure for setting up a Community system of aid'. The discussions which followed led to a High Authority decision in February 1965 authorizing member states to grant certain types of aid to the coal producers. For oil and natural gas, the six governments 'expressed a wish to establish, under the Treaty of Rome, a common policy ensuring widely diversified supply at the lowest and most stable prices possible and by arrangements adaptable to the circumstances. More specifically, they undertook to promote the development of Community production where this made economic sense : to seek a common stockpiling policy; to abolish progressively any discrimination between their own nationals and those of other member states in the terms and practical application of their national rules; to work out for petroleum fuels a tax system suited to the objectives of the energy policy; and to align charges on other petroleum products'.[10]

The implementation of the broad agreement set out in the 1964 Protocol soon ran into the now customary conflict of interests

[10]*Eighth General Report, op. cit.,* p. 173.

between the Italians and the Dutch, who wanted to maximize cheap fuel imports, the Germans, who wanted adequate protection for coal, and the French and the Belgians, who wanted a mixed programme of protection for their own national coal industries allied to a programme of cheap imports from outside the Community. In the event, the protracted discussions of energy were overtaken by the Community crisis of 1965 and it was not until the beginning of 1966 that the Six met again to consider the next steps to be taken in this field.

The resumption of discussions on energy policy took place against a background of an increasingly serious situation in the Community coal industries as shown particularly in the results for 1965, when in spite of a continuing increase in overall Community energy requirements, substantial state aids to the industry and a reduction in coal output of 10 million tons, the balance sheet for coal showed a surplus of 10 million tons, bringing pithead stocks to the high level of 26 million tons (equal to well over 10% of annual production). But worse was still to follow. At a meeting in March 1966 of the E.C.S.C. Council of Ministers, the President of the High Authority, Signor Del Bo, stated that if the current situation was serious, the medium-term prospects were at least equally bad; according to the High Authority's estimates the demand for Community-produced coal in 1970 was likely to be about 170 million tons – compared with a probable production figure of 200 million tons. Decisions could not be much longer delayed on, first, the rate of cutback in coal production that was possible in the light of social and regional problems; and second, the role of coal in the future. The outcome of the March meeting was that the Council of Ministers recognized the serious situation of the Community coal industry and the urgent need to find and apply solutions.

Shortly after the Council meeting the High Authority issued a memorandum on the coal objective for 1970 and coal policy, in which it put forward the view that for social and security of supply reasons the coal objective for 1970 should be 190 million tons and that measures should be taken, on the basis of a common policy, to limit contraction to this level. To this end, national programmes should be co-ordinated in an objective accepted by the Six who should work together to achieve it. On security of supply, the memorandum argued that the 190 million tons were necessary both in order that the proportion of total Community energy supplies in 1970 provided from Community sources should not be too far removed from 50% of total energy requirements, and to ensure that the production objective for 1975–80 would still be such as to make an effective contribution to overall security of supply. The memorandum suggested various lines of approach to the problem of securing outlets for the 190 million tons. These included joint action for a systematic use of quantitative restrictions varying according to categories of coal; a system of specific aid on a Community basis to maintain the market for coking coal in the iron and steel industry; ensuring for Community coal a substantial share in the power station market by compensating the cost advantage of competing fuels through price subsidization, fiscal concessions or selective electricity tariffs. Since then, in March of this year (1967), the Six have agreed to institute a formal system of national subsidies for all indigenous coking coals to bring their delivered price to the steelworks down to, or as near as possible to, the delivered price of American coal. It is obvious that this measure – as indeed all other forms of subsidy to the Community coal producers – are completely counter to the rules of the Treaty of Paris and the doctrine of a fully competitive and transparent market; it also shows that the Six are prepared – in certain cases at least – to bend the provisions of the treaties that link them as and when required by the necessities of national priorities. The European Commission, for its part, has made little or no further progress on the establishment of a common policy for oil and gas. Common customs duties for oil products (at moderate levels) and gas (at a nil level) were agreed at the end of 1964 but the Commission has not yet resolved the problems posed by the discriminatory French petroleum importing system – despite repeated recommendations to the French government requesting that the French market should be opened up to allow imports of petroleum products from other member countries – and the sales policy for Dutch natural gas – where different prices have been quoted for comparable transactions with internal and external consumers. In short, energy remains one of the main stumbling-blocks in the long march towards common Community policies and while the Community is now committed, at least in the longer term, to an undisguisedly cheap energy policy, present indications are that this goal will be pursued along national rather than along common Community lines.

Agriculture

The second major step forward along the road to the establishment of the common market in agriculture was taken at a Council meeting on 15 December 1964 when the Ministers of the six countries agreed on uniform price levels for grains with effect from 1 July 1967. The following target price levels were then agreed :

Barley	$91.25 per ton.
Maize	$90.65 per ton (with a minimum support price of $77).
Rye	$93.75 per ton.
Wheat hard	$125 per ton (with a minimum price guaranteed to the farmer of $145).
Wheat soft	$106.25 per ton.

In order to compensate German and Italian farmers for this accelerated move towards common grain prices (the date originally envisaged was 31 December 1969), the Council agreed that the Commission should make the following direct grants to farmers in these two countries from Community funds :

	In $ million		
	1967–68	*1968–69*	*1969–70*
Germany	$140	$93.5	$46.75
Italy	$65	$44	$22
Luxembourg	$1.25	$0.75	$0.5

The agreement on the common grain prices meant that as from the middle of 1967 the whole Community would, for the first time, 'constitute a single agricultural marketing area'. Within this area all grain prices would be the same from 'Sicily to Schleswig-Holstein, and from Bavaria to Brittany'. The agreement provided that prices would be reviewed and determined annually by the Council of Ministers.

Agriculture, as we saw in Chapter Six, featured prominently in the Community crisis of 1965. But if an alleged failure on the part of her five Community partners to honour their agricultural bond was the pretext for the French outburst and consequent boycott of the European Communities in June 1965, the real reasons governing French action were, of course, on the one hand, a determination to clip the wings of the Commission and, on the other hand, undisguised hostility towards the extension of the principle of majority voting from the commencement of the third stage of the common market as provided for in the Treaty of Rome. In fact, the Commission's proposals for the financing and organization of the Community's agricultural market – originally put forward in March 1965 – were accepted almost as they stood except for the important proviso that until 1970 national governments would continue to exercise almost complete direct control over the funds flowing into the European Agricultural Guidance and Guarantee Fund. Within a few months of the Luxembourg compromise of January 1966, the Council had accepted the Commission's proposals – in essentially the same form as they had been prepared before the crisis – for a common price level for milk and milk products, beef and veal, sugar, rice, oilseeds and olive oil as from 1967/68 as well as for 'the criteria to be adopted for the establishment of a common policy for agriculture'.

On the vital issue of the financing of the common agricultural policy, the Commission in July 1965 (*i.e.,* after the French walk-out) submitted to the Council of Ministers a revised memorandum on agricultural financing and the independent revenues of the Commission. The main feature of the revised proposals was the suggestion that there should be a transitional period extending from

1965 to 1970 and a consequent postponement in the introduction of a complete common market until 1 January 1970. The Commission's proposals dealt successively with expenditure, revenue and the question of its own financial autonomy. On expenditure, the Commission began by saying that half of the agreed expenditure on price support and structural improvements in agriculture had already been taken over by the European Agricultural Guidance and Guarantee Fund (E.A.G.G.F.) for the year 1964/65. The share of the costs that would have to be borne by the Fund (*i.e.,* as opposed to direct contributions from the member states) each year from 1 July onwards clearly depended on the date on which the movement of agricultural products was completely freed. On the assumption that this date would be fixed for 1 July 1967 – with the Fund taking over all costs from that date on – the transition from part-Fund, part direct grant (by national governments) financing to complete E.A.G.G.F. financing would have to be made in three stages. If, on the other hand, the single market for agriculture were not to come into effect until 1 January 1970, then the transition could be made in five stages.[11]

On revenue, the Commission proposed that 'the burden falling upon the Agricultural Fund should be apportioned among the member states in accordance with a scale fixed by the Commission in the light of suggestions made during the Council negotiations of 30 June 1965; this scale took into account particularly the fact that Italy's contribution to the expenditure of the Fund should not be greater than its economic development allowed. The Commission also applied the principle established earlier that member states importing substantial quantities from outside the Community should bear a rather heavier burden than other member states. Lastly, the Commission selected the factors by which payments would be calculated in such a way that member states' contributions for 1965–70 could already be worked out exactly – leaving no room for uncertainty as to what must be paid in the future. The Commission suggested the following apportionment:

Belgium:
  8.51% in 1965/66 (8.13% in the second half of 1969).
France:
  30.59% in 1965/66 (26% in the second half of 1969).
Germany:
  32.45% in 1965/66 (32.37% in the second half of 1969).

[11]Actual expenditure by the E.A.G.G.F. rose rapidly during its first three years of operation:

	1962/63	1963/64	1964/65	*In $ million* *Total*
Guarantee section	28.4	55.0	167	250.4
Guidance section	9.5	18.3	56	83.8
Total	37.9	73.3	223	334.2

Italy :
18% in 1965/66 (22.93% in the second half of 1969).
Luxembourg :
0.21% in 1965/66 (0.21% in the second half of 1969).
Netherlands :
10.24% in 1965/66 (10.36% in the second half of 1969).[12]

On the vexed question of independent revenues, the Commission suggested that the 'Community's expenditure should normally be financed in this way from 1970 onwards'. One possible way of overcoming this problem was the establishment of an equalization fund for the period 1967–70 – to even out the burden which would otherwise fall unfairly upon certain countries, and in particular the Federal German Republic – leading to a system of completely independent revenues for the Community from 1970 onwards.

The Commission's proposals were discussed and broadly accepted by the other five member states – in the absence of the French delegation – at Council meetings in July and October 1965. At a further meeting in April 1966, where the French were present, the Council agreed to accept as a 'working hypothesis the principle that the calculation of expenditure to be borne by the Fund should be based on the total gross exports of the member states to non-member states (*i.e.*, without offsetting the corresponding gross imports)'.[13] It is worth noting that out of the first allocation of aid from the Guarantee Section of the Fund, covering the year 1962/63 and amounting to 28.7 million units of account, no less than 24.5 million units of account, or over 85% went to France. Aid paid out by the Guidance Section for the same period amounted to some 9 million units of account and was rather more evenly divided.

Agreement on the financing of the Community's agricultural policy was finally reached, later in 1966, on the understanding that as from 1 July 1967 all financial expenditure, whether for market support, refunds on exports or modernization and improvement of production, marketing and distribution, would be centrally financed from a single fund; that for the two years 1965/66 and 1966/67 the cost of the common farm policy would be met entirely by means of percentage contributions from the member states to the E.A.G.G.F.; that as from 1 July 1967, 90% of the amounts charged in levies on imports of agricultural produce from outside the Community – expected to cover about 45% of the total expenditure incurred in operating the common agricultural policy – would be surrendered by the national governments to the European Agricultural Fund; and that the balance would be made up by contributions to the Fund from the exchequers of the six member states in the following ratios :

[12]*Ninth General Report, op. cit.,* p. 194.
[13]Ibid, p. 195.

Belgium	...	...	8.1%
France	...	...	32.0%
Germany	...	...	31.2%
Italy ...	...	...	20.3%
Luxembourg ...	...	0.2%
Netherlands ...	...	8.2%

and that these ratios would apply until 1 January 1970 when the total income arising from the levies would have to be paid into the Fund. Further discussions on the mechanics of the financing of the common agricultural policy will therefore take place in 1969 and will afford an opportunity to review the percentage contributions to be paid in the Fund by individual member states. The total income from levies and customs duties to be paid into the Fund is expected, once the common agricultural policy is fully established, to amount to some $1,500 million (£535 million) a year.

The date for the completion of the common farm policy, including the abolition of customs duties and the application of the common external tariff on farm products for which there was no common market organization, was fixed, like that for the completion of the common market for industrial goods, for 1 July 1968.

Development of relations with the Associated States

Despite the generous provisions of the Yaoundé Convention, trade between the Six and the African Associated States has not shown any significant increase (imports by the Six in 1965 at a little over 1,000 million units of account were in fact marginally below those in 1964; while exports from the Community to the Associated States at some 800 million units of account were practically unchanged from the previous year). The Commission has consequently put in hand a number of studies designed to promote sales outlets within the Community for commodities produced by the Associated States. The first survey of this kind covered coffee, cocoa and bananas and included an analysis of 'the conditions governing imports, transit processing, distribution and price formation for those products; it also included the results of a survey carried out among consumers, and projections of consumption levels in 1970'[14] while a second report was devoted to an examination of further outlets for tropical oleaginous products.

The first European Development Fund – set up under the original Implementing Convention annexed to the Treaty of Rome to finance economic and social projects in the Associated States – to which 581 million units of account had been allocated by the six member states had been fully committed by 31 December 1965. During 1965 the first allocations were also made under the second European Development Fund established under the Yaoundé Con-

[14]*Eighth General Report, op. cit.*, p. 327.

vention and endowed with a total of 730 million units of account. In this connection the Commission estimated, in its *Ninth General Report,* that for the next eight years at least the total annual financial contributions to be made by the Community to the Associated States would be of the order of 100 million units of account. In addition the Community would provide a steadily increasing number of traineeships, scholarships and other educational and vocational training schemes. Thus, for the 1964 academic year, the Community's scholarship scheme provided for a total of 1,400 places for students from the Associated States compared with 713 in the previous year (these numbers do not of course take account of various national schemes financed directly by the member governments).

One major difficulty that has arisen, however, is the number of contracts for work in the various associated states and financed by the European Development Fund, that have gone to the former metropolitan, or colonial, country. Thus, in 1963, no less than 52% of all supply contracts went to France. The main reasons for this tendency to continue to deal with the former colonial power appear to be, first, the problem of language (*i.e.,* almost all the African Associated States are French-speaking) and, second, the fact that it is normally the former colonial power which has by far the largest number of companies, enterprises or representatives on the spot. The Commission is seeking to ensure a fairer distribution of contracts financed out of the Development Fund by greater publicity for any new calls for tenders, but has so far achieved only modest success.

At the time of signature of the Yaoundé Convention, the representatives of the six member states declared 'their readiness to negotiate in a sympathetic spirit agreements with any non-member countries who so requested and whose economic structure and production were comparable to those of the associated States. Such agreements could take the following forms : (a) Accession to the Yaoundé Convention . . . ; (b) Association agreements with mutual rights and obligations, particularly in matters of trade; (c) Commercial agreements to facilitate and expand trade between the Community and these countries.[15]

Since then, several African countries have sought to make their own arrangements with the Community, notably Nigeria – which signed an association agreement with the Community in Lagos in July 1966 (under which Nigeria obtained duty-free entry to Community markets for all her products except peanut oil, palm oil, cocoa beans and plywood – which are subject to quotas – and, in return, gives tariff preferences on 26 Community products); and Tanzania, Uganda and Kenya – who are still in the process of negotiating with the Community.

[15]*Cf. Seventh General Report, op. cit.,* pp. 225–6.

The Community in the future

The achievements of the Community since the compromise of January 1966 have been important and solid. While there are sections of the economy, such as energy, where progress has been insignificant, over the broad field of industrial, agricultural and general economic matters, the Community is now well on the way to establishing the complete customs union called for by the Treaty of Rome. As from 1 July 1968, the last remaining tariff barriers will have fallen and there will be one vast Community industrial and agricultural market. Less spectacular but still solid progress towards harmonization of national provisions or legislation has also been made in such diverse fields as transport, monetary policy, taxation, social security and working conditions. While the 1966 compromise was bought at the price of a diminution in the powers of the Commission, the Six have proved quite clearly over the last eighteen months that negotiation between, and co-operation among, governments, within the framework of a generally accepted set of objectives, can work perfectly well without the spur of a supranational Commission or an international Council acting on a qualified majority vote basis. This has been the case particularly since the fall of the Erhard Administration in Germany and its replacement by the present coalition government under Herr Kiesinger, which has made Franco-German co-operation the keystone of its foreign policy. But with the establishment of the full common market now assured, with generally sound if not actually booming economies, stable finances and reserves and growing economic strength, there has come to the Six – largely at the instigation of France – both a realization of the potential power of the Community and a determination to play an increasingly important role in world affairs. This enhanced role of the Community has been evident both in the Kennedy Round tariff negotiations in Geneva and the recent discussions among the Finance Ministers of the Western world on the need to create additional international liquidity if the growing volume of world trade is to be satisfactorily financed.

The Kennedy Round as originally envisaged was designed to secure a reduction of 50% in tariffs for all goods and products for which commerce between the United States and Europe (i.e., the Six plus the United Kingdom) accounted for more than 80% of world trade. In fact these negotiations conducted within the framework of the G.A.T.T. amounted to a trade confrontation between the Americans and the Six. The problems involved were legion. There was first of all the fact that American tariffs on a number of products were so high that even a reduction of 50% would have left a formidable margin of protection. European tariffs, on the other hand, tended to be much more 'bunched', i.e., the disparities in tariffs between different types of goods or produce are much less marked, so that a 50% reduction in their case would have resulted in a much more substantial increase in trade. On agriculture, the Americans, in addition to proposals for lower tariffs and provisions for increases in trade, tabled a plan for sharing the cost of aid in the form of deliveries of cereals to the under-developed countries whereby the non-Communist world would undertake to supply some 10 million tons of cereals a year to the under-developed countries. Of this quantity, 40% of the cost was to have been borne by the United States, 25% by the Community, and the balance by the other main importing countries, *i.e.*, including Britain and Japan. This plan, understandably enough, was greeted with little enthusiasm. Within the Six, however, it was felt that if the Americans were unable to gain acceptance for this plan, they would put increased pressure on the Community to reduce its degree of self-sufficiency in cereals. The Community, on the other hand, made the review of the American Selling Price a *sine qua non* of the successful outcome of the Kennedy Round negotiations (under the American Selling Price the level of import duty charged by the American customs authorities is based not on the actual delivered price of the product in question but on the price of comparable American products). Agreement on the main element of the negotiations was finally reached in Geneva late in the night of 15 May 1967; instead of a 50% reduction in tariffs – regarded in many quarters as excessively ambitious – an average reduction of about 35% was achieved, while a more modest figure of $4\frac{1}{2}$ million tons had been substituted for the original 10 million tons of cereals to be provided in the form of aid for the under-developed countries. But the significant feature of the G.A.T.T. negotiations – whatever their eventual trade effects – has been the ability of the Six first to adopt a common attitude and, second, to put up such a forceful and unyielding front in the face of intense American pressure.

The impact of the cohesion of the Six has been no less marked and influential in the recent international monetary discussions. Until recently the leading industrial and financial countries of the Western world were deeply divided over the question of how to overcome the problem of the insufficient level of world monetary reserves in recognized international trading currencies (*i.e.*, the dollar and the £ sterling). There was first of all the position of the United States and the United Kingdom, both of whom favoured the creation of a new currency reserve unit to aid the dollar and the £ sterling in carrying world trade exchanges. Opposing them was France, who maintained that the creation of an additional reserve currency would merely postpone the issue and that a major review and study of world liquidity arrangements is required. Somewhere between the Anglo-Americans and the French were the 'other Five' with a compromise proposal for 'contingency planning' –

i.e., without any actual commitments – for an additional reserve unit. At their meeting in Munich in April 1967, however, the Ministers of the Six agreed that 'the member states of the E.E.C. must occupy in the international monetary institutions a place more in keeping with their effective responsibilities, their growing economic solidarity, the development of their trade and their economic and financial influence with third countries. This fact cannot but lead these countries to seek to formulate a common attitude in the present discussions on the reform of the international monetary system and to maintain in future a close degree of co-operation so as to be able to jointly safeguard their legitimate interests.' In other words the Six, while agreeing to continue to differ, for the time being, on the solution to be adopted, did agree on the need to maintain a common front and to seek a say in the affairs of the International Monetary Fund commensurate with their joint economic power and influence.

It is clear that in the longer term this extension of Community co-operation and solidarity – from which all Six stand to gain – can only act to the detriment of smaller units such as Britain and Japan. It is important to realize, however, that this increased influence and sense of power of the Community in economic and financial affairs in the world reflects a rapidly growing economic – and therefore ultimately political – reality. Industrial production is soaring. Large economic units, usually of a distinctly national character, but sometimes also with an international (*i.e.*, intra-Community) flavour, are being formed in industry, banking and other related fields. Already the trend towards bigger units in the steel industry has left the largest current pre-nationalization British companies far behind. The current banking revolution in France and the recent reform of the Paris Stock Exchange is bound to lead to a dangerous challenge to the financial European pre-eminence of the City of London. Above all, the Community is leading to the fusion of European companies, a European system of law, European patents and European organizations over which countries like Britain are able to exercise little, if any, influence and from which they can ill afford to be excluded.

Paradoxically, it is this very increase in the economic and political strength and influence of the Community which is sowing the seeds of potential problems in the future. The six countries of the European Economic Community have – largely as a result of French political action – entered into a phase of intense nationalism in which national priorities have replaced common Community policies and objectives. In certain cases, such as for example the Kennedy Round and international currency reform, the Six may find it to their advantage to adopt a common attitude. In other cases, such as N.A.T.O. and, above all, the question of German reunification, their interests are often utterly divergent. Thus, in the latter case, the interests of

178

France and Germany are completely opposed. However conciliatory and responsive to French interests the policy of the present German government may be, its avowed ultimate aim is the reunification of West and East Germany – an aim which is completely irreconcilable with the maintenance of French predominance in the Community. As long as the government of France remains in the hands of a strong man like de Gaulle, there is little danger of an open assertion of German objectives or an attempt by a German government to enlist the support of the Community in its quest for reunification. But the present external image of a strong France is largely dependent upon the character and presence of one man and it would be dangerous to speculate upon the maintenance of France's present privileged position long after the departure of President de Gaulle. The fear of German economic and political power in the longer-term may indeed well prove to be a powerful argument in convincing the French government of the need to reconsider its former attitude towards British membership of the Community.

As matters stand today any attempt to look into the future of the Franco-German relationship and its effect on the development of the Community must inevitably be speculative. All one can do is to point to the very real difficulty of reconciling the Community as it exists today with the primary German objective of the reunification of their divided country. It has been suggested in some quarters that German reunification could best be encompassed by a wider European union in the course of which several Eastern European countries, such as Poland or Hungary, for example, could one day join the European Community. Such a development, while perhaps possible in political terms, would of course require a major realignment within the existing economic and political European structure.

The establishment of the European Community of the Six has created a new situation, the longer-term repercussions of which cannot be accurately gauged or foreseen at the present time. Its immediate effect, however, has been to give an impulse to Community industry, agriculture, business and trade, whose dynamism cannot be denied or ignored. It is to this change in the economic and political balance of the Western world that has been brought about by the success of the Community of the Six that we must look for the explanation for Britain's new moves to gain admittance to the European Communities.

CHAPTER 8

Britain and the Common Market: the next round

The Gaullist veto of 14 January 1963 tended inevitably to push the issue of British membership of the common market into the background. It was, however, significant that even during the immediate and bitter aftermath of the French veto there were virtually no constructive or economically realizable proposals for the establishment of an alternative trading group. It was indeed the lack of economic alternatives to the common market which constituted one of the main weaknesses of the Conservative Government between the time of the breakdown of the common market negotiations and the 1964 General Election.

Notwithstanding the brave words of Conservative Ministers in the months immediately after the veto that Britain, despite the French rebuff, would not 'turn her back on Europe', it was not until the early months of 1965 that Conservative leaders began once more to turn overtly to the common market as a major plank in their overall political and economic strategy. The new Labour Government, elected in October 1964, soon began to warm to the European theme and began seriously to reconsider its previous, on the whole, rather mistrustful attitude towards the common market. Thus, less than two years after the brutal veto of 14 January 1963 which many people had thought would effectively 'kill' the possibility of British membership of the common market as a major issue in British political life for at least a decade, all three main political parties were either wholeheartedly, or well on the way to declaring themselves to be, in favour of accession to the common market. What, it may well be asked, were the reasons for this apparent obstinacy on the part of the British Government. *The Times,* in an article published almost exactly two years after the veto of January 1963 and entitled 'Toward Europe again', had the following comment to make: 'Some Continental reasoning gives a cold political twist to the answer. For twelve months Europe has watched both major political parties locked in an electoral struggle, before the election and since, without seeing either put any significant emphasis on the need for European unity and Britain's part in it. As an election issue Europe was, in

Sir Alec Douglas Home's unhappy phrase, a dead duck. The election was then followed by the first hundred days in which the new government not only did everything conceivable to annoy France and other members of the Six, but antagonized our fellow partners in E.F.T.A. to a degree that threatened the whole organization.

'The Concord affair, the surcharge, the unbelievable handling of the first meeting with E.F.T.A. . . . and the Labour Government's general lack of interest in European affairs were watched with growing dismay on the Continent. Now apparently all is sweetness and light again. The Concord is on; the Channel tunnel project is to be pursued; the import surcharge is to be brought down before it has had any chance to work; the Government wants to get closer to Europe, and the Opposition chooses this time to launch itself into a major pro-European campaign.

'It has all apparently been a little too sudden for the Continent. The suspicion that Britain becomes conscious of Europe only when in economic difficulties has again raised its head. This is natural. There are other explanations too. The Labour Party has obviously had to learn some quick lessons, in diplomacy if nothing else. The Foreign Secretary has, therefore, said some soothing words in Brussels. He wants growing co-operation with the Common Market. He would like to see the rough edges removed from the relations between the Common Market and E.F.T.A. and the tariff barriers lowered between them. He is also keen to use Western European Union as a forum where Britain and the Six can thrash out their differences.'

The British Government's reasons, in 1965 as in 1961, were both political and economic. With the growing strength of the Common Market there had been an evident shift in the political balance of Western Europe from Britain to the Community. It was an undeniable fact that the voice of the Six, whether speaking from Brussels, Paris or Bonn, counted for more in Washington, Moscow or Peking than that of Britain. It was also a fact that no British Government could afford to ignore. Economically, the power discrepancy between Britain and the Six was even more marked and was increasing all the time. Industrial production, Gross National Product, investment, mergers, concentrations, road building, the application of automation and remote-control techniques, the computerization of industry, economies of scale were all increasing at a very much faster rate in the Community than in Britain. While the Six themselves readily admitted that it was impossible to assign a definite part of their increases in industrial activity to the establishment of the common market, few economists cared to dispute the fact that this was the key and determining factor in the continuing and rising prosperity of the Six.

It was, however, not until 10 November 1966 that the Prime

Minister announced the government's plans for a 'high-level approach' to the Six. The government's plans included arrangements for a meeting of the Heads of Government of the E.F.T.A. countries to discuss the problems arising for these countries in the light of their accession to the common market, to be followed by visits by the Prime Minister and the Foreign Secretary to the capitals of the six Community countries between January and March 1967 in order to ascertain whether in accepting the Treaty of Rome the vital interests of the United Kingdom and the Commonwealth could be safeguarded. The government would then decide, in the light of these discussions, whether to take a decision to apply once more for membership of the European Economic Community.

The visits to the six capitals – and Strasbourg, where Mr Wilson delivered an impressive and convincing address to the assembled Parliamentarians of the Council of Europe – began with Rome, on 16 January, and ended with Luxembourg, on 8 March. The position at the end of the discussions with the political leaders of the Six during these visits appeared, according to press reports, to be broadly as follows : on the British side it was categorically stated that membership could only be achieved if certain conditions were realized : these included a relatively short transitional period to allow for the implementation of the common agricultural policy, revision of the Community price for certain agricultural products, special permanent arrangements for New Zealand, and some amendment of the system of levies as at present operated by the Community. Mr Wilson and Mr Brown allegedly also referred to British fears lest the free movement of capital, which was specifically written into the Treaty of Rome, should result in a severe loss of reserves; at the same time they vigorously asserted the British Government's determination to defend the position of the £ sterling as a major international reserve currency and denied that there was any danger that the Six might be called upon to come to Britain's financial assistance. On the side of the Community, attitudes varied considerably from one country to another : Belgium, Italy, Luxembourg and the Netherlands declared themselves wholeheartedly in favour of British membership. France, in the person of President de Gaulle had, predictably, sat on the fence, pointing to the many difficulties raised by the British request, particularly the difficulty of reconciling the international role of sterling and the strain this put on Britain's financial reserves with her commitments and obligations under the Treaty of Rome, but refusing to give a definite positive or negative answer. Finally, the reactions of the German Government, while positive in welcoming the prospect of British membership, was apparently at least partially affected by the much-publicized remarks made by the Foreign Secretary a few days before the visit to Bonn about possible recognition of the Oder-Neisse line (as the frontier of the Federal

German Republic) as well as a number of other political problems over which Britain and Germany had substantially different views. While apparently generally flexible in their approach to Britain's problems, all six governments were at one in insisting upon the inviolate nature of the Community's agricultural policy.

The British Government's probe did, however, make it clear that the problems of 1967 differed to a surprising degree from those of 1962. Pierre Uri, one of Jean Monnet's original disciples in Luxembourg, and now a well-known consultant on Community affairs, wrote in January 1967 :

If one looks back to the days of the Heath negotiations, the situation appears much simpler in three respects : The Commonwealth countries either partly look to other markets than Britain or have already felt their way towards association with E.E.C. which they spurned four years ago. And the Canadian or Australian experience as well as that of the E.E.C. countries show how overrated the notion of traditional channels of trade may be, how fast exports can increase as soon as they are redirected to new markets.

Great store used to be set on the provisions for economic union as distinct from a pure customs union. Justified as this may be, little progress has been made in Brussels in the field of so-called harmonization, or co-ordination, be it on taxes, capital movements, transport, cartels or rules of competition. The *Journal Officiel* is almost entirely absorbed by detailed decisions on agriculture, which anyhow has to be considered separately. The rest usually relates to such matters as tariff quotas, the setting up of additional committees, or recommendations on stabilization policies. Thus, nothing much is either lasting or final or very binding. Even if the British Government does not want to say so in so many words, there is nothing much to reject – or even to accept. . . .

The better part of the detailed provisions which were tentatively drafted in the Heath negotiations rested on the hope that Britain would align herself with the previous members by 1970, the prospective end of the transitional period. Now, and especially with the acceleration of the customs union, this is obviously out, so that a special transitional period has to be provided for anyhow : nobody on either side would want to eliminate overnight all tariffs between the U.K. and the E.E.C. in its present borders. . . .

This adjustment period may well offer more opportunities than is commonly realized. To begin with the most debated point, even the agricultural issue should cease to look like one which has to be settled entirely in advance. What a gradual adjustment to the E.E.C. system would mean for Britain is

183

clear enough; there are already some import levies in cases where the gap to be met by deficiency payments is too large; it is a matter of raising the former, reducing the latter. Even the most precise calculations on the cost of this change-over leave out a potential element which could completely alter the terms of the debate : an increase in world agricultural prices, which already makes itself felt, and which should continue if the Eastern countries go on buying or if some constructive food aid policy is devised and pursued jointly by the main producers. This would go a very long way towards closing the gap between the E.E.C. and the U.K. systems. . . .

Anyhow the fundamental decisions on agriculture have not yet been taken : how far Europe is content to be self-sufficient or whether it also wants to produce to feed the hungry; how fast and by what methods the agricultural population can be reduced on the Continent. Britain would be a member when this stage is reached. As to the financial regulations, which are the essence of the present system they are firm only as far as 1970. Nobody will require that Britain should have no vote or should refrain from using it.[1]

The probe was followed by a short period of digestion of results and impressions, but by April both Mr Brown and Mr Wilson, in speeches to private meetings of the Labour Party (but which were subsequently widely reported on in the Press) made it clear that, as far as they personally were concerned, their minds were made up : Britain would apply a second time to join the European Economic Community. George Brown, in his address, emphasized Britain's organic links with Europe : 'Europe is the continent in which we live; we have had centuries of other experience and communications, but in the end it has always been in Europe that we have been forced to establish the basis of our power and influence and in which we have often invested men, money and blood.' But there were also solid, even vital, economic advantages to be gained : 'If our future prosperity is to be assured, then industry must expand. Until we can establish a steady and assured rate of growth without internal inflation and external balance of payments bedevilling us, we cannot do this. Industry needs the assurance of a market big enough and the opportunities of a profitability attractive enough to make it worthwhile to the investors. If anything at all would give a stimulus to the industrial development we need, it is this. The change in scale would be dramatic, and this would be a market composed of sophisticated and developed peoples.'

The Prime Minister in his address to the Parliamentary Labour Party on 27 April 1967, was at pains to stress the political arguments

[1]Extracted from M. Uri's article in *The Times,* 17 January 1967. These and other extracts are reproduced by permission of *The Times.*

184

in favour of joining : 'My own view . . . is that, whatever the economic arguments one way or the other, it is the political arguments which can be decisive . . . I do believe that Europe could be on the verge of a great move forward in political unity and that we can – and indeed must – play a part in it. When something is at stake of this degree of importance for Europe and for the world, the role of Britain is on the field and not on the touchline, casting praise, blame, or even bottles at those who are doing a job in which we should be involved as full participants. . . .

'Our purpose is to make a reality of the unity of Western Europe. But we know that this will be an empty achievement unless it leads first to an easing of tension and then to an honourable and lasting settlement of the outstanding problems that still divide Europe, Western Europe from Eastern Europe. This indeed is something that I have striven for for many years; and I am convinced that if Britain is a member of a united European Community our chances of achieving this will be immeasurably greater. . . . We in Britain are the loyal allies of one of the two great world powers, the United States; and we seek the closest and most friendly relationship, economic, commercial, cultural, with the other great world power, the Soviet Union. But, because we seek this friendly relationship with both the great powers, we do not accept the notion that all great issues should be left for settlement direct between those powers because we in Europe are not sufficiently powerful economically – and therefore politically – to make our voices heard and our influence felt.

'That is why we believe in the need to make effective our enormous potential industrial strength by giving that strength a chance to operate on a European and not a national scale – or a series of national scales. It is only if we do this that we can exercise everything that goes with industrial strength and independence in terms of Europe's influence in world affairs.'

Before proceeding with an application for membership one more hurdle remained to be cleared : the approval of E.F.T.A. A meeting of the E.F.T.A. Ministerial Council was consequently called in London on 28 April 1967 and ended by giving Britain a virtual *carte blanche* to proceed with her own endeavours to join the common market. The official communiqué issued after the meeting did however make the following safeguard : 'The change from the present division of Europe to a single market should be as smooth as possible. Were the U.K. or any other member of E.F.T.A. to apply for participation in the E.E.C., the process of negotiation and of ratifying any ensuing agreement could hardly be short. In addition, it would be the purpose of the E.F.T.A. governments that, should it be necessary in order to give reasonable opportunity to their partners in the free trade area to conclude negotiations, sufficient transitional periods should be provided for, with a view to avoiding disruption in European trade patterns.' The terms of this statement tended, however, to disguise the very real concern felt in at least two of the E.F.T.A. countries, *i.e.,* Portugal and Switzerland, about the effect on their economies of British accession to the common market and the consequent dissolution of E.F.T.A.

The last act before the second application for British membership of the European Communities was formally handed over by Sir James Marjoribanks, the Head of the U.K. Delegation to the European Communities, in Brussels on the morning of Thursday, 11 May 1967, was an immediately preceding three-day debate in Parliament. Despite some fractional opposition on both sides of the House, the Government motion 'That this House approves the statement contained in the Command Paper Membership of the European Communities' was carried by the overwhelming majority of 488 for to 62 against – by far the largest majority on any major controversial issue in modern times. It was a vote which reflected unmistakably the conviction of a majority of men in all three major British political parties that it was in membership of the European Communities that Britain's political and economic future lies. In the words of *The Times* leading article of 12 May : 'The mood in which Britain makes its second approach to Europe is therefore more sober but also more realistic and committed than it was the first time. The hopes are more measured but the fears are fewer. There can, indeed, be no doubt about Mr Wilson's victory in the Commons debate. Out of all the quibbles over figures, and the disagreements over terms and details, there came no effective challenge to the view that British entry into the Common Market on reasonable terms will make infinitely more sense for Britain, for Europe, for E.F.T.A., for the Commonwealth, and indeed for the world than any conceivable alternative.'

What membership would mean to Britain

That the impact of membership of the common market upon the life and position of Britain will be far-reaching and fundamental cannot be disputed. The traditions of five centuries of separate development and expansion and expression in essentially global terms will be replaced by a return to a European community and a closer compact unity with the countries across the Channel. It is a step that must affect industry, agriculture, the standard of living, foreign policy and the attitudes and outlook of ordinary people. In the longer-term it must mean the substitution of Europe for the Commonwealth as the immediate arena for British political and economic activity. It is in fact one of the most extraordinary features of contemporary British life that so many people have, in the course of the last decade or so, come to accept almost unquestioningly that it

186

is with Europe that this country's future lies. British industry has, consistently, been one of the most fervent advocates of entry. For the younger generation the old mystique and aura of Empire is little more than a memory, and in the loose multi-racial Commonwealth of today they see little to cherish or share in common. Equally, the Anglo-American partnership of the immediate post-war era has in their eyes little appeal. It is not simply a question of Vietnam and the moral problem this appears to pose for so many, but the obvious and overpowering disparity between the real effective power of the two countries. It is today an inescapable fact that countries like Britain, France and Germany can no longer, individually and alone, play a leading role in world affairs. The success of de Gaulle in France, although more apparent than real, in playing a part of some consequence in world affairs has derived mainly from France's position within the common market. The lesson for Britain is clear. Not only economically, but politically also, the common market is today the second power of the West, and it is only by joining it that Britain can hope to recapture and maintain a direct and major influence in determining European policy. For Mr Wilson, as we have already seen, the political argument is paramount.

Nevertheless, there does not exist, at the present time, either a political union among the Six or even a common attitude with regard to a majority of world problems. Thus, whereas the Six adopted a common line in the Kennedy Round and – for the time being at least – in the discussions on monetary form, and had, in consequence, a strong position, they are disunited, and therefore comparatively weak, in such matters as the reform of N.A.T.O. or the development of a European nuclear deterrent. Progress to date has been concentrated essentially in the economic field and it is to the impact of membership of the Community on Britain's industrial economy that we turn first of all.

The Confederation of British Industries in a recent report[2] on the advantages and disadvantages of British entry into the common market came down firmly in favour of membership. The main disadvantages, which were seen as 'pressures on internal costs, particularly as a result of the common agricultural policy, at a time when external competition from within the enlarged Community and without is likely to increase sharply' and 'some potential danger to our Commonwealth trade' were considered to be outweighed by the beneficial effects resulting from 'the speedy ending of tariff discrimination against us in the E.E.C. and consequent unimpeded access to a wider market; the long-term economies of scale that this may offer' and the 'disadvantages of isolation from the Community'.

All these factors, political, economic, industrial, agricultural, were reviewed in the Prime Minister's momentous statement to the House

[2]*Cf.* C.B.I. : *Britain and Europe,* Vol. 2, p. 49.

of Commons on the afternoon of 2 May 1967 in which he declared to the world that Britain was the second time to seek admittance to the European Communities. It was not fully six years since Mr Macmillan's no less historic statement of 31 July 1961.

The Prime Minister's statement set out not only the motives but also the major issues for the negotiations : British agriculture, Commonwealth interests – particularly the position of New Zealand and the Commonwealth sugar producers – and, to a lesser extent, the position of the E.F.T.A. countries, the question of capital movements and freedom to promote regional development. In view of its importance as evidence of the official position of the British Government, the full text of the Prime Minister's statement is given below :

Her Majesty's Government have today decided to make an application under Article 237 of the Treaty of Rome for membership of the European Economic Community and parallel applications for membership of the European Coal and Steel Community and Euratom.

As the House will recall, I stated on 10 November last that the Foreign Secretary and I would embark on 'a series of discussions with each of the Heads of Government of the Six for the purpose of establishing whether it appears likely that essential British and Commonwealth interests could be safe-guarded if Britain were to accept the Treaty of Rome and join E.E.C.'

These discussions took place between January and March. Since then the Government have carried out an exhaustive examination of all the issues involved, resulting in the decision I have just announced.

The reports I have made to the House have made it clear that during the discussions in the six capitals we were not engaged in negotiations. But the Foreign Secretary and I, and indeed the House, have reason to be grateful to our hosts for the very frank exchanges which preceded today's decision.

These exchanges have enabled us to identify the major issues which we, for our part, shall wish to see settled in the negotiations.

On the Treaty of Rome itself, as I informed the House on 10 November, we have throughout our discussions taken the view that, as I then said, '. . . the Treaty of Rome is not in itself or necessarily an impediment. There are anxieties . . . but the treaty need not be an obstacle if our problems can be dealt with satisfactorily, whether through adaptations of the arrangements made under the treaty or in any other acceptable manner'.

In short, as I said then, 'the Government would be prepared to accept the Treaty of Rome, subject to the necessary adjustments consequent upon the accession of a new member and provided that we receive satisfaction on the points about which we see difficulty.'

Our discussions in the capitals of the Six have confirmed the validity of this approach in terms of the practical working of the Community and its institutions.

It is in this spirit that the Government intend to embark on the negotiations which must precede entry. The House will, I am sure, agree that they ought not to be unnecessarily complicated with lesser issues, many of which can be best dealt with after entry.

Agriculture

It is our hope that the negotiations will be followed through swiftly, and will relate to the small number of really important issues which have been identified through our recent discussions, issues on which agreement should be reached if the House and the country are to be satisfied that essential British and Commonwealth interests will be safeguarded.

This is the spirit in which the original partners to the Community conducted their own negotiations over ten years ago.

Our recent meeting with our E.F.T.A. partners has confirmed that they too view the matter in the same light. They will, we hope, also be making their approaches to E.E.C.

I now turn to the major issues which it must be our purpose to resolve during the negotiations.

First, there are the problems associated with the operation of the common agricultural policy of the Community – the problems of its potential effects on the cost-of-living and on the structure and well-being of British agriculture; problems of the budgetary and balance of payments implications of its system of financing; and certain Commonwealth problems with which I will deal in a moment.

As I have already made clear, publicly, we must be realistic and recognize that the Community's agricultural policy is an integral part of the Community; we must come to terms with it. But the Government recognize that this policy would involve far-reaching changes in the structure of British agriculture. This will require suitable arrangements including an adequate transitional period to enable the necessary adjustments to be made.

It is also the Government's view that the financial arrangements which have been devised to meet the requirements of the Community's agricultural policy as it exists today would, if applied to Britain as they now stand, involve an inequitable sharing of the financial cost and impose on our balance of payments an additional burden which we should not in fairness be asked to carry.

Commonwealth

There are also highly important Commonwealth interests, mainly in the field of agriculture, for which it is our duty to seek safeguards in the negotiations. These include in particular the special problems of New Zealand and of Commonwealth sugar-producing countries, whose needs are at present safeguarded by the Commonwealth Sugar Agreement.

We have, as the House knows, been in touch with all our Commonwealth partners, and will make special arrangements to keep in close consultation with them, as with our E.F.T.A. partners, throughout the negotiations.

Regional Policy

Again, as the House knows, capital movements raise questions of special importance. Our discussions suggest that these can be dealt with by suitable arrangements.

Another important issue is the question of regional policies. Here, too, we had to satisfy ourselves that we should be able, as members of the Community, to continue to take the necessary steps to ensure the industrial and social development of those areas of the country with which this House is always and rightly specially concerned.

Our discussions with the heads of the governments of the Community, not least the information we were given about the policies currently being pursued by member countries, have reassured us on this score.

As I have said, these are major and important issues, but I can tell the House that the Government believe that there is nothing either in the Treaty of Rome, or in the practical working of the Community which need make them insoluble.

I have gone into some detail about certain specific economic issues, on which hon. members are rightly concerned. But the Government's decision has been motivated by broader considerations of economic policy and still wider arguments to which I will turn later.

On the economic arguments each hon. member will make his own judgment of the effect on exports and imports, on industrial productivity and investment. Equally, every hon. member must make his own assessment of the economic consequences of not going into the Community and, in an age of wider economic groupings, of seeking to achieve and maintain viability outside.

But all of us are aware of the long-term potential for Europe, and therefore for Britain, of the creation of a single market of approaching 300 million people, with all the scope and incentive which this will provide for British industry, and of the enormous possibilities which an integrated strategy for technology, on a truly continental scale, can create. I am glad to say that the Foreign Secretary and I found that this concept has made a great impact throughout Europe.

Europe's Role in the World

But whatever the economic arguments, the House will realize that, as I have repeatedly made clear, the Government's purpose derives above all from our recognition that Europe is now faced with the opportunity of a great move forward in political unity and that we can – and indeed must – play our full part in it.

We do not see European unity as something narrow or inward-looking. Britain has her own vital links through the Commonwealth, and in other ways, with other continents. So have other European countries. Together we can ensure that Europe plays in world affairs the part which the Europe of today is not at present playing.

For a Europe that fails to put forward its full economic strength will never have the political influence which I believe it could and should exert within the United Nations, within the Western Alliance, and as a means for effecting a lasting détente between east and west; and equally contributing in ever fuller measure to the solution of the world's north-south problem to the needs of the developing world.

Provision for debate in Parliament

It is for all these reasons that we intend to pursue our application for membership with all the vigour and determination at our command.

The House will of course wish to debate this decision at the earliest opportunity, and arrangements will be made for a three-day debate next week, when the House will be invited to pass a motion approving this present statement, which will be presented as a White Paper. We shall seek to meet the requirements of Parliament for the fullest possible information over the coming weeks.

A first paper dealing with agriculture will be available later this week and we shall take the opportunity of the debate, and of further White Papers which will be laid, to enable Parliament, and public opinion generally, to form a full, fair and informed judgment of the great issues involved.

For all of us realize that this is an historical decision which could well determine the future of Britain, of Europe, and indeed of the world for decades to come.

In this statement the Prime Minister was once again at very great pains to stress the political importance which the United Kingdom Government attached to British membership of the European Communities. Clearly, a united and strong Europe will be in a position to play a much more important and, at times, determining role in world politics than the individual states of the European continent or, indeed, the existing Community. At the same time it must be recognized that once Britain is a full member of the Community she will no longer be able to follow a purely national foreign policy. Community policies will be thrashed out, shaped or determined at meetings of the Foreign Ministers or, perhaps occasionally, the Heads of State of all the member countries of the enlarged Community at which most, if not all, of the participating countries may have to modify their own national viewpoints. To the extent therefore that membership of the common market will inevitably involve joint discussion and elaboration of foreign policies – extending, as the occasion requires it, to such vital and intimate sectors as defence (*i.e.,* Britain's role East of Suez) and the formulation of a common attitude to, say, the United States – there will be a loss of national sovereignty that seems likely to be much more evident and keenly felt than in the case of the acceptance of a majority view within the Council of Ministers on matters affecting trade in industry or agriculture.

In considering the broad economic advantages and disadvantages for the United Kingdom of membership of the common market, we have attempted to divide the vast field of application into three main headings : markets and trade; agriculture, and related factors, including transport; social policy and financial and monetary questions.

Markets and trade

The main argument put forward by British industry in favour of joining the common market is that this would give British exporters access to a dynamic and rapidly expanding market of over 200 million people (some 280 million if all the E.F.T.A. countries were to join) and offer invaluable opportunities for economies of scale and co-operation, mergers or collaboration with enterprizes in the other member countries.

In joining the Community Britain would remove her tariffs for all goods imported from the Community, gain unimpeded access for her own goods in the Community and adopt the common external tariff of the existing Community for imports from all third countries (subject to any derogations that might be negotiated on a temporary or permanent basis for certain Commonwealth products). Thus, French or German motor cars imported into this country, and which at the moment are subject to an import duty of 24%,* would come in duty-free; while British motor cars exported to the Community, and which will be subject as from next year to the common external tariff of 18%,* would similarly enter free of duty into the member states of the Community. It is from the removal of tariffs and quotas – in both directions – and the adoption of the common external tariff that the main challenge to British industry will arise : thus, although the tariff treatment of raw materials is broadly the same, *i.e.*, basically free or with low duties, in the United Kingdom as well as in the existing Community, there are both high rates and significant differences in the broad range of manufactured goods. In this respect the recent C.B.I. report stated that while 'textiles and clothing also generally are charged the same rates except where textiles contain man-made fibres; in this range the United Kingdom duties are higher and often much higher. Other goods for which the tariffs are broadly in line are films, furniture and motor vehicles, though here again the C.E.T. is generally slightly lower. The United Kingdom tariff on machinery generally is somewhat higher than the common external tariff (about $17\frac{1}{2}\%$ compared with 13%). Over a wide range of chemicals there is a marked disparity, *i.e.*, $33\frac{1}{3}\%$ compared with 16/20%, although in some important sectors of the chemical industry the tariffs coincide, and for plastics the United Kingdom duty of 10% is well below the C.E.T. United Kingdom tariffs on iron and steel products are broadly similar, but United Kingdom rates on some ferro-alloys are higher, as are those on miscellaneous consumer goods such as pottery, jewellery and fur products. The biggest discrepancy is in the field of optical and scientific instruments, where the United Kingdom tariff ranges from 20 to 50% compared with the common external tariff of mostly 13%.'[3] Clearly, industries which have until now enjoyed a level of tariff protection of 20 to 30% will take unkindly to the very much keener and fiercer competition which the abolition of tariffs must and will bring about. Lenses or cinematograph cameras, for example, bear at the present moment import tariffs of 50% and 25/50% respectively. Once we join the common market not only will these protective duties have to be abolished – unless special arrangements are agreed in the negotiations for entry – thus enabling German products to enter duty-free, but the degree of protection *vis-à-vis* Japanese lenses and cameras will be reduced from the ruling United Kingdom tariff to the existing common external tariff (*i.e.*, from 50% to 13 or 14%). The reaction of the C.B.I. was, broadly, that British industry would be able to take the removal of British protective tariffs in its stride, *i.e.*, that the loss of protection on the

*Both these figures and those quoted in the following extract from the C.B.I. report will, of course, be affected to some extent by the reductions that were agreed in the Kennedy Round G.A.T.T. negotiations.
[3]Ibid, Vol. 2, pp. 9–10.

home market would be more than offset by the gains made in Community markets, and that any special cases of difficulty could be dealt with during the transitional period that would preface full British membership of the common market : 'Given the opportunity of competition on reasonably equal terms, tariff changes should not in the main impose any intolerably adverse effects on industry. A great deal would clearly depend, however, on the length of the transitional period that was available. During the Brussels negotiations the kind of transitional arrangements being contemplated were that, on acccession, Britain would immediately have matched the internal tariff cuts to other E.E.C. members already made by the Six and aligned tariffs to third countries to the C.E.T. to the same degree, subject to any agreed decalage for Commonwealth imports. The situation that would confront Britain in any new negotiations would be different in that the common external tariff would be fully established, and the likelihood that the Six would be willing to tolerate one of their partners having substantially different tariff provisions for any length of time is remote, quite apart from the substantial technical difficulties that would result from such a situation. However, traditional arrangements over some period of time would clearly be necessary.'[4]

In addition to the loss of protection in their home market, membership of the European Economic Community will, inevitably, mean for British manufacturers loss of preference in E.F.T.A. – *i.e.*, whether the other E.F.T.A. countries join the Community or not, British exporters will be on exactly the same footing as other Community producers – and in Commonwealth countries. Total exports to Commonwealth countries and South Africa (which although no longer a member of the Commonwealth has continued to grant Commonwealth Preference on British imports) in 1965 amounted to some £870 million. The degree of preference enjoyed by British goods in Commonwealth markets has, however, been steadily eroded during the whole of the postwar period. Certain Commonwealth countries, particularly India, Pakistan and the African countries, grant little or no preference to British goods, and it is in the white former Dominions that the loss of Commonwealth Preference would be most severely felt. Thus, in New Zealand, where Britain enjoys preferential tariffs on some £80 million worth of her total exports of £125 million a year, the average preference margin is as high as 20%. In the case of Australia about 85% of total British exports enjoyed an average margin of preference of the order of 12%; while in Canada about 60% of British exports (including such items as metals, clothing and motor cars) enjoyed a margin of preference of about 13%. These margins, despite considerable erosion over the past ten or 20 years, have been valuable assets to

[4]Ibid, Vol. 2, p. 15.

British exporters and their loss cannot be lightly dismissed. On the other hand, the goodwill built up between British exporters and their traditional customers constitutes a powerful commercial factor which should survive the dismantlement of the Commonwealth Preference system.

Despite numerous estimates and studies, the equation between the commercial advantages arising from access to the common market and the commercial disadvantages resulting from the loss of protection on the home market and preference in Commonwealth and E.F.T.A. markets remains unresolved. It is indeed questionable whether if it were simply a case of weighing up gains and losses in tariff changes the majority of British industry would be so emphatically in favour of accession to the common market. The decisive factor is the need in our contemporary society for industry to be able to participate in, to plan its investments and its future policy as well as to operate against, a commercial background of adequate size and promise. The C.B.I. report on joining Europe was completely dogmatic and emphatic on this point : 'In the world of today and of the future an advanced industrial country needs, almost more than anything else, free access to other large and dynamic industrial markets and full exposure to the resulting competitive forces. Western Europe offers the challenge and opportunity which Britain needs; and the favourable trends in Britain's trade with Europe and especially with the E.E.C., in the last decade are sure signs that British industry is competitive with her neighbours and potential partners. IT IS THESE CONSIDERATIONS AND THE OPPORTUNITIES FOR EXPORT AND FOR LARGE SCALE OPERATIONS WHICH, IN THE (C.B.I.) VIEW, FAR OUTWEIGH THE SHORT-TERM PENALTIES WHICH MEMBERSHIP OF AN ENLARGED COMMUNITY MAY BRING.

'The efficient growth of modern industry is powerfully influenced by the extent to which science and technology can be brought to bear upon all facets of industrial activity. Partly because of unco-ordinated foreign and defence policies, the present scale of technological development in Western Europe falls a long way short of the efforts and investment of the other major industrial powers, notably of course the United States, which has already made large inroads into European industry and trade. The creation of an enlarged European Economic Community, embracing all the present Common Market countries, Britain, the Republic of Ireland and the majority of the E.F.T.A. countries, would offer the best prospect of generating the resources and the collaboration which alone could ensure Western Europe's competitive efficiency in the future.'[5]

A C.B.I. survey among 1,700 British firms – but of which only just over half replied – showed an overwhelming number in favour of

[5]Ibid, Vol. 1, p. 2.

the earliest possible entry into Europe. Even so, only about a third of the companies which participated in the survey expected to reap marked gains from unrestricted entry into E.E.C. markets, while 15% expected a marked loss as a result of the loss of protection on the home market. About two-thirds of the companies believed that entry into Europe would create opportunities for growth or increased sales. About a fifth of the companies expected costs to rise as a result of entry – but a roughly equal number expected them to decrease. This, in the words of the C.B.I. press hand-out on the survey, seemed to suggest 'that companies are looking to an expanded volume of sales and lower unit costs to offset the effects of the common agricultural policy on wages and of other cost pressures. This hypothesis is strengthened by the fact that 49% foresaw economies of scale; 41% expected operations to be more profitable.' About three-fifths of the companies expected entry into the common market to result in a marked increase in new capital investment, either at home or elsewhere in the Community. Finally, only about one-sixth of the companies expected major problems of adaptation.

The reaction of the very wide range of companies covered by the C.B.I. survey appears to have been considerably more decisive about the short-term advantages than the voluminous earlier C.B.I. study to which we have already referred. This very much more cautious attitude to the balance of advantage during the years immediately after British entry was strongly reinforced by the reported conclusions reached in an analysis completed in the early part of this year by the Society of Motor Manufacturers and Traders. This study, according to press reports, accepts the fact that in the short-term of, say, three to five years, the industry might well lose financially as a result of entry into the common market. The arithmetic of the survey went as follows : a loss of some £22 million as a result of the abolition of Commonwealth Preference; a loss of some £13 million as a result of the dissolution of E.F.T.A.; a gain of about £18 million as a result of duty-free entry into the Community; in total, a loss of some £17 million. In addition, of course, there would be the loss of protection on the home market – which could be expected to result in a reduction in sales of British cars in the United Kingdom market and a possible narrowing of profit margins both in order to meet Community competition in this country and as a result of intensified competition over the enlarged Community area. Against these potential, indeed probable, short-term losses must be set, first, the increased efficiency, the wider and above all rapidly expanding and more prosperous market that the enlarged Community can be expected to provide, and, second, the very bleak outlook for the British motor car industry in the years ahead if it remains excluded from the European or any other major trading bloc. It is this fear of economic isolation that runs like a *leitmotiv* through the

196

attitude of the whole range of British industry, *i.e.*, the feeling that in order to survive and compete in the modern world, British industry needs a wider base than that provided by the home market or even E.F.T.A. alone. But industry is only one of the two major elements in the European equation. The second element, and one where Britain must inevitably lose rather than gain, concede rather than acquire, is the acceptance and application of the Community's common agricultural policy.

Agriculture

The National Farmers' Union in a report on British Agriculture and the Common Market, published in November 1966, concluded that if the common agricultural policy of the existing Community were accepted, and applied, as it stood, to British agriculture, farm income for about 75% of British farmers would decline. Thus, while there would in all probability be a sharp rise in net return to producers of wheat, barley and fat cattle, for all other commodities net receipts could be expected to decline.[6]

The favourable situation with regard to wheat and barley is due to the high intervention price fixed by the Council of Ministers for cereals generally – a decision due in turn to political pressures arising from the big discrepancies in costs between France on the one hand and Germany and Italy on the other. Community farmers – attracted by the high price for soft wheat – are tending to increase the amount of acreage devoted to wheat growing with the result that the Community as a whole is rapidly moving into a position of a major excess producer. It is hard to see, therefore, how the present high prices for wheat and barley can be expected to continue indefinitely – even less so if other countries with large potential soft wheat growing areas (*i.e.*, the United Kingdom, Ireland and Denmark) were to join the Community.

For beef and veal, pigmeat, eggs and milk, the application of the existing Community regulations would almost certainly mean a reduction in the net income received by British farmers. The position would, however, be especially difficult in the case of fruit and vegetables where the relatively unfavourable climatic conditions in this country – compared with certain Community countries – added to the higher cost of farm labour, would jeopardize a substantial part of British production. This in itself is of course no matter for surprise. The Community's agricultural policy was drawn up to meet the political and economic objectives, compromises and concessions of the Six. It is aimed, deliberately, at giving the Community's farmers a privileged and protected position. It

[6]*British Agriculture and the Common Market,* published jointly by the National Farmers' Union, National Farmers' Union of Scotland, and Ulster Farmers' Union, November 1966.

constitutes, moreover, one of the fundamental elements in the fabric of the Community and cannot lightly be renegotiated by the Six without endangering many other parts of the whole. The full acceptance by Britain of the common agricultural policy on the other hand would inflict a heavy financial burden on this country and one that might well jeopardize the delicately-poised balance of gain and loss from entry into the common market. It may well be, as some experts have affirmed, that the National Farmers' Union have, wittingly or unwittingly, under-estimated the efficiency of British agriculture – which is among the foremost in Europe – and its ability to compete successfully with its Continental rivals; and that it is to some extent dazzled by the virtues of the existing, and admittedly highly efficacious and advantageous guaranteed price system, to the extent even of failing to see clearly some of the possible advantages and opportunities offered to it by accession to the common market. From a national point of view there is also the long-term factor to be taken into consideration that world food prices cannot be expected to remain indefinitely at their present low levels and that as the general standard of living throughout the world rises, so the cost of primary foodstuffs may be expected to increase. It is nonetheless clear that, if the United Kingdom joins the Community, its food will cost a great deal more.

The conclusions of the N.F.U. report included a formidable list of disadvantages that would arise for British farmers in the event of unconditional acceptance of the Community's agricultural policy. These were listed as follows :

1. The general stability provided by guaranteed prices together with long-term assurances and a long-term production policy would be abandoned. Greater fluctuations in prices, with no assurance that they would be around higher levels, would be experienced by large sections of the industry, especially pigs and eggs for which an enlarged Community would normally be self-sufficient.

2. The termination of some of the direct production grants, e.g., the hill cow and hill sheep schemes, the calf subsidy and the beef cow subsidy, if they were deemed incompatible with the Common Market, would have serious consequences for a large number of producers.

3. There would be substantial increases in the cost of grain for animal feed which would be particularly harmful to producers of pigmeat and eggs.

4. Higher grain food costs would also more than offset the slight price advantage of the target price for milk compared with the pool price. Moreover the target price would be likely to be under pressure owing to the tendency to surplus milk production and the high consumer prices for milk products

resulting from the application of the milk and milk products regulation.

5. Large sectors of the horticultural industry would be jeopardized. The risks to horticulture of unconditional entry have been specifically recognized by the Government.

6. There is as yet no regulation for potatoes. Growers of early potatoes would lose protection against imports from countries with earlier marketing seasons; the buying-up operations of the Potato Marketing Board would be likely to be incompatible with the Common Market.

7. For sheep and wool there are no regulations. Imports of lamb would be subject to tariffs, but since it is not known what special arrangements might be made for New Zealand lamb the outlook for sheep farmers is uncertain. Imports of wool would be free of restriction and the guaranteed price for wool would be abandoned.

8. The opportunity for the industry to influence the formation and execution of agricultural policy would be greatly diminished.[7]

According to the N.F.U., therefore, the acceptance of the existing Community regulations on agricultural produce would have disastrous effects on British farmers. They considered it vital that any new British approach for membership of the common market should include 'an appraisal and an adjustment' to the Community's agricultural regulations in order to safeguard, at least in part, the position of British farmers and horticulturalists.

The N.F.U. report also acknowledged, albeit somewhat grudgingly, certain fortuitous and possibly only temporary advantages for British farmers, *i.e.*, a greater measure of control – virtual exclusion would be nearer the mark – of imports from low cost producers; the possibility of cheaper farming equipment and machinery as well as other goods and services, as a result of keener competition in the industrial sector; initial higher net incomes for producers of grains and beef; and, finally, enhanced export prospects, *i.e.*, at attractive prices, for producers of cattle, lamb, grain and 'certain' horticultural products.

The N.F.U. report made an attempt to assess the additional expenditure that would be involved in paying for this country's agricultural imports under the existing Community farm policy. Prices for a number of commodities could be expected to rise sharply; some even dramatically. Thus, the application of the Community's guide price for cattle would involve an increase in beef prices in this country of 'at least one-third', while 'retail butter prices would be likely to be about double the current prices for New Zealand butter'. In short, the increase in Britain's food import bill as a result of the

[7]Ibid, p. 34.

adoption of the Community's agricultural policy as it stood was expected to be of the order of £685 million – and this was without taking horticultural products into account.

The breakdown of the N.F.U.'s estimated cost increases is as follows :

Commodity group	Effect on cost of living (£ million)
Cereals	90
Dairy produce	210
Meat	320
Eggs and poultry	35
Sugar	30
Total	685 [8]

This, according to the N.F.U. report, would mean an increase in the weekly food bill for a family of, say, four people, of 25/–. The N.F.U. report did not accept that the adoption of the common agricultural policy and the consequent abolition of the present system of price guarantees would result in some relief in direct or indirect taxation, since any savings the Exchequer might make as a result of the cessation of guaranteed price payments would be swallowed up by the annual payments the United Kingdom would have to make to the European Agricultural Guarantee and Guidance Fund – indeed, the drawback would be doubly serious since any such contributions would inevitably constitute a direct drain on our balance of payments. In this connection the N.F.U. report referred to the statement made in the House of Commons by Mr Wilson on 10 November 1966 when he said that '. . . on the basis of present Community arrangements and present world prices, suggest that, after any transitional period, the adverse effect on the United Kingdom balance of payments might be of the order of £175 to £250 million. . . .' This clearly is no light price to pay.

It is not unlikely, as we have already indicated, that the N.F.U. report on Britain and the Common Market takes an unduly pessimistic line. It is interesting to note that in a memorandum included in the C.B.I. study, prepared by the private firm of Unilever, the increase in the cost of food to the consumer in this country – by 1975 – on the assumption of course that Britain will by then have joined the Community – is estimated at £500 million a year, i.e., some £200 million less than in the report prepared by the N.F.U. Moreover, out of this sum, only some 33%, or £165 million, would be expected to represent additional foreign exchange expenditure. The remaining 67%, or £335 million, would be available for redistribution to the British taxpayers 'who meet the

[8]Ibid, p. 29.

present cost of agricultural support (over £240 million in 1965/66)'. The Unilever memorandum went on to say that 'the £165 million increased cost on the balance of payments represents increased payments to Community farmers for their produce and the payments to F.E.O.G.A. (*i.e.*, the French initials for the European Agricultural Fund) in respect of levies on imports from non-member countries. The figure of £165 million is arrived at after adjusting import levels for changes in consumption and domestic production, resulting from the E.E.C. price levels. The change in the cost of butter on joining the E.E.C. is expected to be by far the largest single item in both the extra cost to the balance of payments (£90 million of the total £165 million) and the increase in the cost of living (£95 million of the £500 million)'.[9] The Unilever memorandum added that while the figure of £165 million made no allowance for any payment into the European Agricultural Fund over and above the levy contributions, any such contributions could probably be offset by the grants that might be made from the Fund to promote structural improvements in British agriculture. This, however, seems a somewhat excessively optimistic hope.

The Foreign Secretary, in his statement on the common market at the private meeting of the Parliamentary Labour Party on 6 April had this to say :

As to the impact of the Community's agricultural policy on ours, the issues here are threefold :

(a) The effect on our cost of living. The figures are around 10% to 14% on the retail cost of food and $2\frac{1}{2}$% to $3\frac{1}{2}$% on the cost of living. This is a very serious issue, but how serious it is depends on the time it takes to absorb the increase and the validity of the assumption that there are no changes in world and Community prices.

(b) Some of our farmers would suffer. Small livestock producers, not easily turned to cereal production, would be hit, but on the other hand, East Anglian farmers, for instance, would do extremely well, and over all I think the prosperity of British agriculture would be just as good and perhaps a little better. But many agriculturalists would have disagreeable changes to face and there would be distortion in the pattern of our agricultural production. Here again the time factor is important.

(c) The effect on the balance of payments. If financing arrangements stay the same, then it would be a blow to our balance of payments. We would pay twice as much as Germany and very nearly as much as the rest put together. This is inequitable if it stays as it is, but in 1969 the present financing

[9]*Cf.* C.B.I. *Britain and Europe, op. cit.,* Vol. 1, p. 28.

arrangements come to an end and the new system to replace it will be negotiated.

It is, of course, impossible to assess clearly and accurately the exact additional costs that acceptance of the Community's agricultural policy will involve for Britain. Not only must it be assumed that at least some concessions – even if they are few in number – will be wrested from the Six in the course of the negotiations, but the effect of the common agricultural policy upon British farming practice and production patterns remains at least in part a matter of conjecture. It is nonetheless absolutely clear that this is a sector where membership of the common market will cost this country dear. Probably a figure half-way between the N.F.U. report and that of the Unilever memorandum would constitute as near a guess as any that can be made at this stage. This would still leave us with an increased food bill of some £600 million a year; an increased outflow of foreign exchange of some £170 million; and a sobering realization of the harsh realities that await this country under the common agricultural policy.

Two essential factors to be borne in mind before we leave the subject of agriculture are, first, that Community agricultural prices are not immutable; they are of course subject to review. Similarly, the percentage contributions that are required from each member country are due to be reviewed in 1969. Second, that in any negotiations between the United Kingdom and the Community, major and far-reaching agricultural concessions will undoubtedly have to be made by this country as a measure of reciprocity for the industrial advantages which it is hoped membership will bring.

Related factors

As we saw in Chapters Four and Seven, the Treaties of Rome and Paris go far beyond the simple abolition of tariffs, quotas or other trade barriers for industrial or agricultural products, or even the establishment of a common external tariff and market organizations. There are provisions for common policies in transport, energy, finance, social matters, taxation and many other aspects of the economic life of the nations that make up the European Economic Community. The difference is that whereas for industry and agriculture the common policies, whether it be a matter of tariff removal or common market organizations, are largely agreed and in operation, they have, in many of these vital related fields, not yet passed beyond an essentially formative and therefore still malleable stage. In the energy sector, for example, the Community's efforts to formulate a common policy have so far failed signally and there would be virtually no rules or regulations for the United Kingdom to accept covering the levels of oil or coal consumption or the degree of protection that should or should not be afforded

202

to indigenous sources of supply. For transport, the position would be more complicated since the Community have made substantial progress in ensuring some degree of publicity for rail and road transport rates. In the United Kingdom both British Rail and the road hauliers have complete freedom to negotiate the most attractive commercial rates and are under no compulsion to respect the rule of non-discrimination. It is difficult to see – particularly in the light of the concessions which the United Kingdom was prepared to make during the previous negotiations for membership of the European Communities – how this country could avoid acceptance and implementation of the Community's transport policy as at present applied. At the same time, it is worth recalling that the Community has itself still to agree on means of achieving publicity for inland waterway rates and that it has never even attempted to tackle the problem of publicity for sea freights. This latter aspect will of course assume very great significance if and when Britain joins the Community and the Channel becomes a vital artery in the European transport network. In the social field, the United Kingdom will be called upon to accept the principle of freedom of movement for labour and services, the application of the principle of equal pay for men and women, the gradual alignment of its social security provisions upon those in force in the Community. In practice, however, the powers of persuasion or enforcement of the Commission, although so substantial on paper, have proved only moderately successful. Of considerably greater consequence are the Treaty rules and regulations on competition and restrictive practices – as well as recent developments with a view to developing a Community system or formula of company law (*i.e.*, the Commission has only recently submitted to the Council of Ministers a memorandum calling for the establishment of a 'European' company status) – and, to a lesser degree, the harmonization of industrial property law and commercial contract law.

Some changes would also have to be made in British law and practice in order to fall in line with the Community's policy on cartels and concentrations. Generally speaking, the British Monopolies and Mergers Act is considerably more restrictive and limiting in what it permits than the operative Articles of the Treaty of Rome. As we have seen, the current trend in the Community is towards the formation of bigger units and is in fact steadily accelerating. In the United Kingdom the Government has stated its support for mergers or concentrations that 'are in the public interest' but retains the power under the Act to refer to the Monopolies Commission any merger which gives the firms concerned control over more than one-third of the total internal availability of the products in question or total assets exceeding £5 million in value. Since British accession to the common market would almost certainly lead to increased pressures towards mergers and concentrations – if only to enable British firms to match up to their Continental counterparts – some change in legislation would be necessary. Similarly, in the field of taxation, membership would require a substantial change in Britain's present system. The Community, as we saw in Chapter Seven, has recently reached agreement on the substitution of the French type added-value tax for the various forms of indirect taxation that are at present in operation. In Britain's case this would involve the replacement of the existing purchase tax by the newly agreed Community added-value tax.

In the wider monetary field, the position is considerably less clear. The Treaty of Rome is careful and discreet in its references to monetary policies. At the same time it is difficult to see how a truly unified common market can be achieved without a common and integrated financial and monetary policy for all the member states. The Six – and not only the French in this case – have already made it clear that they would not be prepared to find themselves in a situation where they would be expected to provide financial support to maintain the £ sterling as a major world reserve currency. It was for this reason that Mr Wilson and Mr Brown in their tour of the capitals of the Six stated that Britain, if she came into the Community, would be prepared to give an assurance that she would not invoke Article 108 of the Treaty (which provides for financial assistance on an intra-Community basis) in the event of new financial difficulties due to the international role of the £ sterling. One possible solution, in the medium or longer-term, might be the absorption of sterling in a new European reserve currency, which could be expected to attract support in all the financial centres of the Community. Already the six existing member states are tentatively, and with great care, feeling their way towards a limited common monetary policy. M. Marjolin, one of the Vice-Presidents of the European Commission, has apparently commented that this will become a reality within the next two years. This seems excessively optimistic – and depends too, of course, on what exactly is understood by a common monetary policy. If by this term is meant a single currency for all six countries, together with a single central or federal bank or even a federation of central banks, then M. Marjolin's statement does indeed smack of extreme, even unbelievable optimism. If, on the other hand, the growing confidence among the Six in the stability of exchange rates between their various currencies and the increasing and now almost unlimited freedom of capital movements – and the financial confidence which these conditions are generating – are taken as the external symbols of a common monetary policy in the process of creation, then – seen in this light – M. Marjolin's statement is not far wide of the mark. The repercussions for Britain in the monetary field may therefore be expected to be severe : for quite apart from the problems that could arise from the lifting of restrictions on capital movements by British residents into Community equities and by existing E.E.C. residents in and out of sterling, there would undoubtedly come a reappraisal of the position of the £ sterling as a world reserve currency. Monetary policy, as the events of the last few years have shown only too clearly, cannot be looked at, or effective, in isolation. To be successful it must be used in conjunction with other economic means or weapons. But the Six in general, and the French in particular, will not easily agree to the City of London's promotion to the rank of the financial centre of the enlarged Community – with all the advantages this would bring to the United Kingdom. It would indeed be surprising if the role of the £ sterling as a major reserve currency were allowed to pass unquestioned into an enlarged Community.

Finally, there is the question of regional policy. The difficulties involved in granting preferential treatment to under-developed regions or areas appear, however, to have been exaggerated right from the beginning. The Rome Treaty specifically calls for the harmonious development of the whole of the Community area and provides for special measures and financial assistance for backward areas. All six member states, moreover, are at present actively engaged in national – as well as Community – measures specifically designed to improve the standard of living in certain under-developed regions. There is therefore no reason to suppose that any one of the Six – or the Commission – would raise any objections to a similar policy on the part of the United Kingdom; indeed, the position could well be the reverse, since failure to act on the part of the British Government could well lead in the longer term to a direct drain on Community resources.

The Commonwealth and E.F.T.A.

It is clear that the problems of the Commonwealth and E.F.T.A. will play a very much less important role in any new negotiations than they did in the Heath negotiations. In 1962 discussion of decalage procedures and special arrangements for the under-developed Commonwealth countries constituted a dominant theme throughout the negotiations. Mr Wilson, on the other hand, in his statement of 2 May 1967, mentioned only two specific items of Commonwealth trade, i.e., New Zealand and the Sugar Agreement. But it already seems clear that there will not be a repetition in 1967 and 1968 of the detailed and comprehensive negotiations over Commonwealth trade that were such a feature on the previous occasion. What arrangements the British Government has in mind to safeguard or protect at least temporarily other Commonwealth countries or trade, one can at this stage only conjecture. For the

African and Caribbean countries, association with the enlarged Community must presumably remain the most likely and satisfactory arrangement. For New Zealand and the Commonwealth sugar producers the Six may well prove understanding and agree to special arrangements to safeguard their trade either with Britain alone, by means of quotas, or on a broad Community basis. For India and Pakistan the proposals of 1962 would probably remain largely valid. The main problem would appear to be for the industrially advanced Commonwealth countries such as Australia and Canada – and South Africa (which has of course remained in the preference area). All three of these countries, but Australia in particular, have during the past five years striven hard to diversify their patterns of trade and to reduce the degree of their dependence upon the United Kingdom market. Even so, an abrupt loss of preference combined with the sudden application of protective duties and measures, would have a severe and untoward effect upon the economies of these countries. None of them are likely to be acceptable to the Six as candidates for association with the E.E.C. and it is therefore in the general direction of temporary safeguard measures, designed to avoid too rapid a transition from the present system of Commonwealth Preference to the application of the Community's common external tariff, that the most acceptable and probable solution may lie. At the same time President de Gaulle's overriding concern to maintain and promote the position of French life, culture and presence throughout the world could well be reflected in a readiness to agree to more generous conditions for Canada than would otherwise be the case. A not dissimilar feeling of sentiment as well as the existence of traditional ties on the part of Germany, Belgium and Holland, for South Africa, could well result to that country's advantage. Such developments, if they materialized, would clearly leave Australia in a particularly exposed position.

The position of the other E.F.T.A. countries has not figured prominently in the various lists of common market problems that have been released or discussed during the past few months. Several of the other E.F.T.A. countries would, undoubtedly, follow Britain into the common market. Recent press reports in Switzerland and Portugal have clearly suggested that these countries at least have been left with the uncomfortable and unwelcome – even if on the whole rather unjust – feeling that Britain would, if necessary, leave them in the lurch and make her own terms with the Community.

The constitutional and legal position

One question which was often raised during the previous negotiations and which appeared to give many people in Britain cause for concern was that of the surrender or abandonment of national sovereignty. To what extent, for example, would the supremacy of Parliament be affected by the provisions of the Treaty of Rome? Would existing laws need to be amended? Would membership of the European Communities mean a massive change-over from British common law practice to Continental law based on the strongly codified Napoleonic system?

An up-to-date and complete answer to these questions – and one that should resolve the fears of most people – was given by the Lord Chancellor in his opening statement on the legal implications of membership of the common market in the debate in the House of Lords on 8 May 1967. The following summary of his statement was published in *The Times* on the day after the debate : 'He (*i.e.,* the Lord Chancellor) said membership of the European Communities involved acceptance of a body of law derived from the treaties. Some of its provisions were required to be given effect in the member states by national legislation or other appropriate means. Much of it, however, took effect directly as law within the member states.

'Membership involved a transfer of legislative and judicial powers in certain spheres to the community institutions and an acceptance of a corresponding limitation of the exercise of national powers in these spheres. Apart from the impact of community law on Britain's present and future national law, adherence to the treaties would, broadly speaking, have the effect of transferring to community institutions the power of concluding treaties on tariff and commercial matters. Adherence to the treaties would involve a considerable body of implementing legislation. A number of existing Acts would require to be amended. The United Kingdom legislation would be an exercise of parliamentary sovereignty, and community law, existing and future, would derive its force as law in this country from it. The community law so applied would override national law so far as it was inconsistent with it.

'Under the British constitutional doctrine of parliamentary sovereignty no Parliament could preclude its successors from changing the law. It was, however, implicit in acceptance of the treaties that the United Kingdom would not only accept existing Community law but would also refrain from enacting future legislation inconsistent with Community law. Such a restraint on our legislative system would not be unprecedented.

'There was in theory no constitutional means available to make certain that no future Parliament would enact legislation in conflict with Community law. Some risks of inadvertent contradiction between United Kingdom legislation and community law could not be ruled out, but if Britain joined the Community, they would be taking part in the preparation and enactment of all future Community law and their participation would reduce the likelihood of incompatibility.

'The Continental origin of Community law would not necessarily make it difficult to apply in the United Kingdom. The principal matters dealt with were the subject of modern legislation in many industrialized countries and no difficulty had been found in connection with these subjects in applying the same statutes to England and Scotland in spite of the wide differences of the two legal systems. In the task of applying the law, the United Kingdom courts would be assisted by the European Court to whom it fell to give authoritative rulings on the interpretation of the treaties on references from national courts. If we acceded to the treaties we would expect to be represented on the Bench of the European Court.

'Community law had little direct effect on the ordinary life of private citizens. In so far as it imposed obligations, it did so mostly in relation to industrial and commercial activities and did not touch citizens in their private capacities. The main impact of community law would be in commerce, customs, and restrictive practices. It would also affect the operation of the steel, coal and nuclear energy industries. An important safeguard for the protection of those affected was that all decisions imposing penalties were subject to a right of appeal to the European Court.'

On the basic issue of loss of nationality, moreover, there is as we have had occasion to see both in relation to the supranational provisions of the Treaty of Paris and the qualified majority voting procedure of the Treaty of Rome, a very wide difference between the wording and original spirit of the Treaties and the reality of Community life. Membership of, and participation in the Community, will, inevitably, mean a much greater degree of involvement – and, consequently, greater restraints upon our freedom of action and decision – than membership of N.A.T.O. or of the G.A.T.T. But these are questions of degree. The Community, as it is operating today, is governed by the Council of Ministers representing the six national governments in which the decision-making process is one of persuasion, co-operation and negotiation – and not one of direction.

The institutional position

British accession to the Community would of course mean British participation in the Institutions of the Community. Until recently the nine-man European Commission was made up of two Germans, two Frenchmen, two Italians, one Belgian, one Dutchman and one Luxembourger. The United Kingdom would no doubt claim and obtain the same importance of representation as the three largest countries of the existing Community. It is difficult at this stage to see exactly what form this might take. The Community countries have themselves agreed in principle on the fusion of the three European Executives and their replacement by a single Commission of fourteen (to be reduced later to nine) members. If Britain and several other E.F.T.A. countries join the Community, some way will presumably have to be found of assuring adequate representation for all the participating countries without at the same time rendering the work and operations of the unified Executive too cumbersome by turning it into too large a body. There would of course also have to be British judges appointed to the Court of Justice, British officials in the European institutions, and British parliamentary delegates to the European Parliament. Here again, the weight of British representation or participation could be expected to be roughly equal to that of France, Germany or Italy. Finally, British Ministers would take part in the regular meetings of the Community Councils of Ministers – where each country has one and theoretically equal vote.

What are the alternatives?

What, it may be reasonably asked, are the alternatives to the common market? What should Britain do if her second application to join were to be rejected – or if the conditions required of her were too onerous or humiliating to make acceptance possible? Is it after all so obvious that joining the common market is the best answer to Britain's problems today?

Let us consider for a moment what these alternatives are. There is, first and foremost, the suggestion – popular in some quarters – that Britain should link up with the United States. There is a common language, a common history and, of course, a host of common liberal traditions. Such an arrangement could, furthermore, be extended fairly easily and logically to embrace Canada, New Zealand and Australia and so form a world-wide and immensely powerful English-speaking bloc. It is a proposal with undoubted appeal and could, no doubt, be made to work if the need arose. But there are drawbacks too. Prime among them is the massive preponderance and geographical advantage of the United States in any such union. How long would it be before British industry, stripped of its tariff walls, became completely Americanized – in terms of capital, control and direction? Such are the power and resources of American industry that it is difficult to see how in a union of this kind a rapid expansion of American industrial colonialism could be avoided. In such a system Washington would inevitably become the capital and the laboratories, workshops and universities of the United States the Meccas of our graduates and entrepreneurs.

Then on a more limited scale there is the possibility of a revival of the old Anglo-Canadian free trade area scheme. But there is no evidence that the Canadians would view such an arrangement with any more enthusiasm today than they did in 1959. Another possibility is the merger of E.F.T.A. into some wider Atlantic union. But even if Britain were to decide that the entrance fee for membership of the common market was too high, there can be no guarantee that some of the other E.F.T.A. countries (and, notably, Austria and Denmark) would not succeed in coming to some kind of settlement that would involve, *inter alia*, their withdrawal from E.F.T.A.

There is, lastly, the argument that we should seek to 'go it alone'; that we should be prepared to see a lowering in our standards of living in order to maintain our national identity and right and power of self-determination. Unfortunately for those who hold this view there is – besides the obvious question of whether many people in this country would be prepared tamely to accept any lowering in their standards of living while those of their neighbours around them rose – the fact that a Britain living and working in isolation, outside the framework of a major economic organization, would become rapidly weaker in relation to all the larger economic powers and groupings and so find herself reduced, comparatively quickly, to the position of a relatively minor and backward economic and political power.

One other idea that has been mooted is that of a Pacific 'area of co-operation' which is reported to be the diplomatic objective of the Japanese. The Japanese plan would in essence involve the creation of a free trade area between Japan, Australia, New Zealand, Canada and the United States – but could conceivably include Britain also. Such an arrangement would in fact add Japan to the world-wide English-speaking union which we discussed above and, like it, would almost necessarily lead to American industrial domination. Japan, with her lower labour costs, would in fact be better placed than Britain – at least in the shorter term – both to resist American penetration and to compete with British or American goods in the Canadian, Australian and New Zealand markets.

To conclude, any meaningful alternative regional grouping to the common market must include the United States; and this, in turn, cannot but lead to American industrial – and agricultural and financial – supremacy. Nevertheless if, despite her second attempt to join the common market, Britain were once again to be spurned, the only workable and possible alternative would appear to lie in some form of association – whatever its perils – with the United States. In an enlarged common market, on the other hand, Britain would find herself with other European powers (*i.e.*, France, Germany and Italy) with actual or potential economic resources broadly equal to her own. Together, these countries have it in their power and their reach to equal and surpass the economic wealth of the two super-powers. They have it in their power, moreover, to do this in a way which, while calling for full co-operation between them, will allow all of them to retain their national identities and to find in the fusion of their economies and in their common achievement and prosperity, a sense of national and European fulfilment.

The prospects of success

Now that the dice have been cast and Britain's second application for membership of the common market has been made, the question uppermost in most people's minds is, inevitably, what are the chances of success? What is the likelihood of a second French veto?

Broadly speaking, it is probably fair and accurate to say that five of the six member states of the Community, *i.e.,* all with the exception of France, would like to see Britain in. Their motives may differ and sentiment may play a very minor and probably unquantifiable part in their calculations or assessment of the balance of advantages or disadvantages. But this is immaterial. The fact remains that on the whole, and after all has been said and done, five of the six see profit, safeguards or advantage in Britain's accession. But France . . . there is the rub and the ugly question mark.

For France the common market has been a triumphant diplomatic success – one that has probably far exceeded the fondest hopes of its original initiators. Politically, France has recovered a position of influence in the world, due in large part to her pre-eminent role in the common market. It is fully understandable, from her point of view, that she should be reluctant to surrender even a part of her spoils by agreeing to British entry. The position – and decision – is, however, not so clearcut. Compared with Germany, the economic strength of France is pale and unimpressive. France may not be a European paper tiger but she is, as *The Times* so cruelly put it in a brilliant leader article earlier this year, 'a second class power with pretensions above her real strength. President de Gaulle is not Louis XIV; he is Louis XIV from son et lumière; he is not an expression of the greatness of France, but of the greatness he would like France to have. Like all fantasies this gathers energy to itself, but results in practical decisions being taken which are based on fantasy and not on truth. The French position in Europe, the French nuclear submarine, are, viewed historically, symbols of detachment from reality.'[10] Nevertheless, de Gaulle is nothing if not a realist. The big economic battalions are massed not on the French but on the German side of the Rhine. The problem that he and the French government must face and resolve one way or the other is whether the short-term advantages of a second exclusion of Britain and the consequent maintenance of French pre-eminence weigh more in the balance of French advantage or security than the latent threat of German economic power and eventual leadership of a Community limited to the present six member states.

The effective strength of the French position today is no longer that of 1962. Not only has France found that she cannot with impunity ignore the views and wishes of her five partners but the prospect of a strong German government (and a French government

[10]*Cf. The Times,* The energy of nations, 8 April 1967.

without de Gaulle to buttress it) looms on the horizon of the European scene. It was presumably considerations of this kind which led George Brown to say, in his statement to a private meeting of the Parliamentary Labour Party that he did not think that it will be as easy a decision for the President of France to consider a veto on this occasion even if he wished to.

If this interpretation of the French position is correct, then we may expect the French to prevaricate and delay as much as possible, and to play at brinkmanship, but without ever going as far as a second veto. Their objective will be twofold : first, that of consolidating their achievements within the existing common market, notably the hardening of the still fragile mould of the common agricultural policy; and secondly, of extracting the maximum possible advantages for French interests during the negotiations – above all an assured and virtually captive British agricultural market, a diminution in the role of the £ sterling as a major world reserve currency (and of the financial status of the City of London) with the avowed objective of enhancing the claims of Paris as a major financial centre for the Community, the dismantlement of the Commonwealth Preference system, and close technological co-operation between French, British and other Community firms. These terms will undoubtedly be harsh. It will be the unenviable but inescapable responsibility of the British government to weigh up the penalties and the potential benefits.

Nevertheless it must be borne in mind that, however unpalatable the terms may be, once inside the Community, Britain will be well placed to influence its future shape and development; while for British industry access to a large, dynamic and expanding market is a question of life and death. Above all, in her incomparable refinement of parliamentary democracy, her unswerving application of the principle of the rule of law, her fidelity to the exercise of freedom, and her world-wide, oecumenical connections and experience – which no other Community country can rival, her language and culture, Britain has it in her power to make a unique and invaluable contribution to a strong, united and outward-looking Europe.

Despite their differences and their rivalries it is in the ultimate interest of both Britain and France – not to mention other countries of Western Europe – that the United Kingdom should join the European Economic Community. The signs are that this basic similarity of interests is becoming increasingly recognized. If this is indeed so, the forthcoming negotiations may often be harsh, even pitiless – this is regrettable but probably unavoidable, and history may well pass an unkind judgment on those whose economic cupidity is insufficiently tempered by sober realism – but they should also prepare the way for the united Europe which the majority of European peoples hope so fervently to see.

Index